The

by

Mary L. Twitty

Johnson's Valley Printers
Verona, MO 65769

Edited by BJ Typing
Monett, MO 65708

Library of Congress Cataloging in Publication Data
Twitty, Mary, L.
The Dream Trail.
96-91004

ISBN 0-9658872-0-0

This book is dedicated to my husband, Bill, who was at the beginning, and patiently waiting at the end, of every trail. He looked after my every need.

I DIDN'T KNOW HIKING WAS A DISEASE!

It was the year, 1971. I was employed at the local Shoe Factory in Monett, Missouri. One day out of the blue, the shop foreman informed all the employees that if anyone wanted to take a week off, they could. The statement struck me like a lightning bolt because I was having a brainstorm about taking a trip. A very exciting trip.

Without giving it a second thought, I eagerly phoned my husband, Bill, and asked him if he could be ready when I got off work to go to the Grand Canyon. He answered, "Have you been fired?" I explained the circumstances at work and reminded him of how we had always wanted to go. Familiar with my impulsive nature, he hesitated, then answered, "Sure, I'll try to be ready." As I drove home, I was having visions of riding the mules deep into the Canyon. When I arrived, we had to perform a miracle to get our 135 acre farm looked after by neighbors and friends. With that accomplished, we finished loading the pickup and camper with the equipment and necessities we figured we would need and headed for the wondrous Grand Canyon. Little did I know, what was about to happen would change my entire life.

It took a couple of days driving to get there. When we arrived, I was told we needed reservations to ride the mules into the Canyon. Our hearts were in our shoes when they said you actually had to have them *two years* in advance. We had a glimmer of hope, when some man asked which ride we were interested in taking. Like two eager children, we told him the overnight ride to the Phantom Ranch. "Well, be in the office by seven o'clock in the morning and just maybe, someone will cancel," he said. Bill informed the guy how disappointed I was and that we would wait at least *three* days, if necessary.

Expectations were low that night and I was beginning to wonder what the heck we were doing here to start with. The next morning we were in the office thirty minutes early. All reservations were confirmed by 7:00 a.m., so Bill and I got up to leave. Then, out of the blue, the man in charge said, "We have a spot for you folks from Missouri to ride the mules into the Canyon." Needless to say, my heart skipped a beat. Bill said, I jumped five feet off of the floor.

Not only did I feel like I had jumped five feet off the floor but I also felt I had landed on my nose when we were told the ride would cost $60.00 a piece. We had not brought that much cash but I wasn't about to lose this chance. I looked, with a squinted eye of an old time gun fighter, and nervously told the man, "I didn't bring that kind of cash, pardner, will ya' take a check?" I couldn't believe I said it like that, but the westerner must have sensed my sincere desperation and politely answered, "Sure ma'am, no problem."

I had spent little time on a horse's back, but I was determined to make this ride with Bill. At least the little mules weren't very high off the ground. Before I knew it, all the excuses were over and we were on our way down Bright Angel Trail. I began to observe *"backpackers"* hiking into the Canyon. It was the first time I learned people did such a thing.

It didn't cost them a cent and they only needed a permit to hike into the great Grand Canyon. I felt no cough, no breaking out of my skin nor any excessive temperature, but I was being infected by something, something as invisible as any bacteria. The thrill I felt was beyond anything I had ever known. I disguised the real symptom with thoughts like, "It would be a good way to exercise and keep fit." Regardless, my mind was made up. I would look into this *backpacking thing* just as soon as I got back home.

When we finally arrived at Phantom Ranch, I realized it really was possible for humans to be split up the middle. I could hardly stand up when I got off that doggone mule and I still had to endure the trip back up the canyon.

I was so sore that night in the bunkhouse, I swore, that when this was over I would never ride a mule, ever again. Early the next morning, we were on our way up the Kaibab Trail to the finish of this painful adventure. The mule ride had ended, but something else was just beginning. When Bill and I got back home, I realized why going was so wonderful. Being back in my comfortable house never felt so good. There really is "no place like home" . . . . or is there?

GETTING STARTED

As soon as we arrived home, I realized I had been infected with a strange obsession. I found myself reading everything I could find about backpacking, what I needed and what trails there were to hike. Realizing I was no gazelle, I discovered that a 70 year old woman, called Grandma Emma Gatewood had hiked the Appalachian Trail. This grand old lady was my first inspiration. Don't get me wrong, I know she was an exceptional lady but if a 70 year old woman could hike 2,160 miles on the great AT, I could too!

Back then, I was buying all my clothes from the good old Sears catalog. What was good enough for me, was good enough for my husband Bill and son Steve, so I ordered backpacks, rain parkas, nylon tarp for a tent and three sleeping bags, all in the color orange, knowing we might be hiking during hunting season.

There are some hunters that can't tell the difference between a human and an animal. Very few animals are bright orange. It has been proven that yellow or orange show up better than any other color on the highway and in the woods. Now, orange has become the standard color for being in the woods. Personally, I like bright colors and still wear my old parka, even though it isn't waterproof anymore. I also bought a little one-burner Coleman gas stove and a nest of cooking pots. They were to come in real handy as I learned all I could about trail menus, creating some of my own as I became more involved.

Well now, I was all rigged and ready to go and the bug that had gotten into me was gnawing away. The next question was, where do I go? I could not get those hikers at the Grand Canyon, out of my mind and since that was where this terrible urge began, I figured we should go back and start there. No, I couldn't just start whenever I wanted to. But the very next Spring of 1972, a trip west to hike into the North Rim of the Grand Canyon was scheduled. I was like a child planning to go to Disney World and time went by so slowly it was agony.

The big day finally came for us to head west. Everything went well, until we got to the parking lot of the North River. Was it an omen that we had a flat tire on the pickup? Our tires were in good shape and we hadn't had a flat in ages. Didn't matter. Bad omen or not, we headed into that Canyon!

Was it my imagination or did the sun become brighter and hotter after we began the hike? It felt like we had hiked about three miles into the Canyon. Alas, it was only a mile. Bill couldn't get the flat tire off his mind, so we used that as an excuse to hike back out.

As we started back, the evening sun setting in the western sky looked as though it was taking a bath in the many colors of that rugged country. We were feeling pretty proud of ourselves until a young lady emerged from the trail, tired and dragging her tail. She told us she had hiked all the way from Phantom Ranch at the bottom of the Canyon, a total of 12 miles . . . all up hill and she still had *another* mile to hike to the lodge on the North Rim.

We were tired, but elated, when we got back to the parking lot. So we hadn't hiked a hundred miles! We were still having an adventure that we wouldn't have had setting at home. I still felt an itch as we snuggled into our camper bed. The sunset painted a beautiful picture of hope and anticipation for us before turning out the lights in the western sky.

As the sun began turning up the dimmers in the eastern sky the next morning, we were on our way South to the White Sands National Monument in New Mexico. When we got there, we decided to try another hike. Packing up our gear like old experienced hikers, into the Dunes we went. The only marking for the trail were poles that someone had been kind enough to stick into the mounds of sand. We carefully went from one pole to the other.

After about a mile, we decided to really rough it for the night. We began setting up our lean-to tarp for a tent by tying it to sage brush, one of the few things courageous enough to grow in the sand. We hadn't been there long when Bill noticed huge black clouds rapidly coming in from the west. This country is notorious for sneaky storms that can come out of nowhere.

It was scary enough to motivate us to pack our tent and hurriedly hike back to the camper. It wasn't a courageous move, but turned out to be a smart one as the rain pounded us all night. Both our hikes had turned out to be "bummers" I suppose, but we were to find out that was what backpacking was all about. You may go one mile or a hundred, but an adventure will occur. Why? Because you're out there looking for it.

The disease I had contracted was permanent but hopefully, not terminal. You would think the trip west would have discouraged me, but it only made me more stubborn and determined not to ever give up. I would never be satisfied to lead a dull hum-drum life again. It was wonderful to discover this creature hidden deep inside me.

As soon as I got home, I wrote the Appalachian Trail Club and ended up buying their guide book and maps to the Great Smoky Mountains National Park. Bill was giving me some weird looks but in truth, I think he was getting a kick out of the whole thing. When I told him I was determined to hike the Appalachian Trail, he just shook his head.

The guide book tipped me off to a Mrs. W. C. Hochstetler at Waterville, Tennessee, who would help move our rig around the park and look after it until we finished our hike. Bill knew the bluff was over, when I contacted Mrs. Hochstetler and plans were made for a hike in August of 1973.

Bill, my son, Steve and I made our way from Missouri to Tennessee, picking up Mrs. Hochstetler on the way to the Smoky Mountain National Park. Our reservations were made for lean-tos provided by the park and scattered throughout the trail. First stop, Fontana Dam, and the hike north to Davenport Gap.

Sagebrush was one of the few things that grew abundantly in the desert of New Mexico. In contrast, everything grows in the Smoky Mountains. We hiked up to Birch Spring Gap Shelter. I was discouraged and totally worn out and settled down for what I felt was a well-deserved rest. The body was tired, but the mind was alert enough to look over our back country permits. While doing so, I realized there was no way we were going to be able to meet our pre-determined schedule for reservations at the lean-tos.

Failure was looming its ugly head in my mind and that is a word I do not like to include in my vocabulary. However, this hiking business was going to require a lot

4

more preparation, especially physical conditioning. My son and I had done very little walking before going out to the trail. Bill has a wooden leg and it was causing him considerable trouble. In short, we were just too slow. Finally, I decided we had accomplished about all we could for this trip.

A scout master, with his troop, had made it to the Birch Spring Gap Shelter, minus one of his boy scouts. Inadvertently, he came to our rescue. It seems the scout had gotten sick on the trail and had to be left back at Fontana Dam. Realizing our dilemma, he offered us a deal we couldn't refuse. We would go back down to check on the boy. For that, the good scout master would let us have the keys to his pickup that was left at the dam to get back to Waterville where our pickup was waiting.

Needless to say, for me it was a dark day that August 7, when we started back down the mountain, knowing this hike would be finished. As if things were not bad enough, my husband Bill, broke his leg on the way down. The only good thing to be said is it was his wooden leg and not his remaining good one. It is, however, a *complete* wooden leg, all the way to his hip. He lost his leg when he was a young boy. There is barely enough stub there to mount it.

Lest you hate me for wanting him to do this challenging adventure with me and pity him because you think he had to, let me tell you now, no one makes Bill do anything. He is more of a man with one leg than most, with two. That's why I love him so much. He's got *guts* and *deserves* a tigress like me. Lord! I can't believe I said that. This illness I caught at the Grand Canyon is affecting me more than I realize.

Anyway, he tied it together and we made it down to Fontana Dam, picked up the Scoutmaster's truck, then proceeded to Waterville where our pickup and camper waited. We always go the extra mile so we went back to Fontana Dam, fed the young scout Kentucky Fried Chicken and ended up spending the night with him. This made him feel better, but I was wondering all the while if backpacking was like this for anyone else. Our thanks to the good Scoutmaster who loaned us his truck.

It was a wet, dewy morning when we headed for Little Rock, Arkansas, where we were able to get Bill's leg fixed. One thing you have to say about a wooden leg instead of a real one, once it is fixed there's no long healing period afterwards. We did learn one good lesson. Bill would not be going on any more long hikes with me. As you will see, this eventually worked out to our advantage but caused me a lot of lonely hours. Well, another strange hike was duped but I was learning valuable things, like supplies I needed and the complex procedure of how to make reservations for the shelters in the Parks. Though still rough, my animal skills were slowly being honed.

Home was becoming a whole different world. It was like arriving in heaven after each trip, trips that so far were sometimes too full of agony. I knew this would have to change because each day I was becoming more and more consumed with my obsession. There was hardly an hour in my days that my thoughts were not on hiking.

Well, I decided maybe agony needs company. So-o-o-o-o, one day I was telling my story about how wonderful backpacking in the rough is, to a group of young people in my training Union Class at Church. *Innocently,* mind you, and seeing the sparkle in their eyes, I asked if they would like to hike through the Smoky Mountain National Park with me. They all thought it would be great. Really now, I love young people but they need a little agony now and again. Don't they?

June, 1974, I had an eager group helping form plans for the next big hike. Like an old pro, I got them to start doing some workout hikes in order to get used to the gear. Helping them to get their backpacks and hiking equipment together, I ordered six ponchos from Sears, one for each of us. I also bought an Optimus 8R stove to use with the Coleman stove and a larger set of cooking pots. My troop and equipment was coming together. What had begun as a possible fantasy was now becoming a reality. So I need to tell you something about my new partners in crime, er, excuse me, hiking.

Tracy, was the youngest of the group. He had a quiet personality and when he did speak, it was slow and deliberate. A serious fellow who loved to fish, but occasionally exhibited a real sense of humor.

Leslie Ervin, on the other hand, was the oldest of the group. He lived on a large ranch so he was used to the outdoors. I might add, he had no problems speaking his mind. You could tell he was used to doing pretty heavy work because he was very strong. Leslie seemed to have a deep, caring feeling for others. I was banking on that.

Red-haired Rita was athletic, outgoing and a very studious young lady. Because of my red hair and interest in physical exercise, she reminded me of myself and I guess I was a little partial to her. A very easy person to converse with and I believe she could do anything she put her head to.

Sonya was the musician of the group. She had a sweet voice and was quite a talented guitarist. In general, she was an all around good person. She and Rita were best friends and made a pair to draw to.

7

Carla had long dark hair that she kept neatly braided, like a young Indian maiden. Now that I think about it, she had dark skin to match her hair. Her nature was quieter than the other two girls and seemed always to be observing all that went on around her. All in all, our ages ranged from 14 to 16 with one 42 year old kid. Need I tell you who that was?

It was decided that Bill and his friend, Don Miller, would ride horses on the trails designated for that purpose in the Smokys. The parks are very strict about keeping the trails for hiking and horse trails separate, for obvious reasons. The plan was that they would meet us at New Found Gap and again at Fontana Dam. Don Miller was called Poppy by his grandchildren so, for some reason, everyone fondly called him Poppy and the nick name stuck.

The Ozark Mountain Range pales in comparison to the mountains in the Smoky Mountain National Park but we did some short practice hikes in them, in an effort to get into condition before leaving. Each of my young hikers acquired their own backpack, sleeping bag, sleep pad and poncho. The short trails in the Piney Wilderness area gave us a chance to try out the equipment and fix our meals.

I will admit, I ordered the food for my previous Smoky Mountain hike from a company called Chuckwagon foods. One complete meal was in each package. After I learned how they did it, I went to the grocery store, bought the necessary materials and fixed my own.

My little group and I hiked the roads in the Ozarks carrying the loaded backpacks, in order to get used to them. There is an old hikers saying that holds true in the end though, "Nothing gets you in shape for the trail, but the trail itself."

August, 1974, with the practice hikes out of the way and all the preparation that we thought we needed . . . bearing in mind that you always forget something . . . the big trip began. When you travel with that many people, it is always a lot of fun. The trip to the Great Smoky Mountains was made without incident. When we arrived at Cosby Campground, Bill and Poppy unloaded their horses and took them to a back country campsite. They couldn't keep them in the Cosby Campground for hygienic reasons.

The impatience of youth was manifest when we had to wait one long day for the good old park reservations to kick in. I lured the youngsters into a conditioning hike up to a place called Low Gap and back. Really, I just wanted them to work off some of their vim and vigor and kill some time.

Typical of the Smokys, it rained all night. With the ground wet and moisture still hanging heavily in the air, we left early to climb our mountain to Tricorner Knob Shelter. The unwanted moisture fell on us, off and on three-fourths of the way up to the A.T. Bill and Poppy came out of the woods like two specters out of a mist on the way down the mountain.

Bill was hesitant to tell me we should turn around and go back. He explained how mud was knee deep to a small giraffe up there. He told of two rugged, big men who were quitting their hike because of the rain and mud. That wasn't the whole story. They had also spent the night in a primitive campsite and a big black bear had walked all over their camp, tearing open their backpacks and wreaking havoc. I felt sorry for the big, rugged men but I think Bill knew that story would not deter my stubborn attitude. He wasn't surprised when I told him "I have not come this far to quit so early. We're going on. We'll see you at New Found Gap in three days."

Boy, I was glad the young people had decided to come with me. We pulled and tugged each other through the mud and even though the rain was descending on us, we arrived triumphantly at Tricorner Knob. The other hikers there looked at us in bewilderment. I'm sure they were thinking we didn't know what we were doing. I was beginning to wonder myself, as we fixed our meal and hit the sack. The tired I felt was like a conquering warrior must feel after a hard fought battle. It was wonderful!

Early the next morning we were still dragging, but we fixed our breakfast. Like the battle-torn soldiers we were becoming, we were the first to leave the shelter. Yes! It was still raining. I could see why no one else was in a hurry to leave, but the rain did quit by mid-morning.

As we came up on a ridge, I took a step backwards to take a picture. I felt my heel slipping over the edge and caught myself just before falling. This was the first time I almost had a serious accident. It was a lesson I would not soon forget. From that day on, I became hyper aware of where my feet were going, especially when they were taking me backwards.

When I had obligated myself to take this hike with these kids, I wasn't sure I would be able to keep up with them, but they were in better shape than I had anticipated. I was, on the other hand, feeling more like a tiger everyday, so up to this point it was no concern.

The approach to False Gap Shelter was a steep walk downhill and because the trail was washing out badly, required a great deal of caution. When we finally sloshed in, we found a small spring behind the shelter, so all in all, it was a good place to camp. By now, we had established a good routine. Tracy and Leslie always went

10

for water. Rita, Sonya, and Carla helped me cook the meals and clean the pots and pans. By the time we finished, we were all ready to hit the sack.

The third day out was longer than expected. A climb called Charlie's Bunion was covered with gray shallic rock, wet with the previous rain. These varied size pieces of shale could have easily become ice skates. Your feet could slip out from under you in the blinking of an eye, sending you down a slippery slope, covered with nature's little razors. Carefully and intact, we made it over.

As we had prearranged, my trusty Bill and Poppy were waiting for us at New Found Gap. We Loaded up four more days of food, my gang and I headed for Mt. Collins Shelter. By this time, I was experiencing some sadness at not having Bill with me. We had spent a long life rarely being separated, especially at night.

It was a pretty steep climb and some of my kids were beginning to complain. The stress of challenging my weary body and keeping them interested, at the same time, was also taking its toll on me. They had not learned to recognize the wonder of feeling body and spirit rising to challenges such as we were experiencing. It was a relief when we got to Mt. Collins to find it full of hikers of all ages.

That evening my young gang experienced people closer to their own ages, who were going through the same adventure. They forgot how rough it was as they told jokes and stories about how each felt. Two young men from Georgia, who had unique southern accents, were probably never aware how their talk entertained my group from Missouri. They all truly enjoyed themselves and it was a welcome break for me.

The next day we climbed up to Clingman's Dome, elevation 6,642 ft. Bear in mind, we started only a few hundred feet above sea level. You do notice a difference in the oxygen and your breathing gets heavier. Your ears even pop on the steep descent. Remember, Denver, Colorado, is only a little over 7,000 ft. elevation and it's called the *Mile High City*. Look at this way, to hike only 2,400 ft. higher than we were, you would be foolish to hike without oxygen. Thank goodness, we would never hike that high on the great A.T.!

From Clingman's Dome, I was beginning to realize what it was all about. No matter which way you turned, the view was breathtaking. Only the few who brave the struggles we had endured, would see this. Let me feebly try to describe what this moisture-laden country is like. Ferns and mosses were like beautiful blankets everywhere. It was so thick under the trees, you quickly are made aware of why the hiking trails are so necessary. The sun's rays trickled down through the abundance of trees like a tropical rain forest. It was awesome.

The walking was a little easier as we continued to Siler's Bald Shelter. My youthful companions were feeling their oats and eagerly moved out ahead, leaving me behind. When Tracy and Leslie noticed how far I was falling behind, they became worried about me. Graciously, they stopped, allowing me to catch up with them. That was truly sweet. I'll tell you one thing though, for my age, I was getting physically stronger, so it didn't hurt my pride a bit to trail behind these young people. What did bother me was the fact that I was responsible for those whelps so I had to tell them not to get too far ahead of me. Try baby-sitting in the Smoky Mountains.

Most of the Lean-tos, that are provided all along the Trail in the Smoky Mountain National Park, are equipped with wire bunks and a fireplace in one end. They also have a wire fence in front of them with a gate. The lean-tos outside the park are generally smaller in size and lacking the fence in front to close them in. As you will see, the fence is there for a very good reason.

As evening came, we built a warm fire with crackling, leaping flames. It was a fire worthy of sitting around and watching intently as the flames did an Indian snake dance. All of a sudden, a Mother Bear and her two cubs came sauntering around the corner of the lean-to. Had it not been for the fence, they would likely have stumbled right in amongst us.

We couldn't believe our eyes. Partly out of fear and joy, and not wholly realizing the danger, the kids were so thrilled to see the bears, they began screaming at the top of their lungs. Startled, the mother and one cub, thinking they had stumbled into a group of wild banshees, bolted up the hill. The other cub, typical of human children, wasn't so frightened and stayed in back of the shelter.

It was exciting to see the bears but just a bit uncomfortable to find ourselves *between* a mother and her cub. The wire fence and gate, designed primarily to keep the bears out, served its purpose well as the mama bear came back to get her cub. With a snuffing sound like an insult, she and her cubs waddled on out of sight. I was thankful for the adventure and grateful for a fence that kept it from being more than that.

The next day was uneventful and brought us to the Derrick Knob Shelter where we spent the night. That evening the girls opted to wash their hair in the spring. We were all getting just a little bit cruddy but I couldn't stand that cold water on my head, so my hair stayed dirty!

An observant, southbound hiker wandered into the Shelter that night and took notice that I kept a close eye on two of my young people that were dating. He commented,

I was like a Mama watching over her brood. Before we parted he was calling me "Den Mama."

I didn't realize it at the time, but this was quite a compliment. Only the more seasoned packers have trail names. "Den Mama", I thought. "How unique." I really liked it. The stranger's trail name was "Trip" and I shall remember him fondly the rest of my life..

We left "Trip" behind early the next morning and climbed to the summit of Thunderhead Mountain, over 5,530 feet. It was weird on top. The wind was blowing the branches of the trees and an eerie fogged locked us in.

Young people never pass up an opportunity like that to let their imaginations run wild. They began to pretend Big Foot, the Sasquatche of the mountains was coming out of the thick, grayish-white walls of fog. They were even making me feel spooky when a large figure loomed up in the swirling mist. As the figure moved toward us, eyes were big and mouths agape. When they realized it was Trip, who had caught up with us, I think they were disappointed that it wasn't some mythical creature. That was to be the last time I would ever see Trip again. Shortly thereafter we called it a day at the New Spence Field Shelter.

The next day we were going for long distance. My breathing was shallow and the group was concerned for me. Going up and down those steep mountains and the change in altitude day after day, was taking a heavy toll on me. It was a long struggle but we made it down hill to the Birch Spring Gap Shelter late in the evening. Bill and Poppy had ridden in on the horse trail and were waiting. It was a relief to see them but they brought us some unusual news.

President Richard M. Nixon had resigned because of the Watergate scandal. I was shocked at the news but amazed that such humoungous change could occur in only one week of being out of touch with civilization. Imagine, Gerald Ford was the new President of the United States. Well, I doubt that it will make a heck of a lot of difference and life must go on. This was our last night on the trail, at least for this go round. Surprisingly, two of our boys wanted to cook supper. Guess what? We let them and they did just fine! It was impossible not to be in a good mood the next day as we headed back to Fontana Dam.

Like birds of the wilderness, we found ourselves back in the modern world on a hard-surfaced road with only trail signs to indicate where we had been. Pictures were taken of everyone. How can I express the pride I felt for these young people, not to mention myself? We had backpacked 63.4 miles through the rugged Smokys, with only a few minor problems. It was my first really big hike and I couldn't have been in better company. My curiosity was peaked. I was wondering what my young companions thought about their adventure. The answer was not long in coming. I held back tears when, in unison, they asked if they could hike with me again next year. My joyful answer was given with my actions. Just as soon as I got home, I began making plans for our next great excursion into the wilds.

O Lord, our Lord, Your greatness is seen in all the world! Psalms 8:9

15

OTHER HIKES

With great fondness I look back on the years 1975 to 1979. That trip with the youth was duplicated. We went back to the wondrous and mysterious Smoky Mountain National Park and another trip into the majestic Upper Rio Grande area in Colorado. They did not forget what they had learned and acted like old hands. The flavor of children growing up was manifest and it was an ingredient I will miss . . . . for better or for worse. At least I was with them before too much adulthood set in. Both trips were uniquely beautiful.

If I sound melancholy, it's because I found it extremely pleasurable being with vibrant, curious, young people. So much so, July 1, 1980, I took another group of 16 young folks and a few adults from my church on a hike from the South Rim of the Grand Canyon to Bright Angle Camp on the Colorado River.

On the way out to the Canyon, we stopped at Hollbrook, Arizona, and spent the night in a campground. The wind blew so hard it bent the poles on one of our tents. As so often happens, some had to sleep in cars. When you travel close to nature, you really learn how fickle and unpredictable she can be.

On that trip I had another pleasant experience. My oldest sister, Martha, who lives just south of Hollbrook, came up to our camp and paid us a visit. I only had a little while to talk with her since we were all so tired and had so far to go the next day. She understood and we turned in for the night. It was good to see her again.

The next day, July 2, 1980, we arrived at the Grand Canyon Campground. Bill cut a tree to use for a tent pole that seemed to work quite well. I guess that meant we are getting into the creative trail life. The trip took on another treat when my brother, Paul, and his son, Paul Junior, came all the way from California to hike with us into the Canyon. If my obsession accomplished no more than to give me a chance to see my family more often, then I suppose that is a good point, especially when they take part in my new-found hobby.

Knowing the hike down the Kaibab Trail into the Canyon would be steep and tough, I got the bright idea of putting cotton in the toe of my hiking boots. It seemed like a good idea since I had noticed that going down the steep trail caused my toes to push forward in my boots, scrunching them up and causing irritation. I was to regret that supposedly creative idea. You could say my illness was reaching epidemic proportions. This was a pretty good sized group that I had managed to convince to put aside normalcy for, what? Insanity. We'll see.

Wanda was the mother of Sonya, who went on the first hike in the Smoky Mountain National Park. Well, Sonya slipped into adulthood and left childhood fantasy behind. Her mother was obviously trying to regain that lost wonder. As a result she was a great inspiration for everyone. I was so happy she had made this hike with me. It was to be only a few short years before cancer took her to the greatest adventure of all. Her death left an emptiness in me. . . . I miss you very much, dear, sweet Wanda.

Then, there were the twins Lisa and Lori. Lisa only hiked with me once. I guess adulthood must have caught up with her. Her sister, Lori, and mother, Sandi, on the other hand, went on several hikes with me. I've often

17

wondered why some people get old in spirit so quickly, while others can go a lifetime without being infected.

Jeanie and Della were two delightful sisters who just loved the idea of being in the grand outdoors. My kind of people.

Janie, mother of LeNae and Sherry, was in part, responsible for helping get this group inspired to go with me on this trip to the Grand Canyon.

Bill S. and Karen, his wife, are my neighbors and got too close to me and whatever this infection is, rubbed off on them. Jeff, John and Jason, their three sons, sort of got trapped into the deal by genetics, because they usually hiked with me as a family unit. On this trip, the three boys couldn't decide to ride the mules with Bill and his friend or hike with me. I was happy they decided to hike.

For our sanity, I'll call my husband's friend Bill B. I'm sorry but the folks in the Ozarks like names like Bill, a lot and it drives me nuts. What are you going to do? Bill B. a bachelor, took up riding horses as a hobby. He's a very quiet person so we won't be mentioning too much conversation from him. He's a popular contractor who builds high quality homes. Later on, after this hike, he started dating a sweet girl, Patti and eventually married her. She was to hike with me on down the road on the magnificent Appalachian Trail.

After all the Bills, I'm glad to say there was my brother Paul and, oh no! his son, Paul Junior. Well, it was a pretty good group when you get past all the same names.

Back to the trail. Janie, Sandie and Sherry decided to stay on the rim and do their sightseeing from there. About halfway down I couldn't blame them. All the adults' legs were feeling the effects of the continual downhill walk, in one way or another. Let's face it, the human body is not conditioned for that constant abuse. As we reached

18

the bridge over the Colorado River, everyone was in pain, with the exception of the younger of our group. They seemed to endure the punishment so well that by the time we made camp by a stream, they were splashing and playing as if they were at the beginning of the trip. Later on in the evening, a curious skunk paid us a visit. Fortunately, everyone had the where-with-all not to bother the bold little creature and he kept his scent with him, where it belonged.

The elevation on the South Rim was 6,860 feet. By the time we got to Bright Angle Camp it had dropped to 2,400 feet. The temperature was an unbearable 100° going into the Canyon. Finally, old man sun took mercy on us and turned the thermostat to a more comfortable 80° that night. My toes were throbbing and I couldn't tell if it was pain, numbness or both. From now on if my boots don't feel comfortable, I will get a pair that fit, but I will never, never put cotton in the toe of my boots again!

The next morning, July 3, 1980, I felt like a battered combatant as we followed our trail, approximately two miles beside the wild Colorado River. Soon we began the climb to Indian Gardens. A pleasant stream kept us company part of the way up. At 11:00 A.M. we arrived at Indian Gardens. It was like a small oasis, half way up to the south rim with a small campground, spring and most of all, port-a-potties. Not long after we arrived, my husband and his buddy, Bill B., rode in on the mules. They were on their way down to Phantom Ranch, and couldn't believe we had been there ahead of them.

Some of us decided to hike out to a place called Plateau Point, (elevation 3,760 feet) to watch the sunset. When the sun sets on the canyon it carries its own artist with it, painting colors so varied and vivid it's hard for a sunset, in any other location in the nation, to compete. As the colors begin to blend on the canvas of the evening sky, they seem to take on a darker hue. The regal beauty would be worthy of the carpets of kings in any castle. It is astounding and most beautiful! The night chill did not need to use great force to send us back to camp. With my sore toes tingling with pain, I drifted into a fitful sleep.

The night's chill continued into the early morning hours of July 4, 1980. Last night had been markedly cooler than the night before. We forced our bodies to start the trip up Bright Angle Trail. Inching closer to the top, the trail was getting steeper and steeper and there were hardly any trees to shade us from the then, hot, blistering sun. The cold of night and that old fickle, schizoid sun burning down during day, made it awfully hard to get out of the canyon, but we finally peeked over the rim.

My brother, Paul and his son moved out ahead of us and reached the top first. I couldn't understand when I found out that they had promptly headed back to California without so much as an attempt to say good-bye. They must have been awfully anxious to get back to the safety of home. By then, I was capable of understanding that urge. Those trips do that to you. Home is a comfortable place and you learn to appreciate it more, after a hike. I found it a little bizarre that he did not wait to tell his hopelessly obsessed sister a tender good-bye. I love you just the same, dear brother.

My husband and Bill B. had ridden up on the Kaibab Trail and arrived a little later with three very tired boys straggling behind. After showering and eating lunch, we headed for Colorado, July 5, 1980. We were all pretty worn out after hiking into the Canyon and decided to spend the night at Cortez, Colorado.

After a well-needed rest, we drove to Mesa Verda, to visit the old Indian Ruins. There were a lot of old cliff dwellings, such as the Spruce Tree House, Cliff Palace, Long House and many others. They were all built into the cliffs, high above the valley floor and yet below the top of the Plateau. The Anasazi Indians lived there from about A.D. 1200 to A.D. 1299, when they migrated south. Then it was off to Pagosa Springs, where the entire group spent the last night together. In the morning, Janie, Sandie, Sherry, LeNae, Lorie and Della decided to return to Missouri.

JULY 6, 1980, the rest of us proceeded to Hansen's Mill Campground, where we spent another night. In the morning, we loaded our packs and hiked to the Wheeler Geological Area. The misery for putting the cotton in my boots was not finished. My toes were throbbing in agony.

Bill S., Karen, Jeff, Jason, John, Wanda, and Jeanie all hiked with me into the Wheeler Area. A tree, my husband had cut for a tent pole, became my steady companion as a hiking stick. When we got to the Wheeler Geological Area, begrudgingly, I donated it to be used as a tent pole again.

This area was unique in that it had a log cabin that we used to cook in when it rained. Using this as a base camp, we spent two days hiking out into the surrounding areas, then back to Hansen Mill Campground. My husband and Bill B. stayed behind in order to spend some relaxing time fishing in the Colorado Streams. They were patiently waiting for our return.

With mixed emotions we headed back to Missouri. I paid dearly for my smart idea of putting the cotton in my boots on that hike into the Grand Canyon. My feet never stopped hurting and I lost five of my toenails as a result. I'll bet, very few hikers have ever figured the price of a trip in toe nails. Still, I was not willing to give up hiking, as you will see.

In December of 1980, an ambitious group of forty-seven, called Hikanation, was hiking across America from San Francisco, California, to Washington, DC. I was fascinated with the concept and when they came through East Missouri, I joined and hiked a day with them. I know, you probably think I'm crazy, but I enjoyed their company and made some good friends that are as infected with this hiking disease as I am. As an example, the oldest man was 68 and the oldest woman was 58. Needless to say, I was impressed.

As we shared our adventures with each other, I told them of my dream to hike the Appalachian Trail in its entirety. An understanding person, called Marce, wrote a note in my log book, "Don't wait too long for the big one, Mary." I can't explain in words how good it felt to meet such a sincere group. It took these dedicated people over fourteen months to complete their hike.

It was becoming more and more difficult to find anyone crazy enough to hike with me. I always used my two-week vacations on the trail and in all fairness, not many people can arrange to be away from home that long. So I turned once again to my son, Steve. It was with some concern because, you see, Steve had been diagnosed as mildly retarded and was overweight. But he is like his father when it comes to courage. We decided to begin the great experience in June of 1984. Starting at Springer Mountain, Georgia, and heading north, the big hike on the Appalachian Trail was on. You will see me write of agony and ecstasy often and that is exactly what I was embarking upon.

The world and all that is in it belong to the Lord; The earth and all who live on it are his. Psalms 24:1

1
STARTING MY HIKE
ON
THE APPALACHIAN TRAIL

It was *June 16, 1984,* 6:00 p.m. when we arrived at Amicalola Falls State Park, Georgia, southern starting point of the Great A.T. By the way, from here on, we will refer to the Appalachian Trail as A.T., for my fingers sake.

The trail doesn't begin in the Appalachian Mountains at all. Its southern point is in the Chattahouchee National Forest of the Amicalola Mountain Range in the beautiful peach state of Georgia. It is a spectacular, continuous marked footpath, extending 2,160 miles from Springer Mountain, along the crest of the Appalachian Mountain Range. Eventually it ends at the northern point, wondrous Katahdin Mountain, a granite monolith in the central Maine wilderness.

Bill, drove our pickup camper. You know, the kind that fits into a pickup bed and is sometimes at the mercy of strong cross winds, especially on the highway. Looking around and checking things out, we drove up a steep, crooked road to a place called Nimblewill Gap, where we spent the night. It rained during the night and cooled things off nicely.

JUNE 17, 1984 - the day I had been waiting for. My DREAM HIKE will start from Springer Mountain, Georgia, elevation 3,782 feet. Bill hiked up the Mountain with us and then returned back to the pickup camper. It was a good 2.2 miles hike one way and the trail was steep, but in good condition. We took pictures at a plaque embedded in a rock near the trail sign. What a wonderful thrill it was to reach the summit of our first mountain.

I was concerned when Bill said good-bye and began his lonely trek back down the mountain. I'm always afraid when he hikes alone, even a few miles. After all, he had broken his wooden leg once and could do it again. What if I was not with him? Oh well, he was pretty good at patching it up.

Nevertheless, Steve and I hiked on. We only dropped to 3,500 feet from the top of Springer when my son and I reached the Cross Trails Shelter. It was small and we were the only two hikers there, in a warm 89° that later cooled to 65°. I had decided to take it easy the first day at least, due to our physical conditioning. Sort of work into it gradually. We still managed to cover 3.7 miles. It was a weird feeling that night without my husband.

JUNE 18, 1984 - 6:00 A.M. Steve and I woke up with a chill that can only be felt in those strange southern mountains. However, we were ready for whatever the day might present. My brave chubby son and I left the comfort of the Shelter and hiked to Stover Creek, where we ate a cold breakfast. It was decided before we left home that we wouldn't carry a stove, in order to keep our load as light as possible. Believe it or not, some foods are fairly tasty without cooking. More an more, I realized we were not in the greatest shape and it did cause me some concern.

This was a beautiful area. We found the campsites at Stover, Chester, and Long Creeks were not too shabby. The rose and lilac rhododendron appeared in profusion with its majestic full bloom of trumpets. There was a virgin strand of ancient hemlock with its poisonous turnip-like, cavernous root hidden below. Where there is bad you usually find some good. This particular hemlock is almost worthless as wood, but the bark is of great importance to the process of tanning.

The falls on Long Creek were swiftly spilling water from recent rains, making a steady sound that was soothing and peaceful. Reaching Hawk Mountain Shelter, we found the opposite of too much to too little water. We ate lunch there anyway. Afterwards, we hiked on to Justin's Creek where we again found adequate water.

Climbing Sassafras Mountain, elevation, 3,336 feet, we then descended the 508 feet to Cooper Gap, elevation 2,828 feet. We spotted Bill just as he was about to leave, but fortunately he heard our jovial son Steve singing all the way down. You would have thought we had been separated for a month, but It was so good to see him, even if only temporarily. Both of us worry about each other. I'll tell you this, my husband and I learned to appreciate each other more out there than we do at home, if that is possible, and I think it is.

The clouds drifted overhead and the temperature was a comfortable 80°. Our little family of three spent the night together, realizing the good Lord was with us, also. My son and I had traveled 10.8 miles.

JUNE 19, 1984 - Steve and I were slow to hit the trail. I think we both hated to leave Bill but the adventure must go on, so at 7:45 a.m. we did manage to bid him farewell. We headed down a rockier trail than we had experienced to this point. A huge tree was lying in the trail where it had been blow down.

Managing the inconvenience of going around it and continuing down a trail of ups and downs, we found only a few occasional steep climbs. Wisely, we skirted around some rugged mountains that had large boulders, some perched precariously. You never know when something may dislodge them and we were not taking any chances. This was not the most beautiful part of the A.T., but we did run across three or four good views of the rugged country.

Bill hiked in to meet us at Gooch Gap, 2,784 feet, where we ran into a group of Royal Ambassadors, a group of boys from a Baptist Church. The boys and their leaders were headed in the direction of Springer Mountain from whence my son and I had come. Wishing them good hiking, we continued on to where we intersected Highway 60 at Woody Gap, still in Georgia. We were not lonely, since there were a lot of hikers there.

We called it quits at 1:15 p.m. I was literally in *"hog heaven"* as I washed my hair and settled down for a good afternoon rest. It was a lazy cloudy, breezy day and I pondered the fact that we had only hiked 8.3 miles. The temperature had been a comfortable 85° to 65° and I wanted to do better than that. Oh well, sleep took away the concern as I drifted into dreamy, imaginary trails.

JUNE 20, 1984 - with renewed vim and vigor at 7:00 a.m., Steve and I hit the trail, knowing that Bill would be meeting us soon. The elevation at Woody Gap was 3,150 feet and we knew that we had to climb 1,311 feet up to Bloody Mountain, an altitude of 4,461 feet. The temperature was not as kind as it had been, rising to a hot

90°. Even though we were going pretty slow, it turned out to be a fairly pleasant climb, all things considered.

We conquered Bloody Mountain at 12:05 p.m., during the hottest part of the day. On the summit we discovered that someone had built a sturdy two-room rock house up there. It was clean and had a rustic fireplace in one room. It was so pleasant we ate our lunch, wishing we had arrived later so we could spend the night.

Bloody Mountain was rocky. The boulders on the trail were worn smooth, possibly from the many hikers who have traveled the Great A.T. in the years past carrying their problems, hopes and ambitions into this ideal dreamscape, or perhaps from the many years of weather. Among the rocks and boulders it was nice to see a mountain laurel blooming. My attention was turned to a descending trail that had become very steep and I needed to watch Steve, as well as where my own feet were going.

I mentioned how rambunctious my husband Bill is. All alone and without anybody pushing him, he hiked up to meet us at the Tilting Rock and then hiked back out with us to Neels Gap and U. S. Highway 19. This should be an inspiration to people who are handicapped. A wooden leg just isn't going to stop him. He then, took us north to Vogel State Park, where we spent the night. We enjoyed one of the most welcome hot showers I have ever experienced. After a whopping 11.3 mile hike, whew, take my word we needed it! Not very many social circles would have enjoyed the aroma of our company. Bill just nonchalantly held his nose and gave me that look that said, "I wonder what kind of a lunatic I am married to."

JUNE 21, 1984 - Returning to Neels Gap where we had left off the day before, we kept the good-byes unemotional. My son and I knew we would only be separated from Bill a short time. We began climbing right off the bat, as we left Hwy. 19. The trail was rocky and some of the climbs steep. In only a mile that felt like three, we reached Bull Gap at 3,644 feet. Then up Levelland Mountain, 3,942 feet. Up and down the trail working our way gradually to Tesnatee Gap, 3,138 feet.

It was interesting to meet Bill for lunch. We would tell him our experiences while hiking and he would describe the other adventure that was occurring with him, as he drove the pickup camper over highways and nursed the heavy vehicle across roads or goat trails, if necessary, to meet us. This helped keep our backpacking load as light as possible. At that point he took the packs, giving Steve and me a break as we hiked over to Hogpen Gap, an elevation of 3,450 feet and conveniently close to Georgia Highway 348.

We then picked up our packs, parted with Bill and continued on. The trail got a lot better, which is a good thing because we were getting awfully tired by the time we arrived at Low Gap Shelter, 3,050 feet. The good Lord was warning us with his thunder most of the way, but he held the rain off until 4:30 p.m. This was just right since we arrived at the shelter after a good 11 mile hike. It was 3:45 p.m. and the temperature went from 90° to 65° because the rain came pelting down. It rained most of the night and its hypnotic, rhythm lulled us into a weary, but satisfying, slumber.

JUNE 22, 1984 - as if on cue, quit raining by morning. We had a good breakfast, but so did a more than friendly mouse that had found his way into my pack. Oh well, maybe was payment for God's excellent timing with the rain storm.

28

The trail was a log road and made good walking until we reached Red Clay Gap. The weather was cooling from 80° - 60° as we carefully worked our way over some rock slides, only to begin the climb to 4,025 feet over Blue Mountain. On the way down, was steep with more rock slides. We were a couple of out-of-condition hikers that were rapidly getting whipped into shape, so it wasn't as bad as it would have been a week earlier. Nothing seems to go perfectly out there, no matter what. Steve broke his glasses and I broke my camera. All in one day! Our bodies were faring pretty well but the equipment wasn't doing so good. No more pictures on this hike.

Bill again, hiked in about 3/4 mile to meet us. We dropped into Unicoi Gap, 2,949 feet, missing by only a few miles, Brasstown Bald, 4,784 feet, the highest point in the State of Georgia. That's one climb I'm glad we passed. We put in 9.6 miles of hiking this time. Not too shabby! And we all got to spend another night together.

JUNE 23, 1984 - we started the climb up Rocky Mountain to 4,107 feet, and a gentle shower bathed us on the way up. Fortunately the trail was fairly smooth without too many rocks. Down and then up again to Tray Mountain, 4,430 feet. Believe it or not, we were in the clouds and couldn't see a thing. We were blind as bats for a while going down the mountain. Naturally, it was a rocky and steep descent.

It was a good time to stop at the Montray Shelter where we ate our lunch. We had a brief conversation with a man and woman camped there before moving on down the trail. The trail was much better as we met a lot more hikers going south. Since Steve and I were heading north we exchanged information with the southbounders about what was ahead and continued on. I was to learn this is a common occurrence on the ever- changing A.T. Wow! There were some of the largest ferns I have ever seen, growing along that section of the trail.

A friendly sky removed the dark curtain over the sun, warming the air to 80°. Working our way to Addis Gap, 3,340 feet, we went another 0.3 miles to the shelter where we found a picnic table with a beautiful stream flowing by. A fire pit in front prompted us to build our first fire to keep the knats away. Someone had written a message on the wall of the shelter. It said, "Iced in for three days, because of an ice storm".

I didn't realize the shelter was so close to a road, until darkness began to descend on us. Cars kept coming in with some very strange people. One group caused Steve and I to be concerned for our safety. They kept whooping and hollering until all of a sudden it was silent. I believe, at that moment, they saw our fire. We were tense and quiet as they seemed to be trying to decide what to do, harass us or leave.

I prayed and truly believe the good Lord kept them from coming over to our shelter. Doors slammed, engines revved and we smelled and heard tires as the cars peeled out of the area. I didn't sleep well after that experience and sometime during the night it started raining again. It was spooky and I could not help thinking of all the animals in the forest and the obvious hazards we had encountered. The greatest fear we felt was from the animal, man. Isn't that pathetic? Pat us on the back though, we hiked 11.7 miles on that stretch.

JUNE 24, 1984 - groggy from lack of sleep and with great dread, we moved out into the rain. Nature's timing was off and I was worried the trail would be slippery as we began hiking. It took us one hour to climb

Kelly Knob, 4,276 feet. Poor Steve was awfully slow, but determined to continue. Jokingly, I gave him the trail name of "Slowpoke". The Trail got a lot easier on the way to Dick's Creek Gap, 2,675 feet. Our eyes lit up as we saw Bill waiting. He was surprised to see us coming in from the rain.

With mixed feelings, I knew it was time to call the hike off, even though we were only eight miles from the North Carolina line and about to leave Chatahouchie National Forest. We only had a couple more days we could hike anyway and I wasn't sure if Bill could reach us where we would end up. We were worn out. It was time to go home. I was so proud of my Slowpoke. He had hiked 72.3 miles with me over some pretty tough terrain. How many of you walk 1 mile a day, on sidewalks?

Not long after we got home, all the bad experiences were fading rapidly as I started planning for 1985. Good ol' Slowpoke volunteered to hike with me again. Practically every Sunday evening, a twelve year old neighbor boy named Todd, walked to church with me. He said he'd like to go hiking. My eyebrows raised with the cunning of a coyote. I'm convinced this disease is catching and I am a willing carrier.

Ha!, another thirteen year old from church, who prefers to be called E.J., was feeling the symptoms that seem to begin with a funny itch. He wanted to go hiking with me also. As a boy scout, he had actually done some backpacking. Guess what? I had my group set up for 1985. Bill and another one of his horse buddies, Glen, would take their horses and ride the side trails while we backpacked. I was as excited as I was the first day this all started.

31

JUNE 16, 1985 - 9:45 a.m., we all arrived at Dick's Creek Gap in Georgia and immediately got organized. The hiking group was son, Steve (Slowpoke) Todd and E.J. Taking up where we left off we began with quite a bit of climbing. More up and down mountains, at last making it to Bly Gap, 3,840 feet. Slowpoke and I were ecstatic at finally entering North Carolina. He and I gingerly stepped over what we felt was the Georgia, North Carolina border. The two boys laughed until we explained how we had just barely missed this experience at the end of the last hike. We were getting a little tired, so we took a refreshing break, enjoying the experience of nature.

After our rest, we began a steep climb up to Courthouse Bald. At 6:30 p.m. we got to Muskrat Shelter. It was an A-frame building with a small bubbling creek running by. After figuring we had actually hiked twelve miles our first day out, we felt justified to be very, very tired. By the time we finished supper and cleaned up our cooking gear, the sun was rapidly turning down the lantern in the Nantahala Forest. Under a beautiful starlit sky and wonderful weather, our talk became jumbled words and deep, peaceful sleep took over.

JUNE 17, 1985 - at 7:30 a.m., we started hiking. The night's rest made the trail feel deceptively easier, compared to yesterday's hike. I told the boys to not get too careless as the trail became extremely rocky upon leaving Wateroak Gap. The descent into Deep Gap was made without incident, where Bill and Glen were waiting at USFS 71 (United States Forest Service Road 71). It wasn't a planned rendezvous, so it was a pleasant surprise, especially since they had some left over fried chicken. Even though it was a little water logged from being in their ice chest, it sure tasted good. Replenishing the food and supplies needed for our packs, we were on our way again. My husband couldn't resist hiking almost all the way to the Standing Indian Shelter with us, before turning back, since it was scenic with a beautiful stream. He loves the mountain streams and it took some effort to get him to turn back. I think he keeps hoping he'll find that stream with golden trout jumping up. After he left, we climbed fantastic Standing Indian Mountain. Wow, 5,498 feet high! Believe it or not, it wasn't a bad hike.

If you ever spend much time in the Smoky Mountains or the Appalachian Trail in general, don't be surprised at how often it rains. It looked like rain again. If it isn't rain it usually mists or fogs, especially in the early morning hours. That's why the variety of floral and other growth is so great. At any rate, we opted for a quick lunch. It did rain later, so whether we liked it or not, we got to use our ponchos.

Like soaked rats, we walked into the Carter Gap Shelter at 3:15 p.m. It was good to get a chance to dry out a bit. After a short discussion, we decided to have an early supper and get a well-deserved rest. We had hiked 13 miles and regardless of how many hours there is in a day, we had reached our limit. Not too bad, all things considered.

Other hikers drifted in, camping out on the hill. Some were south bound, so I talked to a few of them about where we had been and what it was like up ahead. Hikers, even though basically seeking solitude, are generally sociable people. The Mountains in Nantahala National Forest are definitely different than the ones in Chattahoochee Forest in Georgia. For one thing, they are taller. Natures chorus of rain drops falling, played its usual hypnotic lullaby all night long. Sleep came early, as a result.

JUNE 18, 1985 - we had checked into the shelter early, so we got a real early start that morning. The rain stopped as if on cue, making the trail pretty easy and relaxing to walk on.

We were carrying the larger Optimus 111 backpacking stove. I was able to get the cooking done faster on two stoves. I'll tell you something, cooking is a chore when you're home and tired out, but it is not always a pleasant experience after hiking 10 to 15 miles day after day, either. We experienced another form of moisture. It was like rain starting to fall and in mid-course changing its mind and remaining stationary in the air. In short, it got foggy.

Then there was good old Albert Mountain, 5,220 elevation, where we got to experience our first hand-over-hand climbing. Slowly, we helped each other over the rocks. The fog stayed with us all the way to the top. I'd like to tell you about the scenery from that elevation but all I can say is it was like being partially submerged in water with just enough oxygen in between to breathe. There was a fire tower on the mountain. Normally we would have climbed up to increase the view, but the water would have just gotten thicker and the oxygen thinner.

Going down to Wallace Gap near Old 64 Highway wasn't too bad, since we only dropped 482 feet to, 3,738 elevation. Reliable Bill was waiting there for us. Riding in the camper was a strange feeling after all the hiking. We drove to the Standing Indian Campground and upon arriving there I had to wonder whose adventure this is supposed to be. My husband had a bigger story than ours.

It seems he dropped his eye glasses into a hole in an outhouse. I have no idea why he took such delight in telling us such a humiliating story. He and his buddy,

34

Glen, had actually fished them out of the hole. That was one fishing trip I would like to have seen. I kept pushing him away from me, for various reasons, as I told him, "Please don't tell us how big the one was that got away." We had a lot of fun teasing him but weariness crept in and that was where we spent the night. The fact that my little group had hiked 12.8 miles almost got lost after the fishing story.

JUNE 19, 1985 - this morning, Bill took us back to Wallace Gap and at 7:45 a.m. we started hiking under a clear blue sky. The temperature was cool, so we made good time from old 64 to the new Hwy. 64 at Winding Stair Gap. The guys in the camper carried our packs to that point. Picking them up and saying our good-byes, we started our climb up the mountain. The boys and I ate lunch close to a trail that lead to Siler Bald Shelter.

We beat Bill and Glen to Wayah Gap, 4,180 feet. While we waited, a little shower fell on us. We spent the night at Wayah Crest Picnic Area after a healthy 9.1 mile hike.

JUNE 20, 1985 - we rested until 8:00 a.m. and began a climb of 2 1/2 miles. It tapered off for a short while, then climbing to Wayah Bald, 5,336 feet, we found a small park on top with a lookout tower. There were some spectacular views. Lofty clouds between the mountains made the trees below look like armies of pigmies. Streams, that you miss when on a lower level, are easy to see from that high, trickling down the gullies. Bill and Glen surprised us by meeting us there on horse back.

Another exquisite sunny, cool day was inspiring us to move on. The boys were feeling their oats, so we seemed to be making better time. We got into Cold Spring Shelter at 1:50 p.m., elevation 4,760 feet, and I couldn't believe my figures when I checked our miles. We had hiked 10.2 miles. Girls, if you're looking for a real diet program, let me introduce you to hiking.

JUNE 21, 1985 - got an early start on the trail, 6:15 a.m. to be exact. After a quickie breakfast, we hiked .4 mile to the top of Copper Bald, 5,200 feet. Then it was down a narrow, rocky trail to Tellico Gap, 3,850 feet. Gaps are as high as many of the mountains in Georgia. Up again to Wesser Bald, 4,627 feet, where we did climb the fire tower located there.

Beautiful views were making the trip worth the effort. That is what it's all about. Going down the steep, rough hill, we met fifteen boy scouts coming up the mountain. Panting, we exchanged hellos and good lucks and moved on. Eager Beaver Bill hiked up to meet us just past the Rufus Morgan Shelter and then walked out with us. More and more, I realize he really wanted to be with Steve and me all along. The thought made me feel a little bad, but he knew his leg just didn't permit it. Besides that, we were to learn that his backup was almost a necessity and helped get me hiking companions in the end.

Arriving at the Nantahala River, we saw kayakers and rafters enjoying the swift, white water. Our pleasure was dampened as we crossed the bridge. We were extremely tired and knew we were almost finished for the day.

Triumphantly we arrived at Wesser, North Carolina, at 3:15 p.m. Bill and Glen had pitched camp near some railroad tracks close to the Wesser Falls. We were now at 1,740 feet in elevation. The oxygen was rich and helped us to sleep like babies, after a respectable 11.6 mile hike.

JUNE 22, 1985 - eager to get started, we ate and were on our way by 6:15 a.m. Longingly, Bill walked with us for a short distance. Having him with me on the trail was good for a while. The climbs were giving us a real workout as we began to suck air and sweat profusely. About half way up the mountain we had to take a break before climbing the remaining 2,610 feet, to the top of Swim Bald Mountain, elevation 4,350 feet. Sassafras Shelter was a welcome sight with its sweet spring gently running behind it. As rough as it had been, it was only 12:15 p.m. This was still our shortest one-day hike so far, at 6.8 miles. The plus side was, we had all afternoon to rest. You need days like that once in a while. For the next two days, while we finished our hike, Bill and Glen went to the Smoky Mountain National Park to ride their horses.

JUNE 23, 1985 - 6:30 a.m., we made a good climb up Cheoah Bald, 5,062 feet. Even though it rained hard during the night, the views of the mountain peaks were not unlike islands jutting up through an ocean of clouds.

It was warm on the real steep climbs. Breathing was hard, we were sweating again and dehydrating, causing us to drink a lot of water. Water was getting scarce along the trail and we found ourselves sharing drinks from our *botas* or wine skins. We used them instead of canteens. I really like them, but they are harder to fill because of the small opening.

The trail was marked poorly today and there were a lot of trees blown down. One big tree was blown down on the steep trail. We couldn't go around it either way due to the heavy underbrush, so we took our packs off and crawled over it. This sucker was huge! We were carrying a three-man tent. That didn't make it any easier.

At 4:30 p.m. we got to Cody Gap, 3,660 feet and gladly made camp. Slowpoke and I set the tent up, while Todd and E.J. went 200 yards down hill to a nice running spring for water. It had been a hard day and we still hiked 11.5 miles. After a good supper and the luxury of more than enough water for a change, we crawled into the tent early. Make no mistake, we were worn out, but that was not the primary reason for seeking shelter. Bugs were real getting bad. In spite of the little tormentors, we got a good night's sleep.

JUNE 24, 1985 - Slowpoke, E.J., and Todd took down the tent while I fixed breakfast. This would be our ninth day on the trail and our last. At 6:30 a.m., we started hiking, crossing Yellow Creek Road. We came to a burned over area. A crew was maintaining the trail in this area.

Cable Gap, the next shelter, was one of the smallest we had seen. The boys liked it, because it had wire bunks, but we only had time for a break. About one-half mile down the trail, I discovered I had left my wineskin at the Shelter. The boys got another break, while old "Den Mama" went back for it.

It was a big climb up Yellow Creek Mountain, 3,786 feet, where we were rewarded with a fantastic view of Fontana Dam. It was so impressive, we stopped and ate our lunch. Large rocks presented formidable obstacles that we had to get over for the next six miles to the Dam. I thought we were never going to get down that mountain.

Bill and Glen, after their horseback ride in the Great Smoky Mountain National Park, were waiting. Slowpoke and I were the last ones in, our feet were hurting. We enjoyed the free hot shower at Fontana Dam. The two brave boys, E.J. and Todd who had stuck with us, bought some souvenirs before we headed for home.

The hike ended at 1:30 p.m. The last day on the trail had been warm and sunny. Should I say, we were heartbroken to be leaving? Not on your life. That's one of the greatest joys of hiking. It makes you happy when it's over. What is a moment of happiness worth? I was proud of everyone. We had hiked a total of 98.5 miles. Fontana Dam's elevation? For the record, 1,550 feet.

Make a joyful noise unto the Lord, all the earth. Psalm 100:1

1986

JUNE 13, 1986 - hiking must be enjoyable. Otherwise, Slowpoke, Todd and E.J. would not have been so anxious to go again. Even E.J.'s mother, Patti, wanted to go with us. As I said before, some hikers do it for the solitude. Not me, like having someone with me for many reasons, not the least of which is safety.

Fortunately, we didn't have any major problems in 1985. This speaks well of a backpacker, so I feel great. It was decided that Bill and Glen would take their horses to ride the side trails again, so at 5:00 a.m. the following morning, it was good-bye to our home in Verona, Missouri.

We arrived at Deep Creek Horse Camp in the Great Smoky Mountain National Park at 11:00 p.m. It was a long drive for one day but if the rest of the trip went as good, thank the Lord, we won't have any problems. I hiked the Smoky Mountain National in August, 1974, and my goal now was to complete the Appalachian Trail so legitimately I could skip that section, since it didn't mean that much to anyone else anyway.

JUNE 14, 1986 - we drove to the trail head at Big Pigeon River, located by Interstate 40, on the northeast edge of Smoky Mountain Park with an elevation of 1,400 feet. We would head north into the Pisgah National Forest.

Slowpoke, Todd, E.J., Patti, and I started our hike, leaving Bill and Glen behind, to enjoy their horses in the Great Smoky Mountain National Park.

At 8:00 a.m., we began climbing for several miles up Snow Bird Mountain, 4,263 feet. Our condition was manifest on this first climb and we were really dragging. The fact that it was hot and humid didn't help much either. The heat was draining our energy. We did reach the summit and the trail got much easier as we made our way to Groundhog Shelter, our first camp.

It wasn't anything special but it had a picnic table in front and wood floors inside. A small stream was only 100 yards away and it had pretty good water. That was all that mattered. It was 3:11 p.m. and I was disappointed that we had only hiked 8 miles.

Slowpoke reminded me that it had been a hard, but pretty good first day on the trail. We had done worse on previous trips and everyone felt okay, so I wasn't going to discourage anyone. I thought, however, Pisgah National Forest would be easier. This particular trail was like a fickle woman, in that it was sometimes in North Carolina and other times in Tennessee, so It was hard to tell when you were in one state or the other or even on the state lines. Well, I was tired and having trouble seeing my notes. My body said it was time to hit the hay.

JUNE 15, 1986 - Groundhog Shelter had been down the hill from the trail so we hiked the 0.2 miles back up before proceeding up the gradual climb to Deep Gap at 2,900 feet. It was a little less than 2,000 feet to the 3,840 elevation of Haromon Den Mountain.

Something was starting to go very wrong. Slowpoke and Patti were having a lot of trouble hiking and Todd was acting like he had a grudge against the world.

41

This was making progress awfully slow. By the time we reached Lemon Gap at 3,550 feet, my Slowpoke was barely moving. We still had a climb of 730 feet to Walnut Mountain, 4,280 feet elevation, where we would reach our next shelter.

Taking the tent from Slowpoke to lighten his load, I went on ahead, up the climb to the shelter. Leaving my pack there, I went back to get Slowpoke's. What's a mom to do? With no load, he made it the rest of the way up the mountain. As luck would have it, the shelter was full of hikers, so we had to pitch our tent.

The group was worn out and it was late in the evening. To top it off, the spring for water left a lot to be desired. Todd's attitude had improved a little, so he and E.J. fetched the water. Boy, was I glad this day was about over! As soon as we finished supper, we all were glad to turn in with very little conversation. It had been a rough 11 miles and not a bad showing, all things considered. Maybe it had been something in the air, like a pollen or something. Tomorrow would be better, I hoped.

JUNE 16, 1986 - as I got up that morning, I eyeballed everybody carefully to see if there were any signs of the bad omen left over from yesterday. We decided to hold off breakfast until we got to the next stream. The water was terrible at that shelter. It was only 1.7 miles to where we crossed a bubbly brook. Quietly, we fixed our breakfast. There was still some tension in the air. The bunch managed the climb to the summit of Bluff Mountain, 4,686 feet. It was so covered with hardwoods, you couldn't see anything but trees in every direction.

Was I relieved when we met a thru-hiker. (That's a hiker that is hiking the entire trail at one time.) I asked him if he would consider delivering a note to my husband, who was waiting for us at Hot Springs. He graciously accepted my request. I wrote Bill telling him about the problems Slowpoke and Patti were having and not to worry if we didn't make it on schedule. I told him we would spend the night at Deer Park Mountain Shelter. Patti had to rest every few feet and Slowpoke wasn't doing much better. Todd started throwing tantrums again. I just didn't understand this. He had done so well, last year. Hiking is strenuous enough without having to handle a disturbed young boy. Luckily, the trail was mostly downhill after Bluff Mountain.

Arriving at Deer Park Mountain Shelter, to my surprise, everyone wanted to go the 3.2 miles on to Hot Springs. Todd and E.J. got into high gear. They were like horses heading for home. I was glad to see a hostel there. Maintained by Jesuit residents, they only charged us $2.00 a piece for our shower and it was worth every penny. I waited a while before I told my fellow hikers we had hiked 13 miles.

Bill had received the message from the thru-hiker and was worried. I learned something about creating panic, he wasn't expecting us and I knew by the look in his eyes that he was relieved. I never thought I would ever say this, but I was glad to call the hike off, even though we had two more days left. After our showers, we traveled to the horse camp in the Cades Cove Area of the Great Smoky Mountain National Park, where we spent the night.

JUNE 17, 1986 - the horse camp was nestled back in the woods on the north end of Cades Cove. Bill and Glen rode their horses but the hikers were slow getting around. Everyone, but Slowpoke, decided to go sight-seeing around that unique area. Slowpoke wanted to visit all the old homesteads around Cades Cove. Against my better judgment, I allowed him to hike alone.

The rest of us decided to hike out to Abrams Falls. It was relatively easy compared to the actual A.T. The 11-mile loop road at Cades Cove was fascinating and very pretty as it took us past open fields, quaint pioneer homesteads and little frame churches, where mountain people lived and worshipped almost unnoticed for a century.

Late in the afternoon I was getting awfully worried. Slowpoke hadn't made it back to camp. Like a lot of mothers, I knew something was wrong. We found him at the south end of the loop road, so sick he couldn't move. He had taken no water with him, in 80 degree temperature. Taking him back to camp, we laid him next to the camp fire. A Tagamet I gave him seemed to settle his stomach. He needed to be watched closely, since I was certain he almost had a heat stroke because of dehydration.

Can anyone imagine my panic when his eyes rolled up at me and uttered, " Bye-Bye, Mom. I'm gone." Lord, he honestly thought he was dying! It wasn't as bad as he thought, but he was one sick puppy. As the evening shade descended, the Spirit of death decided to leave Slowpoke for another day. The prayers of a mom are powerful!

The next morning, Bill and Glen rode their horses up to the A.T. The rest of us, minus Slowpoke who was feeling much better, hiked up the Bote Mountain Trail to Spence Field Shelter. We climbed the whole 6.6 miles and it was beautiful as we followed Laurel Creek for a while. Then we hiked through beech and birch forests that blended into laurel and hemlock. It was an easy hike back down the mountain. Back at camp, Slowpoke was doing just fine and actually complaining because he had to stay there.

That evening on the far end of the horse camp, we were rewarded with a visit from a mother bear and four cubs, foraging for food. I thought another mama bear had to be lurking somewhere. Four cubs is just too many for one mother. A ranger, we met later, told us that though it is rare, all four of the cubs belonged to her. It was a sight to see the playful cubs with the busy mother doing her best to keep track of them.

We headed for home the next morning. It was some kind of trip, and the last time I was to hike with Todd, Patty and E.J. Patty is still teaching art, E.J. earned his Eagle Scout badge on July 28, 1991 and Todd, bless his heart, still needs help with his behavior.

"You will go out in joy and be led forth in peace;
the mountains and hills will burst into song before you
and all the trees of the field
will clap their hands." Isaiah 55:12

1987

Bill and I spent some time riding horses on the trails in the State of Michigan where our friends, Dick and Lida are residents. I was thrilled when Lida suggested she would enjoy hiking, since I was looking for someone to finish the A.T. with me. They are wonderful people. A deal was struck. It didn't hurt that Dick would be good company for Bill.

Our pastor's son, Rodney, was voicing a desire to go hiking and Slowpoke wasn't about to quit, even though it would have been in his best interest to do so. I kind of wished he had not liked hiking so much, but he is a courageous young man and I guess it is in his genes. After the last trip I had reason to be concerned, so I encouraged everybody to try to get in shape by hiking every day, when possible. Slowpoke was already a problem and refused to physically prepare himself. Yes, I would pay for that stubbornness.

I purchased new backpacks for Slowpoke and myself. They were more rigid than the ones we had in 1972. The one I bought for me is called a *Universal Backpack*. The frame is shaped in such a way as to allow it to stand alone when taken off. It was a real improvement. Slowpoke's was called a Coleman Pack. It fit his back better than the previous one, since the frame was plastic and flexed when he moved.

Even though I would be hiking on ground I had already covered, my plan was to hike back through the Smoky Mountain National Park from north to south. The reason for this was a hope that Slowpoke, Lida and Rodney would enjoy the beauty of the park as much as I did on my first big hike in 1974. Just maybe this hike would infect Lida and get into her blood, as much as it has mine. Slowpoke was ready and willing to hike that section of the A.T. Bill loved riding the horses in the park, so he and Dick would have a ball on the great Smoky horse trails.

JUNE 6, 1987 - we met Lida and Dick at Big Pigeon River just off I-40 in Tennessee, where we set up camp by a bridge. Lida, Slowpoke, Rodney and I began hiking southwest on the A.T. Most of the first day was spent climbing. At Mt. Cammerer, 5,025 feet, we took a side trail, approximately .06 of a mile to a stone tower. There was a breathtaking, panoramic view of the Great Smoky Mountains, much like what angels must see when looking down on we earthbound mortals.

We had to make ourselves turn away and continue hiking down to Low Gap, 4,242 feet, where Bill and Dick had ridden in on the Walnut Bottoms Trail from the Big Creek Horse Camp to pay us a short visit. Seeing Bill, however brief, always made me feel secure that I had a small link to civilization. Our hiking group then proceeded up to the Cosby Knob Lean-to, and gave ourselves a well-deserved rest for the night.

JUNE 7, 1987 - it was pretty good going that day since we did very little climbing. When we got to the Maddron Bald Trail, things looked familiar to me and I realized it was a trail I hiked in 1974, coming from Cosby

Campground up to the A.T. There was one big difference that broke my heart. The timber was dying. It seems there had been a war between the *"woolly adelgid* (a close relative of the aphid) *disease"* and the forest. The forest lost.

The trees, at this ghostly stage of their deaths, looked like huge toothpicks among the green carpet of undergrowth. It was so sad. I pondered Mother Nature's purpose until we arrived at the Tri-Corner Knob Shelter. Unlike the poor forest, our adventurers seemed to be holding up pretty good.

JUNE 8, 1987 - the sun was bearing down, shinning brightly with no special mercy and it was affecting Slowpoke most of all. Our two horse riders, Bill and Dick, arrived ahead of us at Hughes Ridge Trail. Like the cowboys of the long gone past, they had spent the night at Towstring Horse Camp talking over their adventures. Most important, they were our tie to safety so it was good to see them.

On the other hand, we had no time to tarry as we set out for Charlie's Bunion. When we arrived, we took a bypass trail around it. Slowpoke was overheating again, so I told him to slow down. Leaving him behind with the rest of the group, I went on to the Ice Water Springs Lean-To, dropped my pack and went back to help him. He was in good hands with the others, but mothers feel they cannot be replaced. I have been tired before and didn't feel I had any energy left, but still went back for my Slowpoke. When I reached them, they were only a mile from the shelter.

When we got him to the Lean-to, he lay down and the rest of us did our chores. I had never stayed at this shelter before but had heard it was popular with hikers. I could see why. It was a pleasant place with a lovely spring nearby. I began fixing a pizza meal for supper. The crust was some dried toasted bread with a sauce made of tomato sauce that I poured over the crust --- instant pizza. The sauce was too thin and immediately I knew I had way too much.

You can't feed the animals in the park and yet I needed to dispose of the sauce some way. I got this bright idea of slinging the runny stuff over the bushes in front of the Shelter. Sounds gross, but it was effective. Before too long the odor brought an inquisitive bear into the bushes, sniffing around like they do. This caused everyone in the Shelter to line up outside and start taking pictures of the bear. After a while, the creature got tired of all the attention and indignantly wandered up the hill in back of the Shelter to again enjoy solitude. He didn't know he had become an instant celebrity and had been the most photographed bear in the country! He will be spotlighted on the pages of a lot of photo albums. It was an exciting way to end the day.

JUNE 9, 1987 - the rest helped Slowpoke to improve, so we hiked another 3 miles to New Found Gap, where U.S. Highway 441 winds its way through the middle of the Great Smoky Mountain National Park. Bill and Dick waited there with our new supply of food.

Wisdom was crying out to me to make Slowpoke stay with the horse riders. He was determined to go on and it would have taken more persuasion than I cared to invest. Sometimes I can't stand the fact that he is every bit as bull headed as his Mama. Strangely, I respect that and let him go. He did much better to the Mt. Collin's Shelter where we pitched our camp for the night. On into the wee hours of morning, the night owls voiced their opinion that their day was just beginning

JUNE 10, 1987 - things went pretty well to mighty Clingman's Dome elevation of 6,643 feet, the highest point in Tennessee. We were above Denver, Colorado, the "mile high" city. To take full advantage of the view, we climbed the observation tower. Amazing! You could look clear back to Newfound Gap, where we started the day before.

Blanket Mountain to the north and Andrews Bald to the south, were easily visible. You can actually see into seven states on a clear day. Even though our view was awesome, this was not one of those days. Fog began moving in and blocked what view we did have, so we followed a narrow open crest, gradually working our way down. The trail was getting hazardous along the crest, so we chose to go a short distance out of our way, to avoid some dangerous ledges. Finally, we reached the crest of Siler's Bald, 5,620 feet. We then descended to its Lean-To.

Later near sundown, two rangers came by the shelter wearing large head lamps, carrying rifles and walking the trail looking for wild hogs. Evidently the park is getting over populated with the creatures, so they were going to shoot some of them. They said the night hour was the best time to hunt them. One ranger said they would like to get rid of all of them since they can be dangerous to hikers. Jokingly, Lida asked if we could take some home with us. The other ranger stated, "Sure, if they don't take you home with them first." They made the evening less boring and were a lot of fun to listen to.

JUNE 11, 1987 - when we dragged ourselves out into the misty morning, it was obvious we weren't breaking any speed records. Chattering about the evening with the rangers, we made our way to Thunderhead Mountain, 5,530 feet. On the way down, we spotted Bill and Dick in the Gap below. It looked like they were going to try to surprise us. I told the others to keep the talking down so we could sneak up and turn the tables on them. As always, it was good to see them but the element of surprise had little affect. We took time for a short visit, then it was off to Spence Field Shelter. The would-be cowboys rode back to Cades Cove Horse Camp to the west about five miles. The hike to Spence Field was a combination of peaceful meadows and forest.

JUNE 12, 1987 - the hike to Birch Spring Shelter was more downhill so we arrived early in the afternoon. The shelter sat down in a hole and the inside was dark and damp. Later on, other hikers began arriving and the shelter was filling up fast. The buildings are designed to hold twelve people, but by nightfall, we had fourteen. Somehow we all managed to sleep inside.

JUNE 13, 1987 - it was early in the morning when we made our way down the mountain, stopping at the Shuckstack Fire Tower. There was a different view of the beautiful Fontana Lake that we had started from on an earlier trip. The crest line of the Smokys from Thunderhead to Clingman's Dome was spread out before us.

Bill and Dick were waiting for us at Fontana Dam. It was a proud day to have conquered the hike across the Smokys. The shower at Fontana Dam was almost as enjoyable as being in my own bath at home.

Make a joyful noise unto the Lord, all the earth. Psalm 100:1

1988

Lida wanted to hike with me again this year and I am elated beyond belief. Even Slowpoke wanted to go again. Now, the problem is to get them motivated to get out and hike before we go, so that we can accomplish more. At the rate I had been going, I will not get the Appalachian Trail hiked in my lifetime. On the other hand, I don't want to chase off hiking companions.

As a result of my devotion each year I hike, I was getting stronger than the year before. The trail is tough and you need all the strength you can muster! I would like to see all who hike with me getting in the same physical and mental condition.

During my trips, I have noticed other hikers on the trails with dogs. Seeing the wisdom in this, I got a Samoyed pup. Training him to hike with me was quite a chore. The pleasure he was to give me made it well worth the effort. I named him Chief Trail Walker, but Bill and I naturally called him Chief. He had a little red dog pack and he carried his own food supplies. That was pretty doggone good for a six month old puppy and he looked so cute.

JUNE 1, 1988 - Bill and his friend Dick, brought their horses to ride support on the side trails. We started at Hot Springs, North Carolina, where we had ended in 1986. Dick and Lida were waiting and it was so good to see them. A suspicion inside me made me believe some last minute problem would arise to keep them from taking part in this adventure.

It was strange to start a hike in a town. The A.T. runs right through Hot Springs, North Carolina in the Pisgah National Forest. About two miles out, we climbed steep switchbacks to Lover's Leap Ridge. This huge rock face was supposedly named by the Cherokee Indians when an Indian Maid called, Mist-on-the Mountain, jumped from the crag to her happy hunting grounds. It seems her northern lover, Magwa, was killed by a jealous rival named Lone Wolf. What we women won't do for our men.

From that point we had outstanding views of Hot Springs and the French Broad River Valley below. Moving on, we saw some beautiful mountain laurel in bloom as we crossed open meadows. After 10.7 miles, we came to the Spring Mountain Shelter, elevation 3,300 feet. Needless to say, we were all tired out and ready for a rest.

JUNE 2, 1988 - Chief was one happy dog, on a trail most dogs will never see. We went downhill, for the most part, from the shelter to Allen Gap, 2,234 feet. Bill and Dick were so sweet. They had bought us some ice cream from a little, rock store on the highway. Eating the ice cream before it melted, we left the two gallant men behind in order to hike another 1.6 miles to where they had set up camp. It was a small settlement, nestled back in the mountains. Bill met us again by a dirt road where we saw a quaint little sign that read:

RUBINSVILLE
CITY LIMITS
POP - 9
SPEED LIMIT
15 MPH
NO WHEEL TAX

They had their own log church where a circuit preacher came by once a month. It was a neat community. The setting was ideal for me to break the news to Slowpoke that it was a good idea for him to quit hiking. He was just having too many problems and was ready to quit anyway. He is a brave guy and took the advice better than I had anticipated.

Lida and I took a short break, then with a heavy heart, but lighter feet, we continued. Ascending through a strand of white pine trees, I told Lida how much I loved walking through these trees. The needles are like a soft carpet under foot. We got to Little Laurel Shelter that had been rebuilt of stone in 1967. Fixing our meal was enjoyable. Just the two of us talking *girl talk* until drowsiness ended the fun.

JUNE 3, 1988 - refreshed and ready to go, we immediately started the ascent to Camp Creek Bald, 4,844 feet. This was to be the biggest climb of the day as we hiked through a patch of dense rhododendron, that In full bloom are so beautiful. There is nothing like two good friends experiencing nature this way.

At Jerry Cabin Shelter, we stopped for lunch. Without Slowpoke, we were making good time. The trail descended into Chestnut Log Gap, 4,150 feet, then a steep ascent to Big Butt Mountain, 4,898 feet. We came to a blue-blazed trail leading 100 yards to a spring in a ravine, where we got water.

Continuing on to a level spot, we found a single grave with headstones at each end. One read, "Wm. Shelton, Co. E, 2 N.C. Inf." and the other "David Shelton, Co. C,3 N.C. Mtd. Inf." The men were killed here during the Civil War. Their lonely gravestones were erected about 1915. We thought it would be fun to spend the night here so we put up our tent. Like two young girls at a slumber party, we were looking for weird. For me, I think I found just that. Spending the night in that very strange cemetery caused creepy things to happen to the mind. During the night, visions of the battles crept in and out of my mind. Awakening sometime during the night, I could have sworn I heard eerie sounds of a terrible war. Imagination? I don't know.

JUNE 4, 1988 - with daylight at hand and my imagination under control, we packed up early. The trail was pretty easy and made an enjoyable hike. We stopped at New Flint Gap Shelter for a break. Afterwards, while dropping down the mountain, we came upon my old buddy Slowpoke, hiking in to meet us. Bill and Dick met us on down the trail at Devil Fork Gap, 3,107 feet.

Leaving our packs with them, we slackpacked to Sam's Gap, taking Slowpoke with us. It was a steady climb to Lick Rock, 4,579 feet, then a descent by switchbacks to Rice Gap, 3,800 feet. We climbed along a narrow ridge to Hogback Ridge Shelter where we found three older men from a trail crew. They were putting a Bronze plaque on the new Hogback Ridge Shelter and stopped long enough to give Slowpoke a well needed Gatorade drink. A little more than two miles to Sam's Gap we found Bill and Dick. The guys treated us to supper in a little cafe. We liked that! It saddened me that Slowpoke liked hiking so much, but he just wouldn't get himself in shape and that was to be his last hike.

JUNE 5, 1988 - leaving the guys behind, Lida and I hiked back to the A.T. Not long after, we passed an abandoned talc mine. It is a soft mineral with a soapy feel. Climbing a 4,440 ft. knob, we came upon a meadow from which you could see Big Bald Mountain off in the distance. Hiking five more miles, we came to a blue-blazed trail that took us around the southeast side of Big Bald. There was a big sign that said

"DETOUR" - BIG BALD MOUNTAIN PEREGRINE FALCON PROJECT - TENNESSEE'S EFFORT TO SAVE AN ENDANGERED SPECIES - 1987-1989

Following the blue-blazed trail one mile to a place called Big Stamp, we looked back and saw the free-flying falcons over Big Bald. Slackpacking through here made for pretty easy hiking. Descending to Whistling Gap at 3,840 ft., we ascended toward High Rocks, then skirted around a rocky cliff. The trail going down was so steep there was a safety cable to maneuver through switchbacks. A pleasant stream joined us through the woods. Arriving at Big Creek, we found the mournful Slowpoke sitting on a log bridge. It cheered him up a little bit to act as our guide to US 19 W at 3,200 ft., where Bill and Dick waited.

JUNE 6, 1988 - it was a restful night. Lida and my now trusty dog, Chief, and I would slackpack today. Conditioned to carry the heavy packs, our feet felt like they had wings without them. Climbing steeply at times, through lovely rhododendron that abundantly populates that area, the trail was pretty nice for the next 4.5 miles.

At No Business Knob Shelter, there was an elderly backpacker resting. Visiting with him, made me hope I would be as active as he when I reach my twilight years. Dick was highpointing (climbing the highest point in each of the forty eight continuous states) and he only had two left. This pleasant old gentleman had hiked the 2,600 mile Pacific Crest National Scenic Trail from Mexico to Canada and now trying to complete the A.T. What a courageous guy!

It was time for a break, so we stopped near a clear spring. Refreshing ourselves and filling our wine skins, we took off for Cliff Ridge, where we found a gorgeous view of Nolichucky River flowing below. Dick passed us there without any effort. As I watched him disappear down the trail, I doubted that I would ever see him again. This guy knew where he was going and why. How many of us could answer those questions?

Descending down a steep hillside by switchbacks and rhododendrons we crossed Nolichucky River where we found our guys camped close by. Slowpoke said he had walked in and met Dick, the speedy old hiker at the shelter. Old Dick had impressed him as much as he had me. After meeting him he had walked back to camp. It concerned me that he would strike out on his own like that, but he's just that way. I wonder where he gets it?

The weather was a little warm so we took a swim in the river. Chief got his first swim in a river. It took a little coaching! He didn't seem to mind afterwards. We were all refreshed.

JUNE 7, 1988 - we hadn't gone a hundred feet when I got one shoestring tangled in the other shoe hook. As a result, I took a painful tumble into the gravel. Chief took the fall as an invitation to play. Jumping on my poor old body he began licking my face. A young child may have enjoyed that but I had skinned my right knee pretty good and was in no mood. I just wasn't used to that vigorous kind of attention.

57

Shoving him away, I went to the camper, cleaned up my knee and put an ace bandage around it. Animals and I don't usually get very close but I think that goofy pup actually liked me. It would later break my heart. Chief eyed the bandage with his tongue lolling out in glee. He was about to jump me again so I gave him a stern look. After that he was ready to get down to the business of hiking.

We were slackpacking again and the hiking was easy. Since this was our last day, we stopped at Curley Maple Gap Shelter for a break. Walking lazily, we passed a couple of pleasant springs that added to our leisurely attitude. Slowly climbing Indian Grave Gap, 3,360 feet, the wild trio were waiting with the two horses. Normally that was an inviting sight but today there was a sadness. We are going back to Missouri. It was early in the day but this hike, with all its precious moments, was over. We had hiked 75 miles and Dick and Lida were going to meet us again next year to continue north. For us, it would be exciting, uncharted territory!

. . all the earth shall be filled with the glory of the Lord. Numbers 14:21

1989

On *June 3, 1989,* the plan was to meet Dick and Lida at Indian Grave Gap. Bill and Dick would not be riding horses this time. Instead, our jeep would be towed to the site behind the pickup camper. The men would sightsee around the mountains while Lida and I hiked. This guaranteed they would have no problem meeting us at supply points.

Chief was content to ride in the towed jeep. . . for that matter, I think he loved it. After the long drive we arrived at Indian Grave Gap. It was really good to see Lida and Dick waiting loyally. I keep thinking something will keep them from showing, but for now, I know nothing has come up to delay our new adventure.

JUNE 4, 1989 - the weather was cool and crisp and we got an early start. The trail gradually climbed to a natural grassy bald called Beauty Spot Mountain, 4,437 feet. What a pretty name for a mountain. There were splendid views in all directions. We hiked on to Deep Gap, 4,100 feet, where we found a spring, boxed in with concrete on the east side. As we filled our water bottles, I discovered Lida was having problems. She wasn't feeling well and it was beginning to worry me. The hike was just getting underway and the trail is not a good place to get over an illness. I would keep an eye on my friend.

Gradually climbing to the summit of Unaka Mountain, 5,180 feet, Lida improved a little but it was so steep in spots going down, it took its toll on her. It was a relief to reach Cherry Gap Shelter, where we spent the night. It was a concrete block shelter with a wooden floor to sleep on. The spring wasn't flowing very well so we had to take it easy on water. I tied Chief in a way that would keep him on the ground but be by my head while we slept. This was to keep his dirty paws off the floor where the hikers put their sleeping bags.

JUNE 5, 1989 - Lida was always first out of the sleeping bag in the morning. When I heard her, I would get up, put water on the stove for hot instant oatmeal, tea and coffee! Back to the hike, the trail was easy, at first, then it got steep in a hurry going up Little Bald Knob, 4,459 feet. Lida was doing pretty good, so the hiking was going much better. We were even able to enjoy some great views.

We passed a foundation of an old homestead that made me wonder about the people of that day and how they lived in these mountains. I guess I'm like a lot of people who are tired of the hustle and bustle of our times and think they would have been better off in the old days. The old wooden Clyde Smith Shelter was a welcome sight since Lida had taken a turn to the worse. Because of that fact, it was early to bed. I didn't mind, since I was tired out and needed rest too. I could only pray that my friend would be better by morning.

JUNE 6, 1989 - at least the weather was clear when we started hiking but alas, my prayers were not answered. Lida was not getting any better. My heart was heavy as we started a gradual climb, that became much steeper as we reached the cliffs on Little Rock Knob at 4,918 feet. It was hard to enjoy the rhododendron and laurel thickets, since my concerns were always about my hiking buddy.

Dropping steeply more often than not, we finally reached Hughes Gap, 4,040 feet. A steep 1.4 mile climb to the summit of Beartown Mountain, 5,481 feet was a struggle. Down a short way and another whopping steep climb, challenged our handicap to Roan Mountain, 6,150 feet. We passed a site where an old hotel used to stand. All that is left is the parking lot. Roan Mountain is noted for its rhododendron gardens. No one plants or cultivates them, as the term *garden* might imply. They just grow wild in massive groups. Unfortunately, it was too early in the season for us to see them in full bloom. We passed up Roan High Knob Shelter, the highest shelter on the A.T.

Rain was a probability, but the trail was easy going down to Carvers Gap at 5,512 feet. There was a parking and picnic area there so Bill and Dick were waiting. No sooner than we arrived and got our packs off, the sky opened up with a tremendous downpour. We snuggled up in our campers, grateful that we lived in a day and time when such things existed.

The Good Lord had looked out for us but because Lida could not shake whatever was plaguing her, we had to quit hiking this year. It was a terrible disappointment for me, but for Lida, a sacrifice I accepted willingly. My friend's health comes first and bravely she expressed a desire to hike with me again in 1990. That felt good. We had only hiked three days, but even with Lida's illness, we accomplished 24 miles.

My help will come from the Lord, who made the heaven and earth.
Psalms 121:1

1990

Bill and Dick would tow the jeep behind the camper again, leaving the horses behind. Bill enjoyed the mountain roads and it added to his pleasure, having Dick with him for company. It made my hiking much easier in two ways, I didn't worry about him so much and I knew he would have no problems meeting us at the designated points.

JUNE 3, 1990 - the adventure began as we met Dick and Lida at Carver's Gap just off Tennessee State Highway 143. As usual, me and my trusty dog, Chief, were raring to go! Leaving Carver's Gap by way of some stone steps, we began climbing to Round Bald, 5,826 feet. Reaching the top, we discovered pretty patches of rhododendron scattered about. We stopped at Roan Highlands Shelter for a break. It was looking like it might rain. I was glad I had made a small plastic cover to put on Chief's pack. It didn't seem to bother him a bit.

When we reached yellow Mountain Gap, 4,682 feet, there was a blue-blazed trail that led to Overmountain Shelter. This may appear on some maps as Yellow Mountain Barn Shelter. It has a big red barn that allows people to sleep in its loft for a fee. The trail dropped down the side of the mountain, so we passed it up.

A taunting rain held off as we passed a large rock formation on Little Hump Mountain, 5,459 feet. It was cloudy and made the views take on a more spectacular look. Sometimes the clouds looked like waterfalls flowing up the mountains. Pushing our luck to Hump Mountain, 5,587 feet, we passed over some large flat boulders. Wow! What fantastic views our eyes were allowed to see. Several mountain balds were easily seen from this one point.

Many springs and streams along the trail made us feel secure that there was plenty of water, however, most all of it has to be treated. Descending steeply through switchbacks in rich woods, we came to a rock field in a hollow where soon after, the descent became less steep.

In and out of woods, we came to a narrow hollow where it got a lot steeper. At a place called Wilder Mine Hollow, there was a former rock quarry on my left and magnetic iron mines on the right. People are strongly cautioned not to enter any of these old mines. The foul air or poison gas inside the numerous open pits and underground tunnels can cause a person to succumb before they realize they are in danger. Often the roofs fall in. I learned that magnetic ore is the source for natural magnets. The rock here is beautiful pink feldspar, white quartz and green epidote.

Crossing a stream we viewed Apple House Shelter on the left where explosives for the quarries used to be stored, along with tools for the orchards nearby. It was rebuilt in 1984 by the Tennessee Eastman Hiking Club, assisted by the Unaka Rangers. We didn't stop, since we were only a short distance from U.S. 19E Highway, where Bill and Dick were waiting.

Chief wasn't eating very well and seemed stressed out. This had me worried. We all went to a campground to spend the night and Bill and I decided to take Chief to a veterinarian the next day.

63

JUNE 4, 1990 - it had that dark look like rain when Lida and I started hiking. We decided to slackpack to High Point Memorial Baptist Church. Bill was there and had taken Chief to the vet. It seems we needed to put some special high protein meat over his food. This would entice him to eat better. We decided to give Chief another chance, so with backpacks, some caution and a short distance on paved Buck Mountain Road, we turned right and descended steeply into the woods. We had read a piece in the *Appalachian Trail News* about the section of trail we had just hiked.

"WARNING TO HIKERS"

The Don Nelan Shelter in the Cherokee National Forest, along the Tennessee-North Carolina border (guidebook section 5) was destroyed by arson in February 1990. Because of an ongoing investigation of this and other incidents in the area, ATC and the Tennessee Eastman Hiking Club **strongly discourage** *any overnight use of the Trail in this area, from U.S. 19E 2.5 miles west of Elk Park, N.C., on the south, to Moreland Gap Shelter on the north--a distance of 13.6 miles. Northbound hikers are encouraged to stay at Apple House Shelter (0.5 miles south of U.S. 19E) and then walk through the next day to Moreland Gap.* **It is essential that hikers stay on the marked footpath in this section.** *ATC appreciates the public's cooperation until this situation can be rectified."*

There are cemeteries all over that area, a grim reminder of our horrible Civil War. Crossing over plank bridges, there were contaminated water warnings everywhere. We passed close to Elk Park, North Carolina, then over log bridges, steep declines and the ever-present rhododendrons to where the ill-fated Don Nelan Shelter had been.

I was sad to see the shelter in that scorched condition but another experience almost made up for it. The famous long-time hiker, writer and past member of the ATC Board of managers, Ed Garvey was there looking over the damage to the shelter. He had a dejected look in his eyes but I just had to shake his hand. It was easy to see he was in no mood for long conversation and before I knew it, he was gone. Lida and I were hiking at a pretty good clip but this dedicated man was greased lightning.

The trail was lovely but it was water, water everywhere and not a drop could be drunk without purification. There were a lot of rhododendron as we crossed Sugar Branch. Ascending through an old field grown up in briars and over a downed fence into broomsedge field, we came to a level trail.

From that point I had a picturesque view of Hump Mountain on the left (south), Roan High Knob on the right with summits of Little Hump, Yellow Mountain, Jane Bald, and Round Bald in between. It was a scenic trail that crossed over numerous streams, through groves of white pines, beech, oak woods and even larger growths of rhododendrons. Arriving at the Moreland Gap Shelter, 3,813 feet, was a relief. It actually had a non-toxic spring just down a hollow.

We were doing our chores when a strange thing took place. Eighteen hikers came by, measuring the trail with a measuring wheel. I had never seen this before so naturally I was curious and inquired. They wanted to know exactly how far they hiked, right down to the inch. The data was accumulated each time a relocation was made for future guide books. using a van for their backup, they took a short rest and off they went, measuring up a storm. Now that I think about it, it was kind of awesome and I'll bet they only use the most experienced hikers for that job.

I met more hikers on the trail that day than I had met in a long time. Most of them unusual and very interesting. A lot of them would have looked unkempt to the outside world. After saying that, I looked at myself cautiously in the mirror, whenever I was back in civilization. Lord! I was definitely one of them. Chief liked all the hikers around and his diet was working. He appeared to be back to his old self as he snuggled as close to me as I would permit, come bed time.

JUNE 5, 1990 - Lida and I continued easily west along a crest to the highest point in the White Rocks Mountains, 4,206 ft. As we descended on a blue-blaze trail, we found another good spring southwest of some cabin ruins, called the Old Canute Place, in honor of its first settlers.

Crossing a field, we ascended again into woods. We joined a forest service road that came in from our left. It led straight ahead to the White Rocks Mountain Fire Tower at 4,105 feet. Continuing to descend to Dennis Cove Road, Bill and Dick were waiting. They had been having a ball, driving mountain roads all day. Sometimes I envied them for the adventures they were having with a lot less effort.

For instance, they had met some southbound hikers, who told them Bill Irwin was about three days ahead of us. This is a blind man who hiked with his dog Orient. He thru-hiked the A.T. in 1990 and needless to say, I would have loved to have met him, but it was not to be.

It was only a couple of miles to Laurel Falls. Quite a bit of our hike was following an old railroad bed with some of the old trestles still standing. It was originally built for the lumber that was hauled out of this rugged area. I understand the variety of trees included 60% hemlock; the remainder were hardwoods, such as oak, chestnut, poplar, maple, wahoo, cucumber, birch and sassafras.

If you want rough and rugged, this area is every bit of that. We went around the rim of the most terrific gorge you will ever see. Certain times in the year, there are abundant Catawba rhododendron, normally found only on higher mountain tops such as Roan. Carolina rhododendron, mountain laurels and many other varieties of flowers can be seen here in different seasons. It is indeed an unusual, spectacular, strange place.

We stopped at Laurel Falls for our lunch and a thru-hiker stopped and seriously pondered going swimming. Lida and I watched intently to see him turn blue in the cold water. Dipping his hand in, changed his mind in a hurry. Shoot! This definitely would have broken our boredom.

The trail skirted the base of a cliff on a built-up rock walk at the stream's edge then ascended to Laurel Fork Shelter. It was a real mess. People had thrown their trash around with absolute abandon. Lida and I cleaned it up the best we could, given the fact that the trash wouldn't burn very well. It was wet from a previous rain.

Taking turns going to a stream behind the shelter to bathe our dirty, tired bodies, we were oblivious of any danger. Later that evening, Chief's ears stood up and he began barking furiously. This was extremely unusual since he never before barked at anyone on the trail. A lone hiker was coming up from the trail below. We eyed him as close as Chief did, while he took a short break, then moved on as quickly as he had arrived. Chief was coming of age as a watch dog and I didn't mind that a bit!

Crawling into our sleeping bags, Chief started barking again. Lida and I were getting concerned with this bizarre behavior. Following his eyes, looking toward the blue-blazed trail that bypasses the falls, suddenly two policemen appeared with their hands on their guns in a quick-draw position. They cautiously checked the shelter as if someone or something they wanted was still in the area. When they discovered there were only two women and a dog, they relaxed enough for us to have a nice visit with them.

The person or persons who vandalized and burned the Don Nelan Shelter had still not been apprehended. All the shelters, including Laural Fork, were being watched to prevent any repeat of that disgusting incident. Lida and I expressed how comforting it was to know they were checking out the trail. Meanwhile, I gave Chief a proud look and a loving pat. Wondering how dogs can tell when a circumstance is different, I felt pretty cocky lying there with those sharp ears continuously on the guard. Good dog!

JUNE 6, 1990 - the night's event didn't keep us from getting an early start that morning as we walked the 0.5 mile back down to the A.T. An old man had made camp by the stream and was still taking it easy in his tent. Proceeding along a crested ridge covered with pine trees, Catawba rhododendrons and mountain laurels, there was a superb view of the walls of a rocky gorge.

Following the stream, we descended carefully among flowers and pines. On down the stream we found Waycaster Spring, the last dependable water between us and Highway 321. Ascending steeply to the old railroad bed, we were impressed with a view of Buckled Rock and farther down, Potato Top, an unusual formation smack dab in the middle of the gorge.

Reaching the crest of Pond Mountain at about 2,400 feet, we climbed steeply to its summit, 4,329 feet. Disappointed that there was no view due to the overcast we continued our descent, through extremely steep switchbacks. Bill, bless his heart, hiked in part of the way to meet us. When we finally got to Hwy. U.S. 321, there was a service station with a camping area in the back. Our men took us to Hampton, Tennessee where we found a comfortable restaurant with delicious food made even more so, by our not having had a good meal for a while.

I and my loyal pal, Lida, hiked a total of 42 miles over some pretty doggone rough country. Chief turned out to be an excellent watch dog, as well as a fun companion. We quit the hike for that year with memories of Rhododendrons, Mountain Laurels and every kind of tree we could want to see. We were exposed to cliffs, burial grounds, polluted mountain streams, and absolutely fantastic Laurel Gorge with its beautiful falls. By Golly, I think we will come back next year to where we left off. Dick and Lida agreed as we said our good-byes at the end of that year's successful trail on U.S. 321.

Thou are worthy, O Lord, to receive glory and honour and power; for Thou hast created all things, and for Thy pleasure they are and were created. Rev. 4:11

1991

The 1990 trip proved how useful a dog could be on hiking trips and my Chief had certainly shown me his worth. Life is so fleeting. Alas, as Bill was making preparations for this year's hike, the unthinkable happened. He was taking Chief to the veterinarian for his shots. He put my four-legged partner in the back of the pickup on a leash. As he rounded a curve, he heard a frightening thud under the truck. Stopping immediately, Bill observed Chief running out from under the truck. The poor little fellow had been dragged before his leash broke. He was bleeding as Bill loaded him into the truck and rushed to the vet.

The doctor gave him a shot to stop the bleeding. He thought the dog might be all right if he was not injured internally. While I was at work, my husband called and informed me about the accident. The rest of my work day was stressful. Even though Bill had said Chief might be all right, a terrible foreboding crept over me.

Finally, my work day was over and I arrived home to see Chief stretched out on the floor. Looking down at him, I choked, "Hi Chiefee." As he opened those trusting eyes and looked up at me, my dark feeling was confirmed. I knew my dog was severely injured. Stroking him for about an hour, his spirit departed, going to wherever loving animals go. Immediate relief did not come as I sobbed uncontrollably for what seemed like an eternity. I could not believe how hard I was taking this animal's

70

death. Chief was the only dog I had ever called my own. In my deepest thoughts, I feel we will hike peaceful meadows, majestic mountains and bountiful forests in that place my Father has prepared for me. It just must be!

· · · · ·

Faithfully, our friends Dick and Lida were waiting on Tennessee Hwy. 321 at a little store across from Watauga Lake. The owner was kind enough to let us camp behind his store where he had a picnic table and camping area. It was a nice spot. By the way, Bill and I sold the camper and replaced it with a small motor home that we towed our jeep behind. It was so much more relaxing on the highway. You could actually walk from the driver's compartment to the kitchen and sleeping area without stopping. The bathroom was handy too.

Bill and Dick, as before, used the jeep to run the trails and provide our backup. Dick brought an empty horse trailer, just in case he found some good horses. He said, "If I find the right horse, I will buy it." Lida and I spent the rest of the evening getting our packs ready for tomorrow.

JUNE 2, 1991 - saying good-bye to the men, we looked to the south over Laurel Fork Pond Mountain and the memories of the previous hike. I shivered as I was reminded that thoughts of Chief were also mingled in that rugged gorge. The trail skirted the lake crossing a small dam. From there, we again looked back across the lake, to where we had started this new adventure. The temperature was warming up and reached 90° by noon.

The climb up to a mountain crest was pretty steep and while walking through some tall grass, I tripped over a

71

stick. Falling flat on my face I knocked my glasses off. I thanked the Lord, in a very passionate way, that they had not broken and my body was still intact. Missing, was a little white dog jumping all over me. That hurt worse than the fall. At that moment I wondered how long this gut wrenching pain for Chief would last.

Just before we arrived at Vandeventer Shelter, we dropped our packs, took out our water bottles and followed a steep blue-blazed trail one-half mile to a spring. Filling our bottles, we worked up a little more sweat getting back to our packs. It was a good thing it was only a little farther to the next shelter. The heat was telling on Lida and I could see she wasn't feeling well. She began to improve later in the evening, as we sat on some huge rocks behind the shelter. From there we could overlook Watauga Lake and all the lights around the shore; an awesome sight. We returned, eventually, to a nice clean shelter where sleep brought an end to the day.

JUNE 3, 1991 - a fairly restful sleep and meager breakfast, took us back to a pretty easy trail all the way to the Iron Mountain Shelter, where it was time for a break. As clean as Vandeventer Shelter had been, this one was equally dirty. We were willing to end our break quickly.

A mile down the trail, we came to Nick Grindstaff's grave with a stone monument that bore the following inscription -

UNCLE NICK GRINDSTAFF
BORN DECEMBER 26, 1851
DIED JULY 22, 1923
LIVED ALONE,
SUFFERED ALONE,

Old Nick, was a hermit that had lived forty-six years of his life on Iron Mountain with only his dog as a companion. I felt his stone was very contradictory. When I was with Chief, I was never alone. Whoever wrote the words that were carved on that stone must have never known the love of a dog. For the record, It's my opinion that Old Nick didn't live alone, suffer alone and I can't say if he or the dog died last. Anyway, after that emotional outburst, it is sad to read that Nick or anyone would choose to live such an isolated life.

Still pondering old Nick, we arrived at Hwy. 91 where Bill and Dick were supposed to be waiting. They weren't there. An hour later, as I was getting extremely worried, I noticed a note on the north bound trail marker. Fortunately, it was from Bill and it said they were camped up the highway about one-half mile. Lida and I hiked up to that point. Sure enough, there they were.

JUNE 4, 1991 - the frequent threat of rain was present this morning. Lida and I hit the trail early anyway on a fairly easy trail, with only moderate climbing. Light rain did begin to trickle down on us as we observed signs of the previous occupants of this rugged country, such as old rock fences. Thoughts of the old settlers that used to live in these mountains was ever present in my mind. What must it have been like?

Arriving at Hwy. 421 we ate our lunch, then continued on for 3.4 miles where we came upon a small log shelter. It was built in 1934 on Holston Mountain and was the first shelter on the A.T. Mother nature was still pouring forth her gentle mist as if to encourage her blackberry bushes and sparse trees to reproduce. I might add, this included accompanying blackberry briars. Nature seems always to intermingle her blessings with adversity.

Spending the night at Abingdon Gap Shelter, Lida was still feeling poorly. Closing my eyes in anticipation of sleep, I hoped this was not a sign or omen of unwanted news.

JUNE 5, 1991 - dispelling my fears of last night, the hike to Damascus, Virginia, was pleasant. It is a strange feeling to walk from one state into another. I felt like a pioneer from the past as we went from Tennessee to Virginia. It seemed like it took forever to get out of Tennessee and North Carolina. We often did not know what state we were in since the trail zigged and zagged from one state line to another. Often the A.T. is right on the line.

We found Bill and Dick camped in a open field, as we entered the city limits of Damascus, Virginia. Yes, the city was named after the ancient capital of Syria. Originally the location was called Mock's Mill because of a man named Mock who came from North Carolina and built a home and mill in 1821. It is a beautiful mountain setting and must have been inspiring, to say the least, since Mr. Mock had three wives and raised 33 children. I'm going to leave here as soon as possible, it could be infectious!

True to his promise, Dick found a lovely Tennessee Walker horse that he was now the proud owner. Like a child with a new toy, he was having a lot of fun trying to ride it. Leaving the boys to their play, Lida and I walked downtown to the post office and a unique hostel, named The Place, and maintained by the Damascus United Methodist Church. Payment for services is done by donation. Another nice trail called the Virginia Creeper, also crosses through. We finished the day with our husbands, discussing our separate adventures until we were all talked out, then it was time for a well-needed rest.

JUNE 6, 1991 - Lida and I sauntered a mile through Damascus, discussing her doubt as to whether she should continue the hike. It was five more beautiful miles, but a disheartening walk north to Hwy. 58. The men walked into the trail to meet us. Back at the vehicles, Lida told me she had made up her mind and was going home. Darkness descended over me as I realized I was watching Lida slowly lose her hiking spirit. Something about it was continually making her body ill.

I guess the disease I had contracted at the Grand Canyon does not have a long term affect over everyone. My heart was heavy and tears were hard to hold back. Deep inside I knew this would be the last time she would hike with me. Together we had hiked a total of 42 miles over some of the easiest terrain we had experienced, but something about it was too rough on my hiking pal. I lost my pal, Chief, at the beginning of this trip and in another way, I lost my buddy Lida at the end. Still, I shall remember the agony and the ecstasy. What is an adventure without both? As we drove home, Bill did not talk to me for a while. He understood.

My help will come from the Lord, who made heaven and earth. Psalms 121:1

1992

Call me a tough bird. I was already looking for a new hiking partner. I happened to mention the subject in a discussion with my cousin, Norma Jean, who had a nephew, Todd. 28 years old and recently discharged from the United States Marine Corp. He seemed to be an ideal candidate. If he wasn't tough enough to hike with me, who would be? Yeah, I gave him a call and we visited a couple of times. I told him I would like to hike around 145 miles. It turned out that he liked hiking, so he agreed. On the inside I was grinning at the thought that I was now having to turn to the Marine Corp. for people who could hang with me. Arrogant, huh?

Ross, my sixteen year old grandson, decided that since I was going to hike with a strange man, he had better go too, in order to protect me. Isn't that sweet? He is my oldest grandson, very quiet and loves the outdoors but has never hiked. He was raised on a farm, therefore he is no weakling. He might be able to keep up with me and a Marine. Quit that Mary, you're becoming a smart aleck.

Leslie, who was one of my first hiking companions, told me his oldest son, Heath, also 16, wanted to earn his 50-mile badge in the Boy Scouts. He asked if I would mind if he hiked with me. He was also a strong young man and had been brought up on a ranch. I told Leslie I was honored to have Heath hike with me, since his father had been with me before.

Bill and our friend, Glen had been on previous hikes with us and decided to take their horses, in order to ride the numerous horse trails in Mt. Roger's Recreational area. The motor home was capable of carrying all the passengers which included Glen, Heath, Ross and myself, plus pull the trailer with the two horses. Of course, my husband Bill did the driving.

JUNE 1, 1992 - ex-marine Todd met us in Damascus, Virginia. We arrived in the early afternoon and again camped in the little open field. Ross, Heath and I took a walk into town while Bill and Glen took care of the horses. On our way down Main street, a tall red-headed man cordially said "Hello," to us. Continuing on down the street, we found all the people to be very friendly folks. Making our way back to the motor home, to our surprise, we found the tall red-headed man in our camp. Lo and behold it was Todd!

He had parked his car on the east end of town by an old railroad caboose that was near where the A.T. and Virginia Creeper Trail met. With his permission and for convenience, it was decided to use his car on the hike along with the motor home and the horses. So Bill would track us sometimes with the car.

The Virginia Creeper Trail is made up of an old railroad bed that stretches from Abingdon to White Top, Virginia. It is 34 miles long and used for hiking, bicycling and horse riding. This trail runs next to U.S. Hwy. 58 out of town and the A.T. leaves out to the Northeast then crosses Highway 58 about 5.6 miles out. It was one interesting evening before sundown brought a halt to our discussions.

JUNE 2, 1992 - Bill took us out to where the trails left Highway 58, and where we quit hiking in 1991. Todd showed me his backpack that was so heavy, he had to sit on the ground to put it on. There was everything but the kitchen sink in there. He decided to unload about ten pounds of gear from his pack. That still left it awful heavy. The ex-Marine turned out to be an unusual, but nice, young man.

An appropriate beginning was made by crossing a picturesque stream. The trail was gentle to the Virginia Creeper Trail. We hiked on it to the Luther Hassinger Memorial Bridge. Glen and Bill caught up with us on their horses. After a break with them, Bill told us he would see us in the morning at VA 601. We said good-bye, followed the A.T. to our left and disappeared into the woods. A group of eighteen hikers from Backpacker's Magazine was also hiking the A.T. They were only out for a few days, hiking around the Mt. Roger's area, so they strung along with us for a while.

A boxed spring just off VA 601 in a small field, looked like a good campsite. After hiking 5.6 miles closer to the highway we all, including the Backpacker group, set up camp near a place called Feathercamp Branch. It looked like an Indian village right out of history. The day was uneventful and I was anxious to get out into the wilderness again.

JUNE 3, 1992 - Bill arrived early in Todd's car, before we had time to get the tents taken down. Todd unloaded some more of his extra gear into the car. A wise decision. After breakfast, I told Bill good-bye and the rest of us were on our way leaving the Backpacker group behind. At Hwy. 601, the elevation was 3,550 feet. The climb to Whitetop Mountain Road, took us to 5,360 feet.

Crossing some balds revealed appealing views of Mt. Roger's in the distance. We reached VA 600, at 4,434 feet, and continued ascending. We reached Deep Gap Shelter, 4,900 feet and Ross and Heath volunteered to go to a spring to fill our water bag. Virginia Highlands Horse Trail follows close by the A.T. and passed in front of the old shelter. As of this date, the shelter was scheduled to be removed. Sentimentally, our group felt obliged to spend the night here. The 18 Backpackers passed us on their way to a new shelter close to the summit of Mt. Roger's, where they intended to spend their night.

Later in the evening, two interesting thru-hikers came into the Deep Gap Shelter. One fellow, in his 50's, called himself Reno. Yes, he's from Reno, Nevada. The other man, Swede, was from Sweden. His English was awfully poor so he was hard to talk to. We all spent the night in the shelter, with the exception of Swede, who insisted on pitching his lean-to-tent out in the trees. It was evident he was a loner. I suppose because of his communication problem. It must be rough when you're in a foreign country. It cooled off during the night, making my sleeping bag mighty cozy.

JUNE 4, 1992 - 7:00 a.m., after a quick breakfast we started the climb up Mt. Roger's. In a short distance, the heel on my right foot started hurting like I was getting a blister. At the new shelter, the backpacking group was breaking camp. Since there were so many of them, they were considerate in pitching their tents to save the shelter for thru-hikers. The new shelter was a two-story structure. Sure, I could see myself pulling my backpack up that ladder to the second floor.

Just before we got to a rail fence for the Grayson Highlands State Park, we saw a group of wild ponies grazing. Oh, Boy, I loved that! They were so intriguing with all colors including some paints. So much so, it made you want to catch one and jump on board like the Indians used to do. But not with my old body.

My heel was really hurting, but I couldn't see anything wrong with it. I didn't remember getting a stone bruise. Oh well, the open alpine meadows we were crossing at this point, were easy walking with pleasant views. Dropping down to Quebec Branch through dense growths of rhododendrons, we stopped for lunch. Reaching the Scales, a rail-fence corral for cattle and horses, I stopped and put an ace bandage on my foot. But when I put my boot back on, it hurt a lot worse. I took the ace bandage off and tried some moleskin.

After leaving the Scales, we came to where a horse trail crossed the A.T. Bill had left a note there telling me he was camped at the Fox Creek Horse Camp on VA 63. It was beginning to look like rain when we got to Old Orchard Shelter and it was almost full. The backpacking group, that we had been swapping the lead with all day, beat us to the next shelter and some of them had lost their gallantry and elected to stay in the shelter, rather than pitch their tents. Graciously, they had saved a spot for me, but the boys would have had to pitch their tents. This wasn't appealing, especially since I knew Bill was only 1.7 miles further, all downhill.

We all decided to move on, knowing that if we missed Bill, there was a creek where we could camp nearby. It was doing all it could to rain by the time we got to Hwy. 603 at 3,480 feet. Thank goodness the men were there with our motor home. They were surprised to see us, dragging in like lost orphans, Glen fixed our supper and waited on us like we were VIP's.

Bill made my day, when he told us he had heard about a thru-hiker who had been raped near the Nick Grindstaff Monument on May 31. They had not caught the man yet and he wanted me to be careful. I pointed at my three young men and dropped the subject. If I'm not safe out there, I don't know who is.

It was a little crowded in the motor home but since it rained all night, no one was complaining. Being the only woman, I kind of felt like a queen with her own private army. With that fantasy on my mind, I'm sure a smile was frozen on my face when warm slumber crept over me.

JUNE 5, 1992 - Rain settled in this morning, so without backpacks we climbed to the 4,320 foot Iron Mountain Ridge. Bill was supposed to carry our packs to Dickey Gap where we were to meet him later for some delicious sandwiches and pickup the packs. The easy trail would have been a pleasure if we had not had to hurry. The rain that was pouring down. Bill was waiting for us at Dickey Gap on VA 650, but kiss off the delicious sandwiches. They had gotten soggy because of the rain. Yuck! Believe me, we ate in a hurry!

All the road crossings and trail heads had photo-bearing warnings regarding the rape Bill had told us about earlier. It was impressive how quickly the ATC and Tennessee Eastman Hiking Club had gotten the news out for hikers to be on the lookout for the rapist.

The large backpacking group had left the trail before they caught up with us. None-the-less, we quickly loaded our packs and continued on down the trail. We came to a blue-blazed trail that led to the Raccoon Branch Shelter. We were on a roll, so rather than stop, we kept on truckin', excuse me, hikin'. The rain let up and it was only

2.5 miles more to the Trimpi Shelter and we were bound and determined to get there.

It didn't take us long to get a fire built in the welcomed fireplace. As we were trying to dry our clothes out, in came Reno. He was alone and figured, "Swede must have stopped at the Raccoon Branch Shelter." The fire warmed the shelter and while dancing shadows played on the walls, I bid this day farewell.

JUNE 6, 1992 - morning came and the rain was still our unwanted companion. Its continuous deluge would come and go, causing streams all over the area to flow faster and deeper than normal. We were not only getting rained on but also being forced to walk in the accumulating water. Ross and Heath weren't saying much, but Todd was beginning to do a lot of complaining.

When we got to the Mt. Roger's Visitor Center, we pitched our tents up on a hill. Bill arrived and unaware of the strict rules for this area, decided we needed a campfire. He built it for us and left. As we were about to light it, a ranger came by and clearly told us "No Campfires!". Due to a "no trace" camping law I had to tear it all down.

The law means just what it sounds like. You must leave absolutely no trace that you had ever camped at a site. To our relief, another hiker arrived to rescue us. He informed us that the Visitor Center allowed hikers to spend the night on their porch. Reno came straggling in and the six of us spent the night *on the porch*. It rained hard that night, so we couldn't knock it. Even my fantasies couldn't make a pleasant night out of that mess.

JUNE 7, 1992 - Alleluia! The rain had finally stopped. Believe me, the hiking was much easier. On slippery ground we ascended to Glade Mountain, elevation 3,900 feet, followed the crest for a mile, then descended to Chatfield Shelter. Thanks to the abundant rain, there was a nice large creek running in front of it. We were so hungry we cooked our supper meal, and saved the smaller lunch for supper. This was the first time I had reason to switch our meals like that.

Bellies almost full, we made it to Hwy. 11, where good old Bill was waiting to take us to Civilization! A real cafe and showers for hikers were waiting like an oasis in the desert. The showers were $4.00 per person and the boys "just had to have one!" I have not figured out why, to this date, I turned the showers down and bathed in a nearby creek. If you think I've been joking about this fanatical obsession that has infected every fiber of my body, read on. I look in the mirror sometimes at home and don't even recognize the tough lady staring back at me.

Bill told us our buddy, Swede got in ahead of us. He had hauled him into town where he left him at a bar drinking his loneliness and problems into oblivion. After re-supplying and saying good-bye, we hiked under I-81, through some pasture land and ascended to the Davis Path Shelter where we found there was no water. Our other pal, Reno was already there, so we spent the night.

JUNE 8, 1992 - the trail went up and down. Heath, I noticed, had a tendency to be a little mischievous and was directing it at Todd, of all people. I found it strange that Todd was taking it so well and was sure, being an ex-marine, he didn't have to put up with the sixteen year old. I was glad he was so tolerant.

All the creeks were full and running swiftly, which added a little intrigue. We reached VA 42 at 2,600 feet, where there was a nice picnic area with tables and a pavilion. By way of switchbacks, we ascended Brushy Mountain. It was rough and seemed like it took forever to hike 12 miles to Knot Mole Branch Shelter where we found Reno again. He was lonely and spent the night with us. Old Swede was still tying one on back in town.

I don't think Reno liked hiking alone. I could sure identify with that. A girl friend mailed him his food drops. Weird, huh? I didn't dig into his past, so I have no idea if he was self-employed or had a job. He just wanted to hike the entire A.T. just like me. So what can I say. He had a fair personality and was easy to get along with. That was good enough for me. As I prepared to call it a day, I was wishing I had a lady to talk to. Shucks, I'm not a chatterbox, anyway.

JUNE 9, 1992 - the weather improved considerably and was making hiking a whole lot more enjoyable. There was some climbing to Chestnut Knob Shelter. The guide book directed us to get water 1.7 miles before getting there. We filled our five gallon water bag only three-fourths full, to lighten the load to the shelter. Heath and Ross took turns carrying it while Todd and I went on to the shelter, unloaded our packs and went back to relieve them.

Not far from the shelter, I asked Todd to carry the water bag on in. He was one irritated fellow and a short distance later, he threw it to the ground causing it to spring a leak. I think Heath's continual agitating was finally getting to him. Frankly, I wouldn't have put up with it as long as he had. It will just have to play itself out. Picking the bag up and folding it in a way to hold as much water as it could, I carried what was left, on to the shelter. We filled everything we could with the water that was left.

Reno had gone on ahead of us and was at the shelter. He said someone had written in the shelter's log book that there was a spring only a short distance away. Man, after all that hassle and work. A group of boy scouts arrived a little later to find that we had already staked claim on the bunks. I felt sorry for them as they scattered their sleeping bags out on the rock floor. The whole shelter was made out of rock.

Reading the log book, my eyes caught on a statement that read, "beware of mice". This wasn't so shocking. I had already learned to hang the food. A mice problem seemed to exist in all the shelters. The poor boy scouts, who were just starting their 50-mile hike to earn their badges, were unaware and didn't hang theirs.

JUNE 10, 1992 - I hoped the bickering from yesterday was over. Ross, while putting his boots on, found them full of M & M's. Immediately, he accused Todd of the hanky-panky. This adversarial situation was getting out of hand. I explained to him that pack mice store things like candy in places like boots. He just growled. The little mice had a field day with the boy scouts' food, but I was going to have to give my young male companions a good lecture, if they kept up with their nonsense.

Following a ridge to the crest of Garden Mountain, we found a place overlooking Burk's Garden. The view was of an outstanding, enormous cove with beautiful, fertile farm land spread out in the valley below. We were in a hurry to get to the next shelter ahead of the boy scouts, so we didn't tarry too long. It wasn't easy to rush. This was really, lovely country. At VA 623, there was a trash can, so I dumped our water bag and other burdensome trash we had been packing for too long.

That's part of the game, in these restricted areas. I would carry it until I could dump it anyway, but most will not, without laws. Some will litter regardless.

Jenkin's Shelter was a pleasant surprise. Nestled in pine trees, a large stream flowed close by and an honest-to-goodness picnic table. Definitely one of the nicer spots. It was becoming a routine for Reno to beat us to each shelter. Smiling, he said the poor boy scouts were having all kinds of problems. They never did make it to the shelter while we were there. Poor fellows had spilled their hot water for breakfast, couldn't get their gear together and in general had not learned how to get organized out in the rough, which you must master on the trail!

JUNE 11, 1992 - threatening rain was plaguing us again. We got an early start anyway. Reno seemed to sleep about one hour longer than we did, but he could afford to. He was in good condition and an experienced thru-hiker so he always passed us on the trail later. I sensed he was growing just a little weary of hiking. I was right, too. Later on, he revealed that he might hike to the half-way point in Pennsylvania and then quit. He opined that he would come back and finish the A.T. later. I think he was missing his girl friend. I hope so. Maybe he will bring her with him one day and perhaps I will get to meet her. After all, she must love him an awful lot to support him like she was.

The Trail Club had put out signs telling all hikers to take a blue-blazed, alternative high water route. We would have to cross Little Wolf Creek some thirteen times in 2.5 miles, so due to all the rain we opted to follow their expert advice. It was a shorter route that followed an old road bed. It made for some easy hiking. Rain prompted us to keep moving along at a pretty crisp clip. We could hear traffic on Interstate 77 for quite awhile before finally dropping down to U.S. 52.

Bill had the motor home backed into a small spot where he and Glen were shooting the breeze. It was good to see them and let them put up with my bickering babies. Reno had already arrived and Bill took him into Bland for his mail drop. He had become a real friend as he passed me in this journey of life, but I was never to see him again. I still entertain hope that I will one day meet his girl friend.

There was good news. Bill told us, they had caught the rapist. He was in the woods along the A.T., in the same general area where the rape had occurred June 8. Charged with rape and kidnapping, maybe he will be out of society's hair for a while. At least I was happy, knowing all the female hikers behind us would be safe. September 4, the rapist pleads guilty and faces twenty-four years in jail. It's always good to know they got the right guy.

We were all tired, it was raining and patience was at an end. I decided to end this hike earlier than I had planned. There was no rebuttal. All in all, we had covered 125 miles and, for the most part, I was proud of the boys. Silently, Todd loaded his gear into his car and left for home. My suspicion that I would not see him again proved to be correct. Doggone shame too. Without the immature boys, he and I could have covered a lot of country.

Bill and Glen had done a lot of horse riding, so it was chalked up as a good adventure for all. Bill wasn't too fond of driving the motor home on the small highways and rugged back roads, because it was hard on it. Not only had this been quite a hiking adventure, but also a lesson in child psychology as well. I'll tell you ladies something, talk about getting rid of a low self-esteem, this disease is the ticket. So, if you want to get rid of some weight and build one heck of an ego at the same time, contact me and I will do my best to infect you. Deal?

The old heel was still hurting when I arrived at my happy home. The mystery of what had been wrong was finally solved. I had pulled my Achilles tendon. The healing process took about three months and my doctor was amazed that I had endured the pain for so many miles. My pride was still hurting for giving up so early in the hike and I didn't want those feisty boys to pass any rumors that Den Mama gave up.

Sadly, this was the only hike my grandson, Ross, would spend with me. I was so very proud of him and fondly wished he could have gotten the hiking disease like his grand Den Mama. Heath hiked with me later, due to his being in the Boy Scouts. I even became the Backpacking Counselor for Troop 48 of Aurora, Missouri. It was the same troop that he and his brothers, Derrick and Trevor, were members. Heath became an Eagle Scout on December 26, 1995. Den Mama had kept the boys safe on this trip and for that I was thankful.

• • • • *November, 1992* • • • •

Den Mama retired from Wal-Mart in April, 1992. The infection became even worse. Now, I had more time to hike but I couldn't find anyone to go with me in 1993. My husband and I took the Jeep back to Bland, Virginia, where we ended the previous hike. Our goal was to search the A.T. for places where I could hike by myself and meet Bill every evening to spend the night. We drove from Bland, Virginia, all the way into Maryland.

A fall issue of the *Appalachian Trail News* contained an ad from someone called, California Tent

Lady. She wanted a partner to start at Pearsburg, Virginia, and proceed north for a three-week hike. Yes, I answered the ad! About a month later California Tent Lady called to say she would like to hike with me. Needless to say, I think I was happy. She lived in California and was going to fly to her sister's home in St. Louis, Missouri. Her sister would then take her to Sikeston, Missouri. Bill and I were to pick her up on the way to Virginia.

My plan to meet Bill every evening would not be changed. It was good to have another hiking partner. They were getting kind of scarce. That lady knew what it was like to be out on the trail for a long period of time. I was in *Hiker's Heaven.*

When I look at the sky, which You have made, at the moon and the stars, which You set in their places. . . . Oh Lord, our Lord, Your greatness is seen in all the world! Psalms 8: 3 and 9

1993

California Tent Lady set the date for the hike and it would certainly be a new experience for me. It was a lot earlier in the spring than any of my previous hikes. I had no idea what I was in for. Call me gullible, but I was excited to meet this lady under these strange circumstances. Remember, she's sort of like a mail order hiking companion.

Anyway, we picked her up at Sikeston Missouri. She was ten years younger than me and you could tell by her stature that she was no weakling. She had ended a hike on the A.T. at Bland, Virginia, as I had on our previous trip. At least we had that in common. So that was the beginning of this new adventure. I was more than a little bit wary.

APRIL 16, 1993 - arriving at Hwys. 21/52, Bill dropped us off at 11:00 a.m. Wasting no time, California Tent Lady and I decided to slackpack the nine miles to Hwy. 611. The weather was cool, but comfortable. It was weird to see trees without leaves and to start a hike wearing a light jacket. For this trip, Bill and I bought a unique lean-to tent, that fit over the back of the jeep. When the rear door of the jeep is open, it is like one nice size room.

We arrived at our first destination where Bill had made camp at a wide spot on Hwy. 611, right by the trail. The lean-to-tent made a nice shelter so that experiment was turning out well. My husband and I slept in the jeep and California Tent Lady put her free-standing tent inside the lean-to-tent, giving her some privacy. It was a good setup for all. Meeting this new partner and hiking a good nine miles the first day gave me a lot to ponder that night.

APRIL 17, 1993 - to our surprise, three inches of snow greeted us as we woke up, rubbing our eyes in disbelief. It was pretty doggone cold out, so we all slithered back into our sleeping bags. After a late breakfast, we hit the trail around 9:00 a.m. Our camp had been in a gap on Brushy Mountain, 2,720 feet, and we were heading for the summit at 3,101 feet. The trail was in pretty good shape and I found myself walking in front of California Tent Lady. I think she knew she could outhike me and this was her way of pacing herself. That was all well and good, but I was also getting all the cobwebs to boot!

We found Bill at VA 608 in Lickskillet Hollow, elevation 2,200 feet. Bless his heart, he hiked in to meet us. Crossing a new bridge built over Kimberling Creek, we arrived at the jeep. After driving to Walnut Flats Campgrounds, we found a lot of turkey hunters camped there which bothered me more than a little bit. I hoped they were responsible hunters and could tell the difference between us and the turkeys! Bill discovered an old fireplace flue that had been left standing and managed to build a fire in it. It felt wonderful and made sleeping a lot easier.

APRIL 18, 1993 - 7:30 a.m., back to Lickskillet Hollow where we stopped hiking the day before. In a cold 30°, we began the day. Up the trail a ways, we could have hiked 0.3 mile down a blue-blazed trail to an interesting place, called Dismal Creek Falls. Neither of us was in the mood for sight seeing, so we passed it up.

Following Dismall Creek off and on for what seemed like the entire morning, we came up on a washed out bridge. It looked like it had just been built and had met an early end. It was now partially washed down stream. In these cold temperatures, we certainly didn't want to wade the creek. With the fog of our breaths hanging in the cold air, we dragged some logs over to the bank and made our own walkway over to what was left of the bridge.

Call us the bridge makers, it worked good enough to cross over to the remainder of the bridge, high and dry. During that experience, I found out how strong California Tent Lady really was. Following a huge pond surrounded by a levee, it appeared to be a popular campsite. The remnants of campfires and other signs indicated that a lot of people had camped all around the area. At Wapiti Shelter, we stopped for a well-needed break before starting the climb up Sugar Run Mountain. Using the southern slope, there was nice views even though the trees were missing some of their summer garment of leaves.

Bill was waiting at USFS 103, but we continued hiking on to Sugar Run Gap, 3,822 feet. A trail crew there was all excited about something. Turns out, they had discovered a new spring close to Sugar Run Gap. I guess that's a big deal, since water is essential and welcomed by hikers. Meeting Bill again, he took us 0.5 miles to a Woodshole Hostel. Unfortunately, the Hostel was closed and I was rapidly realizing it was bad judgment to have started a hike so early in the spring. Too late to worry about it then, so it was back to Sugar Run Gap and a wide spot by the trail where we set up camp.

APRIL 19, 1993 - things are looking up. Under 70° temperature, we made our way on an exceptionally, decent trail to Angel's Valley and Pearisburg, VA. During the descent by switchbacks to VA 634, two deer peeked curiously out of the trees at us, before scurrying away. I watched them until they disappeared into the trees. I loved that close contact with free, wild animals.

When we saw Bill, he said he would meet us at the Senator Shumate Bridges over New River near Bluff City, VA. This day ended in a civilized setting, motel room, hot shower and fried chicken. It ain't roughing it but, boy, it always felt good. Hey, you have to ease into that rugged life! I laid these tired bones into a real bed, just like yours.

APRIL 20, 1993 - making our way out of the civilization of Pearisburg, VA, we realized Bluff and New River, Virginia were all in the same small area. It didn't take long before we were on the trail again, circling around the edge of Hemlock Ridge, across the Stillhouse Branch into Turnhole Knob. From there, Peter's Mountain stood before us.

Huffing and puffing to its crest, I looked back at the diversion of the occupied areas we had left behind, including a city, that was in the same vicinity, called Narrows VA. From what I could tell, it must be quite a flood risk to live there. New River and Wolf Creek met right smack dab in the middle of it.

Following the mountain's crest about 12.5 miles, interesting combinations of rock outcroppings and meadows kept our vision occupied. Treading the state borders of Virginia and West Virginia, we were making good time slackpacking. So much so, we decided to try for a twenty-mile day. This was not a good decision.

When we reached the high point of Peter's Mountain, a 3,956 foot knob and started a descent for 0.8 miles, we came upon the Allegheny Trail intersecting the

A.T. Newly graded switchbacks had been built to help us down the steep mountain to Pine Swamp Branch Shelter. It was at this point I was really questioning my wisdom at taking on so many miles. My feet were crying out like a howling dog that had just been slapped up beside the head. Huh, I wonder if that's why some people call our feet dogs. Regardless, it was good to have a well graded trail.

Painfully, I reached Pine Swamp Branch Shelter. Bill had hiked in and was visiting with four young men that we later dubbed the "Slow Four". They were out for an entertaining weekend hike and had nothing to hurry about. I was surprised and concerned at seeing my husband until I saw how easy the trail was to the road where he had started. Understandably, he was getting bored and was getting some exercise.

Some of the really wonderful people, who live along the trail, allowed us to camp in their yard. I settled down to a well-needed, healing rest. Bill kept five gallons of water in the jeep, so we didn't have to worry about that.

APRIL 21, 1993 - rain was threatening when we hit the trail that morning. It was a steep climb to Bailey Gap Shelter on Big Mountain. The "Slow Four" had hiked to the shelter and were having a ball fixing pancakes for breakfast. Greeting them briefly, we moved on down a rocky trail to another tough climb to Pott's Mountain. It was 4,128 feet and had an equally steep descent down Lone Pine Peak. Entering Lake Wilderness, we found the War Spur Shelter with a tempting, bubbly stream nearby.

"Sorry little stream, we can't tarry." It was misting rain on us and we were eager to spot my husband at VA 632. What a relief! When we met him, it took no convincing to get us to make camp. He had built us a roaring bonfire, anticipating that we would need it, at least to dry off.

The steep down hill walks took a greater toll on my poor feet than going up. They were in some kind of hurt. The pain was getting disconcerting, but I would endure. Our campsite was at 2,080 feet and the temperature was really dropping. It was a good invitation to crawl into my cozy sleeping bag.

APRIL 22, 1993 - a cold morning greeted us with two inches of snow on the ground. We slept in a while longer before getting up to go into Blacksburg, VA, to do our laundry. It was a pleasant drive and we got to see one of the few remaining old covered bridges. They planted flower gardens around it and made a scenic view even though the flowers were just beginning to bloom. It brightened my day, making the barren trees and snow a little less depressing.

After the laundry was dried, Bill dropped California Tent Lady and me back at the trail around noon. Two tough ladies stubbornly hiked two miles and began a steep climb to Rocky Gap, on John's Creek Mountain, 3,264 feet. With that out of the way, we continued upward to the top of Kelly Knob, 3,724 feet. We weren't invincible yet. The temperature was cool, but comfortable.

Crossing Laurel Creek wasn't to difficult so we made our way through some pasture land to VA 42. Bill was there and informed me to go on 1.4 miles to VA 630. He had found a big grassy spot for our campsite beside the trail in a valley. It was also beside Sinking Creek where we could see the climb to Sinking Creek Mountain that we would make in the morning. As I lay in my sleeping bag I was fighting a foreboding. It was the kind of foreboding you feel when you know the last day of warm summer is gone and dark, cold winter is certainly on its way. The only problem was, it was just the opposite here. Spring was coming and it didn't seem to change anything. One thing was locked in my mind, I will hike later in the spring, next time.

APRIL 23, 1993 - A cold morning was battling a warrior sun, bound and determined it would warm the chill for our hike. Down the trail, an image loomed. The closer we got, the bigger it was. It was a large white oak tree, known on the trail as the *KEFFER OAK,*. 18 feet around it was. Even without leaves, it was beautiful.

Further up the ridge top of Sinking Creek Mountain, we came upon some small fields, where apple trees were scattered. Old-time farmers had piled flat rocks in pyramid shape piles. Having never seen rocks piled in this unique, scenic way, I could only wonder if it served any other useful purpose. I suppose if you wanted to build a cabin or fence you would have ready material.

We had a long straight trail going northeast, then curving back to the southeast. It was picturesque walking with forest on one side and Sinking Creek Valley on the other. Passing Sarver Cabin with a spring for water, then Niday Shelter, it didn't take us long to reach VA 621, at 1,540 feet, where reliable ol' Bill waited to take a break with us.

Pushing on, the trail began to twist and turn like a snake through thick, barren trees sprinkled with occasional, pines along the northwest slope of Brush Mountain. It was rather pleasant. Climbing to a narrow ridge, we traversed several knife-like rock outcroppings before descending steeply to VA 620. Our gentleman overseer had made a camp for us on Trout Creek, near the north rim of Trout Creek Gorge. California Tent Lady and I were both very tired tonight. Climbing over all those rock outcroppings had certainly not done my feet any favors either.

APRIL 24, 1993 - Rising early that morning it looked like it would be a great day to hike. We skirted Miller's Cove, ascended steeply for about 6 miles through rocks to Cove Mountain at 3,050 feet. This is magnificent country but not for the faint of heart. There were a lot of day hikers out who thought they qualified, as they climbed the rocks to Dragon's Tooth, a large rock monolith with views of sandstone ridges and Catawba Valley sprawling below.

Descending through some rugged narrow steep rocks, we reached Catawba Valley. It was both beautiful and tortuous up there and we were glad to get off the rocky steep trail to a peaceful pine grove. At VA 624, the altitude was a comfortable 1,790 feet. This was a good place to share lunch with the waiting Bill.

Climbing Sandstone Ridge was easy and brought us to the descent onto the flood plain of Catawba Creek. The grass was green and lush and there was remains of a little dam left on the creek. Back up again, by way of switchbacks to Sawtooth Ridge on the Catawba Mountain Crest. Up and down was sort of tiring for the next 2.9 miles over steep knolls along the crest.

A gradual descent to VA 311 was welcomed for several reasons. Bill was waiting and we eagerly went to a motel for a hot shower and a good night's rest. Tomorrow would be a long day. California Tent Lady and my proud self have hiked 112.5 miles since we started this trip. Good gracious, I used to think a five mile walk at home was something special.

APRIL 25, 1993 - I was walking pretty confident today after becoming aware of how far this unusual lady and myself had hiked in a relatively short period. We were getting another early start as we ascended on an old wood road most of the way past Catawba Mountain Shelter to McAfee Knob. A descent by rock steps to Devil's Kitchen ended us up at an area of huge, room-sized rocks in the shape of blocks. They looked like some giant child's toy blocks that had been swatted in anger, scattering them all over the place.

There were a lot of rock outcroppings that could have made dangerous hiking, if it had been raining like the other day. Cautiously walking the edge of Tinker Cliffs for 0.5 miles, eventually exposed an overlook with views of another section of Tinker Mountain to the S.E., which we would cross over later. It was great. Brushy Mountain to the south and North Mountain to the Northwest, Carver's Cove Reservoir, Peaks of Otter, Apple Orchard Mountain and looking back to the left we could see McAfee Knob from whence we had come. A good place for lunch.

To air out the boots, rest, and cool our feet at the same time, we pulled boots and socks off. Sitting there, wiggling our toes in the breeze, made for a refreshing rest that we hated to end. All good things must end, so donning the freshened socks and heavy boots, we were off again. Not far, on a downward walk, we came to Lambert's Meadow Shelter. Water from a stream there seemed satisfactory so we filled up and headed across the saw-toothed ridge until we descended to Chimney Rocks. A lot of day hikers were out enjoying the rugged beauty of the area.

With over four miles to go and already worn out, it was a good thing we had mostly downhill hiking to the crossing of Tinker Creek. U.S. 220 and Bill were not far from there. The Knight, with the wooden leg, took us to Troutville, VA and civilization. Motel, shower, good food, the whole works. Soaking my poor, aching feet prepared me for a welcomed night's sleep.

APRIL 26, 1993 - If I had wanted civilization all the time, I would have gone home. I didn't. So early in the morn, up the long climb to Fullhardt Shelter, California Tent Lady and I went. Another lady hiker was camped inside. We had no intention of stopping here, so after a short conversation which made a nice break, we were off again.

The trail was in good shape and we were moving along at a pretty good clip, when we got to the Wilson Creek Shelter. Lo and behold, we found a man still in his sleeping bag. Seeing us, put him in a mood to talk. So not wanting to be ill mannered, we visited with him for a while.

His trail name was Julian, in his early twenties and a very nice looking young fellow indeed. It was his first day back on the trail from a previous hike on the A.T. from Springer Mountain to U.S. 220 and he was plumb worn out. His plan then, was to hike on to Mt. Katahdin that year. I informed him he still had about 1,446 miles to go, so he had better get with the program. He replied that the last climb he had made took his last drop of energy, so he called it quits and went to bed. We told him we were headed the same direction and he said maybe he would catch up to us later. California Tent Lady was getting impatient, wished him good hiking and we pushed upward to the Blue Ridge Parkway.

Bill was glad to see us and drove us to the Peaks of Otter Campground. It was getting colder and trying to rain. The wind blowing made it even colder and didn't make putting up our ingenious lean-to tent any easier, either. Inside was cozy, once the job was done. Finally, getting on the Blue Ridge Parkway that would be our companion for awhile, was exciting in a way. I totaled our miles for the day before going to sleep. We had tacked on another 14.6 miles. California Tent Lady was quite a motivating personality.

APRIL 27, 1993 - 7:00 a.m., back at the A.T., it was cold and windy. Another reminder that I would be starting my hike later in the season next time. Meanwhile, following the Blue Ridge Parkway for 7.4 miles and actually crossing it several times, I got the feeling that the fume-belching automobile traffic had invaded our solitude. That ended when we got to Bearwallow Gap and the trail turned west making us climb to the summit of Cove Mountain at 2,682 feet.

At Cove Mountain Shelter, who should we find? Not Santa Claus, but the young man, Julian. He was confused as he told how he had woke up in the night at the Wilson Creek Shelter where we had left him, thinking it was early morning. So he started hiking, only to realize it was still night time. Now he was at this shelter, sleeping in the daytime again. If he doesn't get his clock straight, he's going to do all his hiking at night. Not a good idea! He had to get back into the grove of hiking. Good luck, Julian.

We traveled five forested miles of Cove Mountain Ridge going over a series of ten knobs and nine sags, before descending to Jenning's Creek at 960 feet. Bill was there and prompted us to take a rest. I think he was getting lonesome. My feet were killing me so I pulled my boots off and soaked my sore tootsies in a cold, cold stream. It must have numbed them because it felt pretty good. Too early to camp though, so we continued climbing up to Fork Mountain, an elevation of 2,042 feet. After that, we descended to a dirt road called VA 714. Lonesome Bill had found a nice little spot to spend the night. The weather had warmed up, making it a dreamy evening. With my sore feet, any night would be a good night to camp.

APRIL 28, 1993 - only 0.3 miles up the trail, we came to a small clearing known as Button Hill. We picked up some buttons. Surprised you, didn't I? Seems that Button Hill got its name from a nearby garment factory that once used the area as a dump. The hundreds of buttons mixed in with the dirt, were mostly like shirt buttons. I'm going to put some on a hiking shirt for a novelty. Isn't it nice that a hill is really named appropriately, once in a while?

Another 3/4 mile down the trial, we came to the New Bryant Ridge Shelter. It was still under construction, nearing completion and what a shelter it was. Three stories high, it could sleep twenty easily and was being built in memory of Nelson Garnett, Jr., an A.T. hiker who died in 1992. I don't know how he left this world but his family felt hiking was so important to him, they made a substantial gift, designated especially for shelters, as a memorial.

We are grateful to Mr. Garnett Jr. The outhouse was awful nice and the small stream flowing close by was appreciated also. Who should we find inside the shelter? Yep, Julian. He was still sleeping and we couldn't resist waking him up. He was wiped out, so it was useless. Boy, this kid ain't ever gonna get his nights and days straight!

Leaving him behind to decide what time of day it was for himself, we climbed to Bryant Ridge at 2,394 feet.

Views of Outstanding Apple Orchard Mountain with its 200 ft. cascading falls, spread out before us. Then more climbing to Floyd Mountain at 3,560 feet. By-passing the Cornelius Creek Shelter near the Blue Ridge Parkway, the trail again followed close to the Parkway for 2.7 miles to Parker's Gap Road at 3,380 feet.

Ascending a rocky trail by switchbacks, we finally reached Apple Orchard Mountain for real. We were at 4,125 feet. No time to stop as we moved on to Thunder Hill Shelter for a welcomed break. Both California Tent Lady and I always liked to write in the shelter log books. Rest was more important to me, so I let her have the honors for us both.

When we got to Petites Gap Road at 2,369 feet, we met Bill. He took us out of the park to the Wilderness Campground where we were glad to get a hot shower, one of the things you learn to appreciate, because you do get cruddy on the trail. Dirt also makes for nasty nightmares occasionally, but that night I was ready for clean dreams.

APRIL 29, 1993 - back to Petites Gap early in the morning. Bill and the Blue Ridge Parkway were left behind, at least for a while. Soon we came to a USFS sign that read, *James River Face Wilderness.* The A.T. traverses this wilderness area for the next 9.5 miles. It was really nice out but strange to be in nature as she was putting on her spring wardrobe. The trees were giving birth to new leaves in the lower elevations and the room temperature of this huge span of the world was in the neat 70's, at least when the sun's lamp was on.

Crossing Big Cove Branch was exhilarating, with several different views of James River, snaking its way through valleys and cutting occasional gorges deeper. Descending to Matt's Creek Shelter with its gurgling creek nearby, was so nice, we had to take a break. Afterwards, only 2.5 miles to James River. We knew Bill would be nearby at U.S. 501 Highway, so we took our time and enjoyed ourselves.

He was visiting with a familiar character. It was our nocturnal hiker, Julian. Bless his heart, his poor tootsies were hurting. He made me feel ten years younger, just looking at him. I broke out the moleskin. Since we had plenty I was glad to share with him especially since he made me feel so youthful.

California Tent Lady and I walked across James River on Snowden Bridge, leaving Bill to nurture poor *old* Julian. Spotting a small dam west of the bridge, we couldn't resist going out a ways. The river was wide but the water was shallow below the dam, with rocks jutting up among the outcroppings of boulders.. Very pretty. James River is the largest waterway in Virginia, flowing 450 miles from the Allegheny Mountains to the Chesapeake Bay. After crossing the bridge at 660 feet, Bill picked us up and took us back to the Campground. We washed our laundry and we settled down to a peaceful evening of restful relaxation.

APRIL 30, 1993 - somewhat relaxed, but feeling the weariness of being on an exceptionally long hike, we started the morning climbing. It gets the blood circulating right off the bat and warms you up quickly. It was a cool new day and upon entering John's Hollow, we passed the shelter of the same name on our way to Fuller's Rocks at 2,480 feet. From there, we looked back on a panorama of James River from the side we had only viewed at a distance, the day before.

As we looked back over the James River Face Wilderness, a sadness came over me. I wished I had started this hiking a lot younger. I wished something in my childhood had motivated me to do so. What would it have been like, say in the 40's? Would I ever pass this way again? What would it be like then?

Oh well, no time to get sentimental. Moving on we ascended to Big Rocky Row at 2,992 feet. It was obvious we would be going up and down in a big way today, as we climbed to Bluff Mountain and discovered we were at 3,372 feet. Going up?

Boy, just as I was getting myself out of a melancholy rut, we found a memorial stone to someone called *Little Ottie*; a simple stone with a few old flowers laying around. Seems a very young, four-year old boy, Ottie Cline, went into the woods in the fall of 1890, a total of 7 miles. I can't believe this! He was actually gathering firewood for his schoolhouse and never returned. His little body was found five months later, nestled among a beautiful group of black spruce, on top of Bluff Mountain. Wow! What's wrong with this story? Can you imagine a child of today, four-years old doing this? I mean, how much wood could the little thing carry that distance? How sad! There's got to be more to this story.

I could only wonder if my mood had been inspired by the spirit of this little thing. I don't know about this subject but I felt awfully strange. It was fortunate the descending trail was a lot easier, since I was deep in thought. California Tent Lady asked me if I was all right. I nodded my head, yes. Her voice seemed off in the distance.

Dropping down slightly to Punch Bowl Mountain and another shelter, it was back to Bill and the Blue Ridge Parkway. After relaying to him what a strange day I was having, California Tent Lady and I marched on a short distance where he met us again on Route 607. We met a couple from England and I eyed them carefully, wondering if they were going to contribute more to this very strange day. Their story was sad, but dull. They had started hiking at Harper's Ferry and were working their way south to Springer Mountain. The wife had hurt her ankle so they were struggling. I told her I knew what she was going through. We wished them luck, bid Bill good-bye and continued our hike on to Little Irish Creek.

On the way, we passed the foot of Rice Mountain. Even though we didn't have to climb the slight elevation, we continued a decline to where we again found Bill. He found us a good campsite by the creek. There were other people hiking and sightseeing in this scenic area. I was tired and we had chalked off another 15 miles today. Sleep came, and my mind was still on little Ottie.

MAY 1, 1993 - Little purplish wild Irish were popping their heads out of the ground. We found them all along the trail. Bill joined us as we hiked over to Pedlar Lake Dam, altitude, 960 feet. The lake is one of the few on the Blue Ridge. The dam was built to make a reservoir to supply water to Lynchburg, VA, 20 miles away. There were some pretty views from the concrete walkway that we used to cross below the dam.

We left Bill behind as we hiked about two miles around the east side of Pedlar Lake at the foot of Piney Mountain. Ascending into Brown Mountain Creek Valley, there were ruins of old homesteads marked by stone chimneys and crumbling rock walls. There were stories here, whispering silently in the wind among the pines, of the struggles of the courageous pioneers.

Old stone wall fences that once contained cattle of the hard working people, dotted the countryside. Decaying timbers of quickly built shelters, where the dreams of slaves still lingered after they had been granted freedom. Looking over the fields that still exist, I imagined cattle and hogs grazing, with children of the past laughing and playing. It was a historical beauty

That melancholy feeling was coming over me again as California Tent Lady and I arrived at Brown Mountain Creek Shelter. We decided to take a short break. Leaving the shelter, we gradually ascended for about three miles along Brown Mountain Creek. Canadian Hemlocks were scattered along its banks. A little steeper climb brought us to Long Mountain where Bill was waiting on U.S. 60, elevation, 2,065 feet

After lunch, Bill joined us as we climbed Bald Knob, 4,059 feet, the highest peak in the area. Years ago it was cleared for farming but you wouldn't know it now with the overgrown underbrush and the dense woods. Nature does inevitably claim her own. Leaving Bill to return back to the highway, we continued down the northeast side of Bald Knob only to ascend Cow Camp Gap. The trail was up and down and we were meeting a lot of weekend hikers visiting the popular area because of its excellent views. It was awesome with creeks meandering to the North and numerous mountain peaks and creeks to the East and Southeast.

Passing Hog Camp Gap, we proceeded across Tar Jacket Ridge to where Bill met us again at Salt Log Gap and USFS 63. The elevation where he had made camp was 3,247 feet. My husband is a good camper, always cleaning up the trail heads wherever he parks. This was an extra messy place before he arrived. Settling down for the night, I calculated the miles we had hiked that day. A tired smile crossed my face. An astounding 218 miles! Not bad for two determined ladies!

MAY 2, 1993 - inspired by our miles, we got an early start. It had been the warmest night for camping since we started. The day time temperatures in the 70's, made great hiking. Twisting our way past Rocky Mountain, at times only one half to three quarters of a mile Southeast of the Blue Ridge Parkway, we came to Twin Springs. East over Porter Mountain was Spy Rock. Supposedly, the Confederate troops used this spot to watch the movement of Union forces in the sprawling Great Valley of Virginia below. California Tent Lady climbed to the top of the rock while I stayed below on the trail. Did that bother me? You bet! It was just too hard a climb for me. I was the kid who wouldn't climb to the tree house. The other kids elaborated on how far they could see, while I squirmed in envy.

Settling down to covering some country, because there was limited scenery when we reached Maintop Mountain at 4,040 feet. It was the same at the summit of The Priest at 4,063 feet, however, someone had carved an Indian Chief head out of an old tree stump. It added to the mystery of the A.T. Why would someone take the time to use their artistic talent in such a remote area? There are a lot of hikers on this trail, and it does do something to the imagination. What better studio to work? The problem is, the artist was anonymous and the work was excellent.

Snaking our way back and forth on switchbacks down a steep 4.2 miles, and then following Cripple Creek for a ways, we found Bill on VA 56 by the Tye River, elevation 997 feet. Another familiar face was with him. You guessed it, dear, confused Julian. Bill had picked him up on his way to meet us. We all rode back to Crabtree Meadows Campground to spend the night. Crabtree Falls, the highest falls on the Virginia Blue Ridge, drops in five cascades, 1,500 feet to the Tye River below. Ancient hemlock trees and rhododendrons actually grow on the levels between the cascades making an unusual and beautiful site. The old A.T. used to come this way. Naturally, it was the trail Julian had taken.

MAY 3, 1993 - Bill took California Tent Lady and me back to Tye River at an elevation of 997 feet. After that he took his buddy, Julian into town for a food drop. Crossing the Tye River on a suspension bridge, it was only a mile further that we came upon two turkey hunters, right on the trail! This sent shivers up my spine because some of these characters really can't tell a turkey from a hiker. We got out of their sight as quickly as possible and then took a short break at Harper's Creek Shelter. With a cautious eye, we watched for the hunters, then headed up to a steep and rocky trail. Julian, with his new supplies, caught up with us. I think he was finally getting his hiking clock straightened out.

He informed us he was going to spend the night at Rusty's Hard Time Hollow, then he was off like a shot, leaving us behind. The shelter was off the trail, so we knew this would not be a suitable stop for us. He had given us a lot of laughs and fun conversation that would be no more. It was the last time we saw him and he would be missed, along with all the other characters that have passed our way. We did learn that Julian had climbed Katahdin in July of 1993.

Passing along a ridge, we saw some interesting rock formations called Chimney Rocks, Balanced Rock and Hay Rock, huge fragments of tilted sandstone layer that makes the backbone of Tinker Ridge. After that, we reached the highest point of Three Ridges at 3,970 feet. It got miserably rocky quite often on the descent. The old feet took agonizing notice of this.

Maupin Field Shelter provided us another short break and we passed up a 1.5 mile hike to a 40 foot waterfall. It was about the same distance on down to Reeds Gap at 2,650 feet, on the Blue Ridge Parkway, so we took off for that destination. Bill was waiting for us. After a brief visit, tired and getting anxious to cover as many miles as we could before evening, we started climbing again on a rough, rocky trail.

Leaving some woods, we crossed the grassy top of Cedar Ridge with spectacular views. We paid little attention because our Knight in the Jeep was waiting at the Dripping Rock parking area. From there, he took us to a state forest campground where two weary hikers were more than willing to spend the night. Mother nature must have sensed that we needed the rest as she spread her dark cloudy hand over the area with a promise of rain. True to her signs, it did. At least I think it did. Restful slumber put me in another world.

MAY 4, 1993 - the Mother of all creatures confirmed that rain would be our companion, at least during the morning. Cautiously, we made our way over rock slides past Laurel Springs Gap and eventually climbed to the flat topped Humpback Mountain, elevation of 3,600 feet. The cloudy hand hovered as a fog, making only the immediate trail visible. There would be no sight seeing for a while. It was all I could do to keep from slipping on the many rock steps on the steep switchbacks.

After going down almost a thousand feet we entered woods so thick that even without the fog you couldn't see anything from Dobie Mountain, 2,700 feet. Crossing Mill Creek, we looked ahead and there was a clean new shelter called Paul Wolfe Shelter. It was a good place to take a break. When we were rested, we started a moderate ascent of Elk Mountain. There was an overlook that, had it not been for the trees and the lingering fog, we could have had a partial view of the Shenandoah Valley.

The trail was easier as we arrived at Rockfish Gap, 1,902 feet where trusty Bill picked us up. We went into Waynesboro, got a motel, did our laundry and indulged in a delicious restaurant meal. Tomorrow we would get a close-up look at the view we had been cheated out of by the blinding weather and trees. We would be hiking into the Shenandoah National Park.

Before drifting off into dreamland in the comfortable motel bed, I reflected back to when I had retired from Wal-Mart in April of 1992. It should have been the beginning of my American dream. My husband, Bill, and I could not just up and leave our farm for a long period.

My dream hiking is limited but Bill is disabled, I am retired, and I should be able to get our business streamlined enough to allow us to spend more time doing what we both love. It's not easy to get rid of all things that get in the way of your dreams. It took us years of hard work to be able to go as much as we do. In the process, the bodies got older and even though we have more time, youth has run off and hid somewhere and I fear we shall never find it again.

Before retiring I bought a new Jansport D-5 backpack. This proved to be a wise investment because it is so much better to carry my rain gear and necessary items. Preparation, that's one thing you must do to accomplish the many miles of hiking in nature's great attractions, as I have done and am doing. My advice to people is to take the time on their vacations to get those young bodies to do something that you feel is a challenge.

Cherish that youth and the little time you have it. Get out and do something just for you.

MAY 5, 1993 - The faucet turned off during the night while my body was recuperating. A beautiful day was spread out before me. We picked up our park Permits at the Shenandoah Park Entrance. Good-bye to the Blue Ridge Parkway. It ends as we enter the Shenandoah National Park and is replaced by the Skyline Drive Parkway that will parallel the A.T. mostly through the park. It also crossed the trail several times so Bill would meet us at those points.

The highest mountain we hiked today was 2,980 feet where a trail called Riprap comes in to the A.T. We were covering some country when Bill picked us up at milepost 87.2 on the Skyline. He took us to Swift River Campground in the middle of the park, where we got a rare treat, a half-gallon of ice cream. We ate the whole thing!

I had a restless night and couldn't get my mind to stop skip jumping. You probably know what I mean. It's when you think of everything else but sleep, even when you know better. Usually I think of the next day's hike but that night I had children, farm and practically everything I could do nothing about, plaguing me into insomnia.

MAY 6, 1993 - My husband drove us back to the trail. While I was trying to wake up, we saw over thirty deer and two turkeys along the Skyline Drive. It was a good sampling of the huge controlled animal population in the park. The deer seemed pretty tame. At any rate, I was about as awake as I was going to be. The first mile that day on the trail, we climbed to Blackrock at 3,092 feet. It

111

was appropriately named since it was extremely rocky, but the trail was well maintained and not so bad.

Bill was supposed to meet us at Brown's Gap Road but he wasn't there. Visions of the worst case scenario began to cross my mind. Why is it we always think the worst when something unusual happens? The fact is, he was almost, always ahead of me.

Putting my thoughts of tragedy aside, I left him a note stating that we would see him at the next crossing. Other than getting panicked, it was all I could do. Needless to say, we covered the next miles in doggone good time. At Doyle's River Parking Overlook, milepost 81.9, the man with the Jack Nicholson smile was there. He wasn't smiling now though as he told how he had hiked in to meet us on Blackrock, and took a blue-blazed trail instead of the white-blaze that we were on. That's how and why he had missed us. I was so thankful that he wasn't hurt, I overcame my frustrated anger. What do you do with a husband with one wooden leg who acts like he has *four* normal ones. Better for me if he was a four-legged animal, then I could put a leash on him!

The A.T. skirted the east side of Loft Mountain Campground. It was no use to us anyway because it was closed. Again, we were too early in the season. We did meet an interesting southbound hiker, who called himself, Sloo-Foot. He had hiked all the way from Maine and told some stories about the trail I would be hiking in the future.

As Sloo-Foot meandered south we came up on an overlook with a perfect view of the wide expanse of Roach River Valley. Sitting on a rock ledge was another cute pair, called Pouch and Padre. Padre was a priest and Pouch, a sweet little poodle dog.

Hikers who may never be social people normally, seem willing to talk on the lonely trail and Padre was no different. He immediately slipped into a spiel about his adventures on his trip all the way from Springer Mountain. As I looked at his little poodle, I could not help thinking of my dog, Chief, with his turned up tail and the black and red pack strapped on his sparkling white coat. Poor Pouch had a sore paw, but Padre said he was doing pretty good, considering.

Bill met us at Smith Roach Gap, milepost 68.6. Padre and his Poodle caught up with us. Pouch seemed to be doing all right with his sore paw. They were running short on food, so in the tradition of good hikers, we shared. We decided to drive back to Swiftrun Campground where we were last night. It had been a lovely 70° day and the Dogwood trees were blooming beautifully. Three deer peeked cautiously out at us.

MAY 7, 1993 - They say you can't catch up sleep and I say that's baloney. After last night, I was an entirely different women than I had been the morning before. The breakfast of oatmeal, tea and a pop tart was pretty standard for us on the trail and seemed to keep my energy up.

I was ready to cover some miles at 6:22 a.m. In 1.3 miles we came to a place called Hightop Hut. The huts in the park, unlike the shelters, charge by the night and are on an honor system. Basically for thru-hikers only and because they charge for their service, they are usually pretty nice.

It was a fairly easy climb to the summit of Hightop Mountain, 3.987 feet. The descent was a different matter and got pretty steep and hairy at times on the way down to Swift Run Gap, milepost 65.5 on Skyline Drive. The drop had been 1,611 feet before heading right back up Saddleback Mountain to 3,296 feet. Trillium flowers, with their tall stems and leathery leaves, were blooming here like they were trying to rush spring along. The flowers were white to pink in color and the variety was a welcome sight from the rhododendrons that were so prevalent all along the trail.

Bill found a parking area on the Skyline Drive where we met him. While we climbed Boldface Mountain, 3,600 feet, he drove to Lewis Mountain Campground where we were to meet him later. It was a pretty easy trail to hike so we were able to relax. Bill was at the campground as scheduled and, as it turned out, it was the only campground open until Memorial Day weekend. Good thing we decided to spend the night there.

California Tent Lady and I decided to hike three more miles to Booten's Gap, 3,243 feet, milepost 55.1, where Bill picked us up and drove back to the campground. It filled up in a hurry, so we were glad we had saved our site earlier. Padre and a policeman from New Jersey, who also had a dog, came in later. Since the campground was full, Padre looked around and spotted us. The Ranger sent them over to our campsite. Lucky for them, we prepare in advance.

Pouch's paw hadn't improved and he was limping worse. Padre was getting concerned as he inspected the little dog. After all that hiking, he found a little rock lodged in the paw that he had overlooked. It turned out to be the problem for sure. Poor little poodle! After it was removed, he did a lot better. We enjoyed a nice evening with our extra guests and other campers, sharing stories of our hiking experiences. Then sleep dictated the end of the day.

MAY 8, 1993 - Bill took us back to Booten's Gap and we continued our hike, climbing to the top of

Hazeltop, 3,823 feet, the highest point on the A.T. in the Shenandoah National Park. Red spruce and balsam trees were plentiful as we continued to Milam Gap for a peaceful break with Bill.

The trail was getting harder and my body was about worn out as we skirted the north edge of Big Meadows Campground. Of course it was closed. Even though it was getting harder to enjoy, there were some beautiful sites. It was good that Bill was able to meet us as often as he did, due to the closeness of Skyline Drive Parkway to the trail. It made the day go by a lot faster.

He picked us up at Little Stony Man Parking Area, milepost 39.1 and we went back to the Lewis Mountain Campground. The pleasant 70° temperature was making for some great weather. It was a good thing because I was rapidly winding down. This had been a long hike for Den Mama.

MAY 9, 1993 - Arising was getting harder but we still started hiking back at the Little Stony Man Parking Area at 6:30 a.m. The trail was very easy and helped to cheer me up a bit.

At Byrds Nest #3, we found a backpack that some hiker had left inside. As we were about to leave, a desperate lady hiker came from a side trail. She was looking for water. We told her about a nice piped spring behind the hut. I noticed she had no pack so I told her, "Boy, you sure do it the hard way!" She was almost crying as she told us she had lost her pack. It felt good to tell her there was one in the hut. She came out grinning like a Cheshire cat. We dropped the subject because she felt silly enough. However, it was her pack.

Leaves were beginning to bud on the mountain tops, catching up with the full blown ones in the valleys. It was strange. This would normally be when I would be starting a hike, not ending it. Off in the distance I could see a target I had been anxious to get to. It was called Mary's Rock. Jokingly I told California Tent Lady "It was named after me." I don't know why she didn't believe me! It was a large rock outcrop and would always be special to me. Anyway, we climbed to the top, 3,514 feet, and the views made the rock worthy of my name. So, I have an ego. I wouldn't have been there if I didn't. Other day hikers climbed up to share *my rock*. That's all right, as long as they keep it clean and presentable.

Approximately 2.1 miles later, reality set in and we dropped 2,307 feet to Thornton Gap. I was ready for Bill to meet us. He had sensed we were ready for a boost. Remembering it was Mother's day, he took me and California Tent Lady out for lunch. I told her this was one of the many reasons I liked this guy. She thought it was real sweet of him.

After the early, well-needed lunch, being partially rejuvenated, we climbed to the summit of Pass Mountain, 3,052 feet. The trees were thick so we had an excellent view of trees all the way to the top.

Bill met us a couple more times. Afterwards, we were wandering through some thick woods when California Tent Lady got excited. This was not like her so I paid particular attention until she shouted "run". Get real!, I thought, these legs can walk, but run, no way! I looked in her direction to see a baby black bear. I told her, "It was no time to run, because she might run right into the arms of Mama Bear." We stood quietly and the Mama bear never came. The baby bear wasn't as fascinated with us as we were with it and continued on downhill, away from us, Thank goodness! As California Tent Lady finally calmed down, we made our way carefully out of the area, without an introduction to Mama Bear. After it was all over and we were safe with Bill at the Keyser Run Parking Area, I kind of wished we had seen the bear's mother.

After telling Bill about the encounter, we all rode on to the Browntown-Harris Hollow Road Parking Area. Bill and I were both tired as we crawled into the jeep for a rest. California Tent Lady did something very unusual, especially after the bear incident, she hid her tent down below the parking area away from us. I was just to worn out to worry about it.

MAY 10, 1993 - my hiking buddy already had her tent packed and by our jeep. It seems deer had circled her tent, snorting all night and, of course, keeping her awake. She said they were angry at her. Bless her heart, first she thought a bear was going to get her and now the deer almost did. One deer was still hanging around letting us know it did not appreciate our presence. I concluded that she had put her tent in their nesting area and they were just trying to move her out.

After that excitement, we hit the trail at 6:00 a.m. It was a lovely day and we were making good time, but California Tent Lady was acting a little moody. When she asked me if I wanted to quit hiking at Compton Gap, it came as no surprise. That would not have gotten us out of the Shenandoah National. I had to tell her I would rather hike to the end of the park, so I wouldn't have to finish it next year. Not only that, but it would make Bill have to come back into the park to get me on the trail later. Reluctantly, she agreed.

After arriving at Compton Gap, mile post 10.4, elevation 2,415 feet and a short break with Bill, we continued on down the trail. Stopping at the Tom Floyd Wayside Shelter, out of curiosity I looked in the logbook.

Padre and his little dog, Pouch, had spent the night there. Sadly, I knew I may never see them again. It was a nice place and I hoped they had rested well.

As we walked on we came to the property of the National Zoological Park Conservation and Research Center. Tall fences surrounded the area for 2.5 miles. We tried to see the various zoo animals, but they never appeared. Crossing a bridge over Sloan Creek Swamp, it was really grassy. Someone had mowed the right-of-way to the A.T.

Leaving the Skyline Drive Parkway and after hiking 6 miles, we reached U.S. 522 where Bill waited patiently. He wasn't the least bit surprised when we told him the hike was over for this year. It was only 1:00 p.m., as we loaded the jeep and took California Tent Lady to Dulles International Airport. We spent the last night with her in a motel, since a flight was not leaving that day. It was an emotional thing to say good-bye to someone you had spent so much time with. However, she did promise to hike with me in 1994, so I was happy. That tough lady and I had hiked a total of 368.8 miles. You just don't forget that. The long trip home to the best campsite in the world, was one of deep thought.

God is the one who made the mountains and created the winds. He makes his thoughts known to man; he changes day into night. He walks on the heights of the earth. This is His name; the Lord God Almighty!
Amos. 4:13

1994

Enough of the hum-drum normal life. It had been nice being home with my friends and family but my hiking pal is waiting in St. Louis, Missouri, apparently as eager as I am to get back on the trail. The trip to St. Louis ushered in a happy reunion as we arrived at the home California Tent Lady's sister. They were good people, inviting us out for dinner and to spend the night at their home.

In those gracious and welcome surroundings, California Tent Lady and I were able to catch up on all that had happened since we last saw each other. Her sister listened intently as we poured over all the exciting things that we had experienced on our adventures. I think I spotted a little friendly envy.

Hiking makes it easy to appreciate other's hospitality, especially when they are not hikers and share the comfort of their homes with us. After all, it is never worse than a tent. In this case, we had a wonderfully comfortable bed and a good night's rest.

APRIL 24, 1994 - early that morning California Tent Lady, Bill and I bid our hosts good-bye and began the long drive to Virginia. I was pondering whatever this trip had to offer as we arrived at Hwy. 522, east of Front Royal, VA at 10:30 a.m. This was to be a different hike in many ways. We would be crossing many major highways, however there would be no parkway along the A.T. or

119

even criss-crossing the trail, as was the case in the Blue Ridge and Shenandoah National Park.

There would be several highways for Bill to meet us, so we decided to leave the large backpacks with him and slackpack the A.T. to VA 55, at Manassas Gap. Ascending and descending, the trail followed the National Zoological Parkland for 2.3 miles. It was magnificent, with wild flowers, dogwoods, and redbud blooming with a wide array of beauty.

We breezed over the 5.3 miles to the Jim and Molly Denton Shelter. Built in 1989, it was dubbed the *Hiker's Hilton*. Wood was already cut and stored neatly in a shed. A table and fire pit under a pavilion made it convenient for burning the wood safely, .

There was a large front patio with solid wood furniture and get this, down a hill by a stream, water from the stream was force-fed through a pipe to a barrel on top of a boxed in shower. You just pulled a chain, the water released, wet you down and you danced like you never dreamed you could. You have to love the outdoors to appreciate this sort of thing. It was really something. They even had daffodils planted along the rock walkway.

We met Bill at Manassas Gap, picked up our packs and continued 2.4 miles to Manassas Gap Shelter where my husband had planned a surprise. He had walked in about a mile to visit with us. This was so sweet and not without a lot of effort, due to his wooden leg.

The shelter was picturesque, with a peaceful spring and a table in front of a quaint building. It was a macaroni-and-cheese supper that Bill and I shared. We had a pleasant evening going over the day's events. Bill had to get back to the jeep and left us in a most unpleasant situation. Mother Nature, in a sour mood, was allowing her dive bombers to attack. The little flying monsters were mercilessly going after our eyes, ears and noses as we tried to go to bed.

The bugs continued to keep us company through the night so I finally decided to put on my bug shirt. It helped. This experience would send all but the most seasoned hikers packing for home but you learn that Mother Nature is not unlike God. You must tolerate the good with the bad. I guess that's what makes us strong.

APRIL 25, 1994 - leaving the flying enemy behind at 7:00 a.m., we were back on the trail. Hiking was easy, as we arrived at a blue-blazed trail that lead to Dick's Dome Shelter. Even though it was 0.2 miles down a hill, off the trail, we decided to visit there and take a break. The unusual geodesic dome structure was worth the effort and the lovely stream passing in front, only added to the charm. It was different, but unique, in a modern sort of way.

Two more miles down the trail, we entered Sky Meadows State Park. It was easy going through there and not long thereafter we reached U.S. 50. Bill was there with his usual good nature and took us to a little restaurant for a good old juicy hamburger.

California Tent Lady had brought a new pair of boots and decided to give them a workout. After putting them on, they felt so good she gave her old ones a heave-ho in the next trash can. Her feet had been hurting her a lot and it was good to see her relieved. On the trail at 2:00 p.m., she made a comical statement about how much more cooperative her feet had become. In my mind, I was thinking how more cooperative she had become. Hiking is difficult enough without a companion in pain.

Some of the obvious differences on this trail were the marvelous variety of trees. Elms, dogwood, beach, maple, hickory, and oak trees, scattered among old stone walls and outdated mine pits made for unusual scenery and, I might add, made the 85° temperature a little more tolerable. Even so, we were pleased to see a nice stream on the path before Rod Hollow Shelter. Unloading our packs at the shelter, we strolled back to the stream for a refreshing splash bath. We were pleased with our 13.6 miles. Not bad for the second day on the trail! The refreshing rinse and the bug population being low caused me to look forward to a restful sleep.

APRIL 26, 1994 - was hot early in the morning and taking its toll on us. It was steep up one mountain and the descent equally so, making the beginning of a hard day's hike. Crossing the many beautiful creeks was a benefit, not only in scenery but also giving us the luxury of splashing ourselves once in a while. Meeting Bill at VA 605, we had a break before struggling on.

Regretfully leaving Bill behind, we finally stopped to soak our feet in a stream before ascending to Bears Den Rocks. From here we had an outstanding view of the Shenandoah Valley. After filling our eyes and brains to overflowing, we descended to VA 7, where Bill picked us up and took us to the Bears Den Hostel.

The quartzite castle, now owned by ATC (Appalachian Trail Conference), was built in the 1930's. It had bunks, hot showers and a kitchen for our use. It was too hot out to pitch our tents, so we slept in the basement of the hostel, and it was so much cooler. At $10.00 per person, it was well worth it. We had hiked 10.3 miles and were in dire need of a good night's rest.

APRIL 27, 1994 - when we arose, the temperature was again rising. Regardless, when Bill put us back on the trail, we left Snickers Gap (VA 7), ascending through pine and chestnut oak that gave us some welcome shade from the merciless sun. This one small blessing made hiking a lot better than yesterday. In 2.5 miles we came to Crescent Rock where we enjoyed excellent views of the Shenandoah River and Valley below.

Three quarters of a mile further was another interesting place called the Devil's Racecourse. It was a deposit of boulders, with an unusual small stream running beneath them. We were making good time as we pressed on. Passing a blue-blazed trail that lead to the Blackburn Center, a light shower of rain fell on us. We didn't mind a bit. It was moist and warm and felt so good.

At 3:00 p.m., Bill met us at W. VA 9 in Keys Gap. Since we had hiked 13.4 miles, we were ready to call it quits. We found a campground in Harper's Ferry with rustic cabins. After acquiring a cabin, we left for a laundromat to do the necessary laundry. A very good meal at a restaurant, which is always a treat, left me in a good mood to call it a day. Upon retiring, I must admit I still would reflect back on what had led me to take on this wondrous hardship.

APRIL 28, 1994 - hiking was easy this morning. The temperature was cool and we were anxious to get to Harper's Ferry. A steep drop to the historical Shenandoah River created an excited feeling in me, as I found myself crossing the bridge where so many famous and infamous had passed before. It didn't hurt to see Bill waiting patiently on the other side.

I knew the Appalachian Trail Company Headquarters was in the area so we drove over to pay them a visit. As the door opened, there was Jean Cashin, author of many articles in the *Appalachian Trail News.*

Having read most of her writings, it was such an honor to meet her. She even helped me decide what guide books of Pennsylvania and New Jersey I would need later. Rather than order the material, I decided to buy it then and there. This turned out to be a blessing in disguise. They were out of new books so a nice sales lady offered to *give me* books that had been returned to ATC. Boy, was I ever grateful. After all, they were in excellent condition. During the process I spotted a rain cover for my backpack so I bought it.

Before we left, Jean took a picture of California Tent Lady, Bill and me for the Appalachian Trail Album. What an honor! It had been a wonderful visit with the special lady and I hated to end it.

California Tent Lady and I couldn't resist sightseeing around Harper's Ferry. Bill went on a trip out to the Harper's Ferry Youth Hostel. We caught up with him later. California Tent Lady and I continued on the A.T. following the white-blaze guides through town. Remember, to complete my hike, I had to walk the trail in town or wherever.

Jefferson Rock, a flat stone supported by red sandstone pillars, rose from a larger rock perched on a cliff. After climbing to the top of the rock, the Shenandoah River spread out before us. To the right, the spire of Chimney Rock was seen rising above Loudoun Heights. The Potomac River sprawled off to our left. It was a haunting sight, when you think of how much of our nation's history had evolved here. Some of the view is now blocked by buildings and trees so I will insert how Jefferson described this same scene in 1782.

From his notes, I quote;

> *"You stand on a very high point. . . .*
> *On your right comes up the Shenandoah . . . .*
> *On your left approaches the Potomac, in quest*
> *of a passage also. In the moment of their*
> *junction, they rush together against the*
> *mountain, render it asunder, and pass off to*
> *the sea. . . .*
>
> *For the mountain being cloven asunder,*
> *she presents to your eye through the cleft, a*
> *small catch of smooth blue horizon, at an*
> *infinite distance of the plain country . . . .*
>
> *This scene is worth a voyage across the*
> *Atlantic. Yet here, as in the neighborhood of*
> *the Natural Bridge, are people who have*
> *passed their lives within a half a dozen miles,*
> *and have never been to survey these*
> *monuments of a war between rivers and*
> *mountains . . . . "*

Moving on past the ruins of St. John's Episcopal Church, built in 1852 and down some stairs a short distance, was St. Peter's Roman Catholic Church, built in 1833. We couldn't resist going inside. It was so beautiful with its old architecture. Down more stairs on the left we found Robert Harper's house, the oldest in Harper's Ferry (1775-1781). It was unique. We didn't go inside but the rock work on the steps where we walked, and the walls, were extraordinary.

I liked the fire-engine house. It was a replica where John Brown made his last stand. Mr. Brown, a Negro, was an ardent abolitionist in the bloody riots in Kansas. He was determined to get the slaves to rise up against their masters.

In 1859 he, and a few of his followers, took over an arsenal in Harper's Ferry. He had all the weapons of war at his disposal and was certain a lot of the black slaves in the vicinity would rally around him.

His plan was to supply the slaves with arms, then send them out to burn the houses and kill all the white men, women and children they could find. He hoped this would frighten the southerners so much, they would abolish slavery. To his disappointment, the Negroes did not come out to help him and the white men of the area surrounded the arsenal, pinned him down until some marines arrived.

It was a sad day for Old John Brown as he was led down the wooden stairs of the fire house. After giving his young child and wife a kiss, he was hanged. The north considered him a martyr, the south considered him a criminal. Some, later, thought he was insane but his acts caused a further division between the north and south until the inevitable Civil War came.

After reading John Brown's story on a sign, I proceeded with mixed emotions. After all, he was going to slaughter innocent women and children. Even so, I felt sorry for his plight.

Following a brick walkway to the G. E. Bryon Memorial Footbridge over the Potomac River, we had another view of the two rivers flowing together. Crossing the Bridge, we stepped into Maryland.

It was flat and easy hiking on the Chesapeake and Ohio Canal Towpath. It was an emotional walking tour of the famous area, but we were glad to finally arrive at Harper's Ferry Hostel, located on the east side of the Potomac, and north of the C & O Towpath.

Bill was involved in a conversation with the caretaker of the hostel when we arrived. It seems, the caretaker felt my husband should have a trail name, since he was such a valuable part of the hike. So because Bill's last name is Twitty and it doesn't take long to discover how fond of pie he his, the caretaker came up with, *Tweety Pie*. I thought it was cute, but strangely enough the handle has stuck to this day.

A tired crew pitched their tents on the lawn of the hostel. The temperature had cooled off and the ever-present bugs were allowing us some peace. I was looking forward to an evening of rest until the Caretaker's wife invited us in to see a video of Bill Irwin, the blind hiker. Needless to say, rest had to wait. The video was so great, I bought one as soon as I arrived home. It capped off an interesting day. Even though we had only hiked 7.6 miles, I felt we had been on our legs the equivalent of a hundred. Besides, you need a slow day once in a while.

My tent was facing a bluff and as I stared out at the timeless stone, my eyes closed with visions of Thomas Jefferson looking over the junction of the Shenandoah and Potomac Rivers and poor John Brown's sad ending. Finally, sleep took complete control, that is until Tweety Pie decided to go to the bathroom. It was sometime during the night after he had taken his wooden leg off. Rather than go through the task of putting it back on, he took off on one leg. Taking a couple of hops, he lost control and was heading for the bluff where he would have become airborne. Fortunately, he has very strong arms and caught himself on a tree. After he took care of the reason for being out there hopping around, he was safe again, I thanked the Lord that he had helped him develop strong arms to make up for the missing leg.

Tweety Pie drifted back to sleep but I was too excited, not to mention, there was a railroad track below the bluff. Trains passed by all night long. Oh well, I thought, Tweety Pie and trains, that's definitely two just causes to keep a person awake. Finally, my dark knight, called slumber, rescued me.

APRIL 29, 1994 - it was 7:00 a.m. and we were late getting the climb up South Mountain started. Lots of beech trees, growing along the trail, made pleasant hiking. A giant one had dates of 1892 and 1899 carved into it. Explorers or perhaps trail blazers. Its fun to try to imagine what they must have been like. It would be nice to have psychic abilities sometimes.

A mother and father, trailing behind an energetic young daughter, caught up with us and soon disappeared on the trail ahead. Arriving in Gathland State Park at Crampton Gap, my husband Bill, now using his new trail name, Tweety Pie, was visiting with the family. Turns out their last names were Little. As we approached, they ended their visit and took off after their fleet-footed daughter.

During lunch I noted that Gathland State Park had a memorial to Civil War newspaper correspondents, appropriately named the Townsend Memorial. The weather was ideal and we moved out, making good time to the Dahlgren Backpacking Camping Area. Here we found restrooms, showers, water and Tweety Pie talking to a man and woman. He introduced us to Herb and his wife, Jolene, a couple from Arizona.

Herb's trail name was Daypack and he was slackpacking the A.T. while Jolene drove the roads to meet him, like Bill does for me. They were staying in a pickup camper and towed a Tracker vehicle behind, as they moved from one campground to another. It was fun visiting with them and then they were gone. It was okay, because we ended up camping with the Little Family that we had seen earlier.

California Tent Lady was so taken with the family, she invited them to hike a quarter of a mile to Turner's Gap to eat at a famous restaurant. It didn't really hurt our feelings that we were not invited, especially since I was beginning to feel some tension boiling up in the California Tent Lady. Tweety Pie built a big bonfire just as it started raining. Fortunately, we had our tent and jeep to sheltered us from the pelting rain.

California Tent Lady returned later on, telling us how wonderful it was, eating at the Old South Mountain Inn that had been host to several presidents in its 200 year existence. I was a little envious but happy for her none-the-less. Enough said!

APRIL 30, 1994 - during the night the rain stopped and the weather was okay. After breakfast California Tent Lady and I had a little climb up to Washington Monument State Park. Built in 1827 and restored in 1934-46, it was the first monument dedicated by our nation to the great George Washington.

After spending a little time there, the trail descended steeply to I-70. Crossing a convenient footbridge over the Interstate, Tweety Pie was waiting with doughnuts. He knew we had a rocky stretch ahead of us and would need energy. It was thoughtful of him.

After the rocky stretch, the trail was much easier as we made our way down to Old Wolfsville Road, MD 153. For some reason, we were all getting stressed out so Tweety Pie made a good decision. We went into Hagerstown, Maryland, and got a motel. It looked like rain again. It was an opportunity to do our laundry and get a good meal at the Po' Folks Restaurant. After 13.8 miles, we deserved home cookin'.

Tweety Pie ran across Daypack (Herb) again. Daypack told him it was pretty rough and rocky from Wolfsville Road and the Maryland-Pennsylvania State Line. It rained pitchforks during the night but we were tucked into a comfortable bed in a motel. I'm sure I was grinning with contentment as I drifted into sleep.

MAY 1, 1994 - on the way back to the trail, California Tent Lady refused to hike the last 10 miles to the state line. I couldn't believe this, since she knew how important it was for me not to break trail. Tweety Pie tried to reason with her by telling her how much this upset me and how much trouble it would be to stop here next year for a measly ten miles. Stubbornly she still refused, so, to Penn Mar on the Pennsylvania state line we drove. I had to make a trip back there again because I simply won't skip 10 miles of the trail. I can only assume that the rain and the rocky trail scared my companion into not wanting to risk that section.

It was 9:00 a.m. by the time we got on the trail again and I was still irritated. Mother Nature was, at least, cooperating. It had quit raining by the time we got rigged into the heavy backpacks. My adrenaline was really pumping and we covered six or seven miles to Antietam Shelter in short order. It was a different beauty in that heavily forested area with the creeks running freely from the recent rains. It became cooler, which helped keep the bugs inactive.

The hard 1,000 foot climb to Chimney rocks, elevation 1,940 feet took its toll on me, even though the trail wasn't too difficult. I was tired and, quite frankly, emotionally drained. We met Bill at PA 233. Knowing me as well as he does, he saw the fact that all was not well with me. The silence could have been cut with a knife as the jeep wound its way to Caledonia State Park. Only 3:30 p.m. and we were quitting for the day.

The trouble I was having, getting over the fact that I had skipped ten miles of my hike, was really waking me up to who I am. My first night in Pennsylvania and it was not what I had planned. I went to bed early with the puzzling thoughts of who was wrong. Was I being too picky about my hiking or was the California Tent Lady a volcano about to erupt? I would just have to get out of my rut and see what the volcano was going to do next.

MAY 2, 1994 - I was somewhat brighter after breakfast as Tweety Pie took us back to PA. 233. The volcano...excuse me, my hiking companion and I then hiked back to Caledonia State Park. We had a break with my husband or at least I should say, I had a break with him. California Tent Lady was sullen and acting very strange. For whatever reason, she was under a strain. But I can't read a closed book and this book was locked shut.

It was a steep climb out of the park, but it was everything in beauty you want on a hike. Pretty streams and lots of pine trees. Twin Quarry Gap Shelter was under construction when we got there. They were putting a cooking area between two shelters making it convenient for we tired hikers.

Making good time to the Twin Birch Run Shelters, there were eighteen young people camped there which brightened up my day. I like young vigorous people and the more time I spent with my strange hiking companion, the more I yearned to have my old youthful buddies back with me. After a brief discussion with them, we moved on, since the shelter was full.

We hiked on to Shippensburg Road, where we found Tweety Pie. California Tent Lady refused to make camp here, so Tweety Pie hauled us several miles to Pine Grove Furnace State Park. where we stayed at the Ironmaster's Mansion Hostel.

Everyone had to pull their boots off before entering the Mansion because the manager kept the place immaculate. I felt like we were in Japan. He was meticulous but, basically, a very nice person. Later in the evening, he gave us a tour, showing us such things as where they kept slaves around 1827. The hostel was then used as a stop for the Underground Railroad when the slaves were being smuggled from the south to the north. George and Martha Washington had even been known to stay overnight, during the wedding of the Ironmaster's daughter. It was fascinating to hear the adventures that took place there, back in those days. It was an interesting place with a lot of history. I was having a modern adventure myself.

A tall, large-boned section hiker, I would guess in her forties, known as Moxie Turtle, came in for the night. She was tough, so it was easy to see where the "moxie" part came from. She said she was from the State of Maine. California Tent Lady hit it off with her immediately. As they talked, I sort of envied their rapport. I have never talked much. In truth I keep my thoughts inside, but Moxie Turtle just blurted out whatever she was thinking.

I lay in my bed going over the day's events and I think I was beginning to figure out why the California Tent Lady was having problems. As my eyelids closed for the night ,a last typical thought crossed my mind, you can't please all the people, all the time. I am what I am and she is what she is. Fortunately, I can put up with almost anyone on the trail. After all, I go home with Bill and he puts up with me all the time. I try to leave my hiking companions at the end of the trail and hope we all had a good time. Darkness took over my mind briefly and the sun rose.

MAY 3, 1994 - Tweety Pie got us to Shippensburg Road at 7:30 a.m. I passed up a chance to climb up Big Flat Fire Tower. They say you have fantastic views from there. On to the head of what was the former Dead Women Hollow Road, Oooh!. Evidently, someone met their demise at some time or another on that road. It is now a winter time snowmobile trail.

Reaching a long descent, we could see Mount Holly and Long Mountain in the distance. As we descended, the temperature was really cooking and so were we. It felt as if I were heading for some destined event and the rule of the day was, keep moving toward the unknown.

It didn't take long to reach the Twin Tom Run Shelters where we came across three women camping out. One lady was trying to cook breakfast on a little wood burning stove and having problems getting it to burn. I gave her some help and their meal was soon on the way to being prepared.

I would like to have taken the Sunset Rocks trail that goes to the southeast of Tom's Run and ends up back on the A.T. but there was an urgency that I was only just beginning to understand. Back into Pine Grove Furnace State Park we had an early lunch with Tweety Pie. We had hiked 8.4 miles, but it had been fast and easy. California Tent Lady kept suspiciously packing away more supplies, as if it were permanent.

On our way out of the park, we passed the ruins of the old Pine Grove Furnace. A little farther was the old charcoal flats which provided fuel for the furnace in the 1700's. About two miles down the trail, we came across a big monument marker that said we were 1,069 miles from Springer Mountain, Georgia, the half-way point! I was thrilled at the realization that I had hiked halfway to Katahdin, Maine, minus 10 miles. Believe you me, I would make that up. My thoughts drifted back to all the people I had met since Georgia.

Tweety Pie picked us up at Green Mountain Road. Moxie Turtle had arrived there ahead of us so we all went to a little restaurant for supper. Tweety Pie took Moxie Turtle back to the A.T. while the Lady and I went to Mountain Creek Campground to spend the night.

MAY 4, 1994 - back on the Trail at 7:20 a.m. at PA. 34. After a climb up Trent's Hill, we descended to PA. 94. Another steep climb took us past the new Alex Kennedy Shelter. I wondered if Moxie Turtle would be there, since she liked hiking late and sleeping in the next morning. Another big difference about me that might bother California Tent Lady. No use in continuing to worry about this. We are all individuals and I can only change who I am so much. It would be a boring world if we were all carbon copies.

We came upon some large boulders that were as big as small houses but we followed the arrows and blazes that directed us through them, with minimal confusion. At last, White Rock Ridge, the end of the Blue Ridge Mountains. We had been following the Blue Ridge Range since Georgia. The hike downhill to Boiling Springs felt great.

The terrain was almost level for a few miles, passing through a lot of pasture land. Tweety Pie met us, but we kept on hiking into Boiling Springs along Children's Lake, where geese were bobbing and swimming with the anxious expectation of full summer. It was a relaxing sight on the way to the Appalachian Trail Conference's Mid-Atlantic Regional Field Office where a break was in order.

The storm, that had been brewing, finally hit. My life and my hike took a big change! California Tent Lady mailed a lot of extra gear home while I waited. Soon thereafter, Moxie Turtle arrived. California Tent Lady was in no hurry to leave and finally stopped beating around the bush. She proceeded to inform me that she was going to start hiking with Moxie Turtle. It wasn't all that big a surprise. I had been sensing this plot for some time.

That doesn't mean I wasn't extremely upset. To say the least, it is highly unethical to desert a companion on a planned hike. In my haste my true emotions came out. In frustration I told my husband I was going to hike on and meet him down the trial. He was puzzled and knew this was not like me at all. And it wasn't!

I was in such disorganized array that after hiking about a mile, I remembered California Tent Lady had a bug shirt and a little stove wrench that belonged to me. Frustrated and completely out of sync, I hiked back to the A.T. Field Office. As nice as I could be, I asked her for the two items. Fortunately, she gave them to me without an incident. Still flustered, I handed them to Bill to put in the jeep. Then like a jet airplane taking off on the runway, I was off again, leaving poor Tweety Pie absolutely bewildered.

Then, doggone it, as I got out of Boiling Springs it dawned on me that I didn't have any paper or pencil to leave notes for my husband along the road crossings. I don't cry easily. My tears are like a stream in the desert waiting, hoping for rain, before drying up in the parched sand. The droplets never made it to my cheeks. Frantically, I scratched my initials in the dirt with an arrow, showing him I had gone on.

A couple of hours passed before I realized, this was just not going to work unless I could get a grip on myself. I found a note from my angel, Tweety Pie, by the trail. It read, "Go on to the next road and I will be there."

Tweety Pie picked me up with the jeep on Appalachian Trail Road. We drove around, partly to look for places he could meet me, but mainly so he could use his simple psychology to pull out my emotions. He reminded me that hiking by myself was not a good idea, so why was I doing it? Stretching the truth, I told him that California Tent Lady and I weren't talking much so we decided to go our separate ways.

He didn't buy it, so I assured him I would quit if I felt unsafe. Bill knew I was holding back. We finally got a motel room on I-81 close to the A.T. It was a sleepless night and I finally opened up to, what seemed to be, my only friend. I told him what I thought had been going on for quite awhile. With tired eyes, I pondered what lay ahead for me. It is a frightening thing to hike that trail alone. Some people prefer to do so. I am not one of them.

MAY 5, 1994 - a meager breakfast, a well-needed cup of caffeine and I was back on the Appalachian Trail Road at 6:45 a.m. Tweety Pie met me several times as I crossed a large valley. It wasn't long before I crossed over the Pennsylvania Turnpike. A few more miles took me over Interstate 81. You would think I would be comforted at hearing the hustle bustle of traffic, instead, I felt a foreboding loneliness.

In a pasture, I sensed the cows watching me as if they didn't like my presence either. I think I was suffering from a terrible inferiority complex that I had no idea had been lurking inside of me. Being a farm girl, I knew to keep my eye on the cattle, especially a big bull that had decided to keep me company. Maybe he sensed I needed some pity but I wasn't taking any chances on another unpredictable friendship. Walking backwards and in a calm voice, on the outside at least, I told him I was mad enough to throw him across that dadgum field. Keeping my eye on him I reached the fence, stepped quickly over the stile (wooden steps built over a fence), to safety on an old road.

At PA 944, peanut butter crackers and a candy bar seemed to build up some sort of fuel gauge in my body and I felt better, especially since Tweety Pie was there. It was too early to quit so I proceeded through one-half mile of valley. As I began the climb to Blue Mountain, I heard the jeep horn blowing. Turning around I saw Tweety Pie driving down the road. When he stopped behind some brush, I couldn't see him anymore. His behavior was strange so I waited a minute, then decided to go on.

The trail had switchbacks up Blue Mountain so it made climbing fairly easy, certainly not as bad as it had looked on the map. Stopping to get a drink of water, I realized why Tweety Pie was blowing his horn. I had left my water bottle behind. Fortunately, I had an empty one in my pack. Looking about, I found water that I didn't trust. Using my iodine tablets, I waited thirty minutes to make certain the water was safe before taking a small drink.

At Darlington Shelter I took advantage of a spring about 200 yards away. Drinking deeply, the clean water made me feel like a small, quivering gazelle by the water hole, waiting for the attack of the predator. It was a refreshing drink. From the shelter, it was mostly downhill to PA. 850. Crossing a stream I began the ascent to Cove Mountain. The trail was extremely rocky, making every step hazardous. Being alone, I watched every step even more than usual. "Den Mama couldn't afford an accident now "

September, 1990, two southbound A.T. thru-hikers, Molly La Rue and Geoffrey Hood were hideously murdered at the Thelma Marck's Memorial Shelter that I was passing. The grim murders that took place were sufficient reason for me to get out of there as quickly as possible. I hated to even be reminded of that tragedy. My heart goes out to their families and my prayers are for their poor souls.

Thank the Lord they did catch the culprit who did it. Paul David Crews is now on death row in a Pennsylvania prison. I believe the trail is safe, but there is the element that can entice a weirdo out there, on occasion. The couple were only the sixth and seventh hikers murdered since crime the 1970's when records were started. However, as I am writing this book, there have been two more women added to the record.

When you think of the fact that three to four million persons use the A.T. each year at different periods, including around 150 successful thru-hikers, that's not a bad record at all. Consider the fact that the trail involves several states and any large city has at least that many incidents daily and weekly.

I wasn't doing too bad by myself, all things considered. Besides I wasn't completely out there alone. For instance, when I got to Hawk Rock, I met a young red-headed, lady day hiker. Tweety Pie had already met her down the trail. Since she was hiking my direction, he asked her to take some water to me. She had agreed. Not only was that a wonderful gesture, she hiked back down the mountain with me, where Tweety Pie was waiting anxiously. This is what made me overlook my sorrows and, for a while, stop pitying myself.

My husband and I spent the night where we left the trail on the south edge of Duncannon, PA. A kind lady in a house nearby gave us permission to camp. Maybe tomorrow I would get it together. All my preparation to have a hiking companion would just have to be forgotten, even though both Bill and I were nervous over me hiking alone. The 20.7 miles by myself sure isn't anything to be ashamed of. Maybe I can do it, was my last thought before sleep spread its merciful shroud over me.

MAY 6, 1994 - an early breakfast and Tweety Pie and I were off to a pleasant drive through the city of Duncannon, across Clark's Ferry Bridge and over the beautiful Susquehanna River. I looked over my shoulder at Hardeman Island and up the river to the north at the smaller West Fall Island. Like the Mississippi, it seems to have a lot of islands, when it's not on the rampage.

Tweety Pie pulled the jeep over in the median between highways. I hadn't followed the white blazes across the bridge so I just assumed the trail went to my right, as my old maps illustrated. It was a mistake and I should have had sense enough to know I shouldn't go over one-fourth mile without seeing a white blaze.

This day was not starting out right but Den Mama went on anyway, following some railroad tracks south. Tweety Pie was keeping track of me along U.S. Highways 22 & 322 that luckily ran parallel to the tracks. Realizing that I was confused and hadn't found the trail, he went down the highway to an overpass that allowed him to come back up the railroad tracks on a service road to meet me.

We both shook our heads knowing each was thinking the same thing. Going back to where I had become a vagabond on the railroad tracks, we found the trail. The A.T. sign showed the trail had been relocated and turned left more to the east. That eliminated a lot of unnecessary hiking. Yes, I know, it didn't help me much. I had been doing an awful lot of unnecessary hiking the last two or three days, but even that's pretty good for an old girl, huh?.

Finally, back on the trail and over the rocky Peters Mountain I went. I now know what Pennsylvania rocks are all about. Sometimes, every two steps I took, I felt like I slipped back one. When it leveled out on top I looked back at the Susquehanna. I could see where it and the Juniata River merged. To the south I saw the Rockville Bridge, the longest stone arch railroad bridge in the world. I guess that's where I would have ended up if I hadn't found the trail.

Passing the Clark's Ferry Shelter, that was only about a mile and a half from the river, it got level and straight on top of the ridge of Peters Mountain. This allowed me to look out over all I could survey. I did enter woods now and then, and it wasn't all rocky hiking.

Before I met Tweety Pie, I could see PA. 225 coming up the mountain on both north and south sides. We had lunch together and it was obvious we were calming down and getting used to me hiking by myself. From the parking area we could look to the south at Third Mountain. Second Mountain was south of that. I guess they ran out of names. After our good-byes I headed east on across the crest. Boy, it's fun walking on the mountain tops when they're straight and level.

Moving along at a good clip, I passed the Zeager Shelter and proceeded to Table Rock Outlook. From there I had excellent scenery of Third Mountain. It is State Game Lands in that area. Just down my mountain I could see PA 325 highway following along with me. It felt good. Only about a mile on the crest was the Peter's Mountain Shelter. They were in the process of building a brand new one. It was large, compared to the ones I had been seeing in Pennsylvania.

After I wrote in the log book and a short walk later, I met a southbound hiker. A tall, thin man whose friendly demeanor prompted me to have a short visit with him. During the course of the visit I found out his trail name was Trail Maintainer. I told him if he met California Tent Lady, to say hello for me. I can't begin to tell what an accomplishment that conversation was for me. The A.T. was making some changes in me that I had never anticipated. After all, I didn't begin hiking to become an extrovert but the changes were taking place and as a result I was becoming a more caring, outgoing person.

Proceeding on down the trail, I felt pretty good about myself and I think I was more light-footed. I believe the fact that I was all by myself with no one to see me if I stammered or stuttered, was doing wonders for my self esteem. At that time, I had no idea how much change I would undergo. At least for the time being, I had handled that meeting so good I was tip-toeing through the tulips all the way to PA 325.

Nine miles that day and it was only 5:00 p.m. When I reached Tweety Pie at the highway, I told him that the crest was so level, if I had flares he would be able to see exactly where I was from the highway, all the time.

The 10 miles of the A.T. I had missed hiking because of California Tent Lady's bullheadedness was bugging me badly. Bill turned the jeep back toward Pen Mar, Maryland. He said he was going to see to it that I hiked it out of my system before we got any farther away. There was no rebuttal from me. It was late when we arrived at Pen Mar, so we bedded down in the jeep by the city park. I'm sure I had a smile on my face when sleep finally ended the day. I'm glad Tweety Pie was so understanding.

MAY 7, 1994 - An eager Den Mama woke up, ate a breakfast bar and gulped instant chocolate. Tweety Pie hiked a little way with me going south, until it dawned on him, that I was on a quest and he was only holding me back. Glancing back, I saw a worried look as he watched me moving off by myself. It was then that I hollered back something strange, "Hey Tweety Pie, I'm on the wings of angels."

In 2.6 miles, the trail became switchbacks and I was climbing steeply over rocks. The old feet felt like the wings had flown off by themselves to the angels to whom they rightly belonged. Luckily, the rough terrain didn't last long. One more mile and I was perched on the highest elevation on the A.T. in Maryland, over 2,000 feet.

Hiking south and feeling pretty doggone good, I passed the Devil's Racecourse Shelter, thumbed my nose and stepped up the pace. Den Mama wanted this 9.7 miles completed, so she could get back to PA and head north where she belonged.

I met Tweety Pie at MD 491 and Ft. Ritchie Road. Four hikers, going south, were just beginning their hike. My husband was giving me some puzzled looks as I authoritatively informed the hikers what the trail was like ahead for them. It felt good being the old experienced hiker but, more than that, it felt good to be able to converse with people.

The other hikers and me switched leads for a while before they moved on down the trail, leaving me behind. That was okay, because it wouldn't be long until I would be heading back north toward the silent voice that kept calling me day and night.

Further on, I met two thru-hikers going north, a lady, whose trail name was Sylvia and a male friend, whose name I neglected to get. More and more I was having a ball talking to the thru-hikers, compare information and if time permitted, trail stories. I can't elaborate too much, how unlike the old Mary Twitty that was.

The trail in this area, unlike Peter's Mountain in PA became more up and down and often very steep. I was one pooped hiker when I met Bill at Wolfsville Road, MD. 17. It's hard to understand why this section of the trail was so important to me. I was out to conquer the entire A.T., so skipping even a mile was like being beaten. I don't give up easily and it only took me four hours and twenty-five minutes to finish that section. At 11:45 a.m. that section of trail was over and maybe, just maybe, my brain could put the whole incident behind me.

A quick lunch and we began the drive north, stopping at Boiling Springs, PA., where we returned to the Appalachian Trail Conference Building. I wanted to check the logbook to see if Day Pack had passed through. That was the guy that we had met several days ago at the Dahlgren Backpack Camping Area.

Unfortunately, we missed him by three hours. Tweety Pie and I both liked the couple so much we decided to phone ahead to different campgrounds in order to locate them. At a campground in Carlisle PA. we were successful. Were they surprised when we knocked on their camper door.

The truth is, I wanted to hike with Day Pack but I was four days ahead of him on the trail, so it wasn't possible. We had a nice visit anyway and I hoped we would meet the Day Pack and his lovely wife Jolene later on.

We drove back to PA 325 and spent the night. The depression I felt, at not being able to hike with that delightful couple, wasn't helped much when it rained all that night.

MAY 8, 1994 - rain was still threatening so I decided not to start hiking here since PA 325 crosses the trail and heads northeast away from it. It would be a pretty long hike to where I could meet Tweety Pie again. I still felt like hiking a shorter distance so we drove ahead to PA. 443. After all, I am a section hiker. You may be thinking, here we go again. I am a section hiker, If I decide to skip to another section, I know I will not go home until I go back to finish that part of the trail. Also I am hiking alone and that dictates a different policy.

At 10:45 a.m. I started hiking and it was easy going until I passed under I-81. Blue Mountain loomed ahead, promising to be a steep climb. However, when I reached the top of the trail, wild lilacs were blooming, spreading their unique aroma all around, acting like a tranquilizer to any difficulty I encountered. Every breath tasted delicious.

Occasionally I could look off to the north and see Interstate 81 swooping off into the pine groves. A little further was Swatara Creek and even further, Second Mountain, to my north. To the south was Monroe Valley sprawling up to Little Mountain. Soon I came to another new shelter appropriately named after William Penn, located at the Blue Mountain Campsite. It was off the trail so I didn't go down. From there, Swope Mountain spread out under the clouds. For that matter it had stayed cloudy all day. It made for a pleasant hike.

A few miles down the trail was Tweety Pie at PA. 645 and a special surprise. Since it was Mother's Day, I was going to get to eat in a real restaurant. We enjoyed fried chicken, mashed potatoes and apple pie, plus extras. This was so sweet of him. I was tired but another 12.1 miles were logged. After that marvelous meal we went back to PA. 325, so I could keep my promise to leave no gaps in my hike.

MAY 9, 1994 - up early, bright-eyed and bushy-tailed I started hiking at 6:45 a.m. The 15 miles that I skipped yesterday should be fairly easy. The temperature had dropped to 38° during night and it was soaking into my bones.

After a big climb up Stony Mountain, I was rewarded with a splendid view of the spillway of De Hart Reservoir that spread out at least 8 miles to the east. Following the crest of Stony Mountain, I came upon an old stage road and stayed on it for 6.8 miles. From it, I got periodic peeks at the reservoir and to the south, Second Mountain. All along its crest is the boundary of a military reservation.

At the end of the old stage road, I came to Old Yellow Spruce Village where I discovered a mailbox with a trail register. Naturally I was curious to see if anyone I knew had signed it, such as California Tent Lady or Moxie Turtle. I wanted to know if California Tent Lady had passed me yet. Still no sign of her, so I signed in, entered my notes and took a break.

The Yellow Springs Village Site had been a thriving coal mining community but now, as so many things of the past, old and abandoned. Rested, I went another 5.6 miles and came to an old strip mining site. Crossing Rausch Creek over an old stone railroad bridge, I was fascinated at the way the stones were placed to form the curve of the arch. Such effort and art to create a bridge made it a wonder to see.

I was glad to finish my hike at 1:45 p.m. at PA. 443. Tweety Pie was waiting and after the loneliness, I had a deeper appreciation for him than I had been experiencing before. It made me realize how much sometimes we take people for granted. We drove to PA. 645 where I had quit hiking on May 8. This is where I would start my hike north. We spent the night in the Game Lands parking lot, sleeping in our jeep. It was dark when we arrived there and I was ready for sleep.

MAY 10, 1994 - Sliding out of the jeep, the weather was cool and I involuntarily shivered while stretching my arms to shake out the night's sleep. I had a good feeling about that day as Tweety Pie drove back to PA 645, where I had quit hiking two days before. I would now head back north. It was a relief to be back on Blue Mountain, picking up where I had left off after the hike from Highway 443. Even though I am a section hiker I still think like a thru-hiker. I wanted to hike straight through to Katahdin.

A brisk two miles put me in the vicinity of some trail history. I passed Kimmel Lookout named after Dick Kimmel, a dedicated trail worker for 40 years who is now an honorary member of the ATC. That brought me to a blue-blazed trail that led to 501 Shelter, named appropriately for the PA highway that crossed the trail there. I was carrying enough water so I continued on down a rocky trail.

Watching my footing, I came to another interesting place called Pilger Ruh Spring which means Pilgrims Rest Spring. It had been a watering and resting place for the colonists as they endured the hardships of settling our great nation. A short distance further I looked down on a place called Round Head with 500 stone steps leading down to a spring. I understand it is a fascinating sight, but 500 steps was enough to make me pass it up.

Less than 2 miles, another blue-blazed trail led down to Shikellamy Lookout, which I also passed. It was a short distance before I crossed a bubbling brook to arrive at the beautiful Hertlein Campsite. An inviting stream meandered by, with graceful fir trees all around. That Pennsylvania scenery is worthy of visiting. Its wonderful valleys and trees defy description for this author.

Another register box had a drinking cup inside and two day-hikers picking up trash and maintaining the trail. I admire people who help keep the trail clean. It is the highest degree of consideration for their fellow hikers. They noticed that I was hiking alone, and carrying that same integrity, walked with me for a little way until I met Tweety Pie, who walked in to meet me with a southbound thru-hiker.

They were enjoying a vigorous conversation. My husband loves to visit with the hikers and will, at any given opportunity, tell them his wife is hiking the A.T. He also adds his famous quote, "She is dumber than a box of rocks." He picked that up from Dick, when Lida was hiking with me.

I was comfortable leisurely walking with Tweety Pie. Hurrying was out of the question, due to his wooden leg and that just served to relax me. We came to the Fort Dietrich Snyder Marker, the site of one of a chain of forts built in 1756, as protection against Indian raids during the Indian and French War. Benjamin Franklin personally supervised the Fort's construction.

Tweety Pie took my picture by the marker. I had hiked 10.1 miles and it was only 12:30 p.m. at PA. 183. It's hard to adapt to hiking by miles rather than time, because you feel like you should go on until later in the day. That can get a person into a lot of trouble and increase the burnout rate. The body feels the miles, regardless of how long it takes.

We ate lunch and then found a campsite to spend the night. After relaxing a bit, I fixed us a supper of noodles and chicken with chocolate pudding and tea, without the ice for obvious reasons. We looked over the maps to plan the next day's strategy. One thing good about hiking alone is visiting with Bill. We didn't have to worry about hurting someone's feelings because we couldn't figure out how to include them.

MAY 11, 1994 - 7:00 a.m., still hiking the ridge of Blue Mountain the trail was okay except for a lot of big rocks. Using the hiking stick that Tweety Pie made for me way back at the Grand Canyon, I managed to balance myself on the doggone things. Regardless, I made good time passing Black Swatara Spring and Eagles Nest Trail.

Somewhere between there and Phillip's Canyon, I met a turkey hunter carrying a large Tom Turkey that had met his demise. Forgetting it was that season again, I quickly turned my rain cover to the orange side, in hopes that some of those guys would be able to tell the difference between me and the poor turkeys. Believe it or not, there are some hunters who shoot at movement rather than form. For whatever it's worth, I don't stand too much taller than a turkey among the trees and bushes.

Reaching Phillips Canyon Spring without being shot was a relief but It was a steep climb out of the canyon. I met four hikers on the way out but I was beginning to get a little anxious to end that hike. All I could offer them was a quick *"Hi"* before moving on. The weather was trying to entice me to remain out longer, just as it was encouraging the leaves to begin popping out in the higher elevations.

Dropping a very steep 1,000 feet into Port Clinton, I met Tweety Pie. He could see I was ready to quit and immediately drove to the Port Clinton City Park where hikers are allowed to camp. In and out of woods, with rocks trying to catch me off guard, I had hiked 15 miles and it was still only 1:37 p.m. It gave us a nice afternoon to rest and I needed it. A gauge I had learned to use on my hikes, is when I get up the next morning refreshed and ready to go, I'm okay. But when that feeling of wanting to quit carries over to the next day, well, its about time to start thinking about heading for the house.

MAY 12, 1994 - It had been another rainy night, so Tweety Pie and I were slow in getting out of the sleeping bags. He was offering me no signs of encouragement to get started, which is another sign that it was about over. In all fairness to my devoted husband, he worries about me hiking by myself over wet rocks and all the other hazards that wait for careless hikers. It's a different stress that eventually takes a toll on he who waits.

There were plenty of slippery rocks, made ten times worse because of the night's rain. I wasn't interested in breaking my neck either, so after our usual breakfast of instant oatmeal, tea and Pop Tarts, we decided to take the day off and drive over to Hamburg, PA to look for Day Pack and Jolene. Checking all the campgrounds in the area, they were no where to be found. It would be awfully convenient to hike with Day Pack, since Jolene was backing him up in the way Tweety Pie was for me. It would be a lot more economical for all of us, but it just didn't seem meant to be. Oh well, the good Lord has been looking out for me and I was getting mighty close to him in my trail loneliness.

We ate our lunch at a restaurant in town, operated by some very nice people and then returned to the Port Clinton City Park. Some friendly town's people came by to pay us a visit. They kept fresh water in the pavilion just for passing hikers to use. The trail register revealed that no one I knew had passed through. This was such an irresistible, relaxing place, we spent another night there.

MAY 13, 1994 - leaving a more than usual, worried Tweety Pie in Port Clinton, at 6:50 a.m., I began climbing by switchbacks up a steep mile and a half to a ridge top with a lot of rocks. Still in the Blue Mountain range, the valley below the Schuylkill River was snaking down to meet the Little Schuylkill River at Port Clinton, then flowing south as one, to the dam near Hamburg Pa. The trail was up and down, but not bad hiking. It straightened out all the way past Pocahantas Spring Campsite. The Y.W.C.A Blue Mountain Camp was to my right.

Soon I reached the Windsor Furnace Shelter, the site of an early pig iron works. I walked over glassy slag still on the trail, straight ahead to where the trail doubled back on itself, then curved back to Pulpit Rock. It was 10:00 a.m., so I took my pack off and enjoyed a break. I truly felt like I was in the arms of Jesus, as I was in awe of the farmland below spreading out for miles. What a delightful sight it was!

My inspiration ending, I moved on up the rocky trail to a place called The Pinnacle. Actually, it was 80 yards out to the Pinnacle and I was getting awfully tired so I passed it up. The altitude was 1,635 feet and even though the mountains in Pennsylvania aren't as tall as in other states, the views are equal. Quickly the trail turned into a two-track old road going mostly downhill. The temperature was a mild 68°. After a low of 38° in the night it felt like excellent hiking weather.

Tweety Pie met me at Hawk Mountain Road and together we went the 0.2 miles south to the Eckville Shelter, a one-room building in back of a farm house. It had a port-a-potty and a pump for plenty of water. There were six bunks and a table with lots of magazines to read and benches to sit on. Hey, what more could you want? I had hiked 15.7 miles and still had energy enough to fix supper. After being in the arms of Jesus it almost felt as good to be in the arms of Tweety Pie. We turned in for the night.

MAY 14, 1994 - belligerently we were still hanging in there as Tweety Pie hauled me the 0.2 miles north to the A.T. It was 7:00 a.m. when I arrived at a bridge and bog boards that took me over and through a swamp area. *A swamp in Pennsylvania!* I didn't have much time to think about that before climbing back up Blue Mountain to Dan's Pulpit, a rock outcrop where a grand old hiker named Danny Hoch conducted Sunday services for wayward trekkers. Good spot for spiritual meetings at 1,600 feet. The views were inspirational.

151

For the next five miles the trail was the same familiar rocky terrain to Tri-County Corner. From there you have gorgeous views of Berks, Lehigh and Schulkill Counties. It's also the site of the very first blazing of the Appalachian Trail in Pennsylvania in 1926, by a crew from the Blue Mountain Eagle Climbing Club.

At 11:00 a.m., I arrived at Allentown Shelter where the trail turned into a comfortable two track. I made excellent time to PA. 309, where Tweety Pie was waiting. We had lunch at 12:30 p.m. and discussed jumping ahead to Bake Oven Knob Road so I could hike back to PA. 309. After driving over, we met a man from The Wildlife Information Center. He watched as I unloaded my backpack out of the jeep. Curiously, he asked if he could video tape Tweety Pie and I conversing about me hiking the A.T. We both have ego's, so naturally we agreed. It made us feel like movie stars making a documentary. He later sent us a copy which we treasure along with all our other mementos.

I was flying high after that, at least for a while. All in all, the trail was good until I got to Bears Rocks. It was like a solid rock wall along the trail and really got scary when I came to Knife Edge Rocks. They were named correctly. Big boulders, like some giant in his anger had chopped them with a sharp ax and then abandoned them, with their sharp edges protruding upward. The rocks attracted a lot of day hikers. They were climbing all over them like ants.

Carefully picking my way through the spectacle, I was relieved when the trail improved all the way back to PA. 309 where Tweety Pie anxiously waited. The large parking area here provided a good place to spend the night. I had hiked 17.6 miles before 3:40 p.m. but the trail was slowly sapping the energy from me. Since it was

Saturday night, we saw several young people carrying ice chests up the trail where I would be hiking the next day. This caused me some concern, since that usually meant a beer party. It's possible my husband and I were both sharing the same vision in our dreams that night.

MAY 15, 1994 - Tweety Pie drove me back to Bake Oven Knob Road. It looked like a promising Sunday morning as I started my trek back north. A half mile up the trail, I reached the summit of Bake Oven Knob, 1,560 feet, when I heard several voices. Sure enough, looking down ahead of me was a group of young people camped right on the trail, some still in their sleeping bags, while others were climbing on the rocks.

I got out my hot pepper spray just in case, but then I realized I would be up against too many for that to do any good. One young man eyed me and to my surprise began picking up the empty beer cans. Seemed like a good enough sign so I nonchalantly proceeded through them with my friendliest smile, hoping I wouldn't ruffle anyone's feathers. Boy, did I give a sigh of relief when I was out of sight. You never know what booze will make people do. Nice people become unpredictable monsters under its influence.

Another group was camped all over the place when I got to Bake Oven Knob Shelter, most of them still in their sleeping bags. The trail register wasn't within easy view, so I promptly went on down the trail. The rocky trail made it necessary to watch my every step. Finally out of all this human chaos, I noticed the dogwood trees were in beautiful bloom as if they took no notice of we humans at all. I wished I could do that.

The trail passed over the Pennsylvania Turnpike, like a gopher through a tunnel far below. Passing the

George W. Outerbridge Shelter, it was downhill now to Lehigh River. Tweety Pie was there and told me to cross over the Lehigh River Bridge to the parking lot where he would meet me.

After lunch, I bid Tweety Pie adieu, then started the climb out of Lehigh Gap. Anytime you start hiking out of a river bed like the Lehigh River, you can just about count on it being steep. This one was very steep with a narrow footpath. At 1,000 feet, it was so tough that I had to do hand-over-hand rock climbing.

My walking stick wasn't doing me any good so I tried to throw it up to the rocks ahead of me. It hit a rock and tumbled down. I heard it falling for longer than I cared to listen. Of course, there was no way I was going to go after it. I saw images of my body as the stick, bouncing off rocks for Lord knows how far. Momentarily laying against a rock, I was more than a little scared. A little prayer passed over my lips and I could have sworn I heard this whispered answer, "The Lord helps those who help themselves, Now Den Mama, get with it." Over the rock I went and sure enough that trail got a lot better. It even turned into another two-track road.

I felt like I was truly blessed until I reached Little Gap. If the Devil has influence over man, here was the evidence. The mountain was barren, all the trees had died because of a zinc smelting plant that used to be on the river. The fumes from the plant had killed all the vegetation. God is slowly nursing it back, but He allows those terrible images long enough to let us know we must care for our home better than that.

Just before I arrived upon this terrible scene at Little Gap, I found a new mailbox with a trail register, that someone had conveniently built. Taking advantage, I wrote a note to Day Pack hoping he would see it. Who knows, maybe California Tent Lady would read it too.

My heart was still heavy when I met my Tweety Pie. His first statement was, "It's supposed to rain. I don't want you out on those rocks after a rain." My thought was, " How nice to have, at least, one human who loves you." I believe it was Shakespeare who said, *"If you leave this world with but one friend, you are a fortunate man (person) indeed."* I was fortunate. My second thought was, "Thanks Father for the healing rain that will erase that mess I just left behind and for the rain that will help cause new vegetation to grow on that poor barren mountain.

After much discussion with Tweety Pie, we decided to quit hiking that year. I had hiked 297.5 miles and experienced a little more heartbreak than joy. A good time to stop hiking, when the pendulum swings too much to the wrong side. With some sadness I went back to the trail register again. I wrote that I was through hiking this year and would love to find someone who has my hiking disease to wander the A.T. with me in 1995 looking for the cure, if there be one.

After arriving home tired and, indeed, ready for rejuvenation, I had a thrill followed by disappointment. It was a card from Day Pack which sweetly said, "I read your lovely notes but I will reach Connecticut before I quit hiking. By the way, I have the disease too." It dashed my dreams and hopes that we would be having the wondrous adventures I had envisioned.

I heard no more from California Tent Lady and yes, I'm sorry that our relationship was not enduring. She will never know how much she boosted my self-confidence. For that, anyone is endeared to me. I am proud of hiking over 150 miles by myself. . . . well, not *all* by myself.

There was Tweety Pie and as always, God.   Thanks,
Fellows!

• • • • •

SEPTEMBER   1994

Tweety Pie and I agreed that I should finish hiking
the A.T. next year, so I put an ad in the September edition
of the *A.T. NEWS.* It was encouraging since we received a
lot of responses. We traveled to the southeast In
November, 1994, and met two potential hikers.

One was called Half-Beard and the other Happy
Hiker.   Half-Beard lived in Athens, Georgia, a retired
pilot, 70 years old and involved in section hiking the A.T.
Happy Hiker lived in Roseland, Florida, also a section
hiker, 67 years of age.   He works at a Boy's Ranch.   Both
their wives were extra nice, but just didn't like to hike.

A lady, who called herself Wildflower, seemed to
be promising, according to our correspondence. So
promising, we worked out dates and plans and decided to
hike together. There was a possibility that Half-Beard and
Happy Hiker would meet us on the trail.   Naturally, like
an eager child, I was ready to go again. It doesn't take
much to restore my heightened expectation in human
beings and I began making plans to finish my *Dream
Hike.*

I even joined a gym to get in better shape. *Ol'*
Tweety Pie worked out with me but his upper body didn't
need too much help, as was proved when he held onto that
tree to keep from going over the cliff. So, the plans were
made for June of 1995! See you then.

Show Your greatnes in the sky, O God, and Your glory over all the earth.
Psalms 57:5

1995

Semi-climax had become an intricate part of my life. Eager as a teenager I anticipated the year I could, *would* complete the Appalachian Trail. With emotion, I again, looked back on 1994 and all the years, the thrills, heartbreaks, wonderful memories of people and the excitement I got from being in the bosom of mother nature.

After purchasing all the food I thought I would need for three months on the trail, the jeep was full. It was necessary to buy a carrier to put on the top. Wrapping food and other supplies to protect them from the weather, we carefully placed them in the carrier. You could say we were full beyond the roof and reaching for the sky.

Saving money, by buying supplies at home, is really a good idea. No matter how nice the people are in the northeast, their cost of living is much higher than in Missouri. It is often more expensive along the trail. After quitting the gym, I concentrated on the exercise I would need the most, walking. Like a child waiting for Christmas, I was ready to get the show on the road.

JUNE 1, 1995 - The drive over familiar country to Pittsburgh, Pennsylvania, was pleasant. We arrived late in the afternoon and I eagerly looked for my new hiking partner. Phyllis, who I will call by her trail name of Wildflower, was waiting and to my delight was as antsy me.

She graciously invited us to spend the night at her home. That was a good sign right off the bat, since it showed our first impression had gained us total acceptance. She had a daughter and a grand daughter staying with her and we had a lot of fun getting to know one another.

JUNE 2, 1995 - Leaving Wildflower's home, we drove through the beautiful rolling, high hills to Lehigh Gap, PA. Finding a motel presented a problem, so we finally had to drive to Palmerton, PA where we found a room at Palmerton Inn. A hot 86° and soaring humidity made the room feel close until a large fan was switched on. Moving the air and stirring the humidity to evaporation, it kept the room surprisingly comfortable.

I decided to phone Half-Beard, to let him know we were near our starting location and my new friend, Wildflower and I were eager to start our hike the next day. His wife, Jolene, answered. She wished us luck and said they would try their best to hook up with us later. The old familiar rain started and served to take a few more degrees off the already tolerable temperature. We were able to get as peaceful a night's rest as possible, when your anticipating an event as big as possibly finishing the great Appalachian Trail.

JUNE 3, 1995 - The short drive to Little Gap, PA. passed quickly. Wildflower and I began our long awaited adventure at 7:30 a.m. As I looked up at the cloudy sky, the rain stopped, as if on cue. That lowered the humidity, but wouldn't you know our hike began in a less than glamorous way, since we had to cross a murky, muddy bog.

With that out of the way, things improved greatly on the steep climb up Talus Slope to Little T, a weathering knob.   Spectacular views greeted us to the south. The little town of Danielsville lay below in the valley with State Highway 946 meandering through it. Country roads winded all over the countryside, some seeming to go nowhere, others ending abruptly.

The rocky climb was a little tough and continued into a rocky trail. It was level, making the walk easier. I was still on the seemingly endless Blue Mountain Crest where I had left off before, tired and depressed. Not so now as Wildflower and I were slackpacking the miles by swiftly, occasionally coming to a clear area like Goose Knob where we could again see the valley to the south.

We ate lunch with Tweety Pie at Smith Gap Road, then put our backpacks on and hiked toward our next destination, the Leroy A. Smith Shelter. Wildflower, an avid bird watcher, pointed at a Scarlet Tannager Bird. It was a beautiful red bird with black wings. This is one of the beauties of individuals. I might have missed that lovely creature had it not been for this lady and her particular interest.

Passing through one area, we had to be careful not to get confused by game land boundary signs. My experience paid off and we made it just fine. Arriving at Smith Shelter, the spring was one-half mile down a steep hill. Wildflower volunteered to go down for water. It was 1:30 p.m. and we had hiked 10.9 miles. Not bad for the first day out.

Another northbound section hiker and a thru-hiker named C.R. (Colorado Rockies) were setting up for the night. Appearing congenial enough they presented themselves as being trustworthy, so we felt safe spending the night in their company. C.R. was about the same age as my son, Slowpoke. His occupation involved computers and since he was between jobs, he decided to use the time to hike the A.T. The other northbound hiker was wearing tennis shoes and seemed to be nursing some very sore feet.

A Ridge Runner is a person who stays at different campsites to help hikers with any problems they may be having with a particular section of the A.T. One came in to visit with us. Believe me it is comforting, since they carry a portable phone, in case they find an emergency situation. Later on the boss Ridge Runner came by, adding to the knowledgeable company. These men are not above keeping rowdy people, who use the trails for drunken parties, in check . On occasion they said they will even remove them from the trail completely. Ridge Runners are usually young college men with an avid interest in the outdoors. The Boss Man was in his late fifties and had a great personality that not only appealed to the younger ridge runners, but also to all the hikers, who meet them occasionally.

JUNE 4, 1995 - we rose at 6:45 a.m. Our male hikers were in no hurry to budge, so off Wildflower and I went on a trail that wasn't too difficult. It remained so for the next uneventful 4.6 miles except for a place called, Pass Hahn's Lookout. We had a beautiful view of Wind Gap Village below and South Mountain in the distance.

A short distance further, before we began the descent, we stopped at Lookout Rocks. The Pocono Mountains loomed way off in an endless sky. In the foreground was Chestnut Valley and the awe inspiring Aquashicola Creek meandering lazily, as if nothing in the world was important.

Down a steep descent, made much easier by switchbacks that ended in stone steps to (PA Rt. 33). We could see Tweety Pie below, with the jeep backed up a steep hill to keep it in the shade. Since it was too early to quit, we took a brief break and prepared to hit the trail, when along came Colorado Rockies. We chided him a bit about two ladies beating him there, then left him visiting with Tweety Pie.

The trail started out rocky and we had to watch every step. Wildflower was nursing a sore foot and my left foot was troubling me some. It didn't take long to reach the crest through a variety of forested areas. I had been dreading Wolf Rocks and not just because of the name. We had been told they were indeed as sharp and rugged as wolves teeth. Fortunately with sore feet and all, we made it over them.

From there we were rewarded with a good view of Fox Gap ahead and to the north, Kittatinny Ridge in New Jersey. The trail gave us a reprieve from Fox Gap, where PA 191 crossed the trail and It turned out to be an ideal place to match up with Tweety Pie.

With ears always open for useful information, he had heard there was an old road that would almost reach Kirkridge Shelter, so along with Wildflower, he took the jeep and hauled our packs to search for it. It was only a 0.6 mile hike on the trail to the shelter, so in solitude I found it without any problems.

When I arrived no one was there, so I walked up to the parking area where, to my amazement, no one was there either. I found the road and hiked down it, getting more worried as I went. Tweety Pie had to go back to Highway 191 in order to drive north to where it curved into this road. He could have had an accident.

When I got to the highway, the gate to the road was locked. Now I knew why he hadn't come up the road. I was relieved that the mystery was solved. Tracking back up the highway, I found our jeep parked with no one near it. All I could do is leave a note on the jeep and hike back to the shelter where the two lost wanderers waited. Tweety Pie, wooden leg and all, had packed my backpack up to the shelter. I was grateful, but couldn't help thinking how unnecessary all this was.

Finally after settling in, Tweety Pie, bless his heart, hiked back to the jeep. It was 3:30 p.m. when all the difficulties were over. Wildflower and I prepared for night in the shelter. We had hiked 13.3 miles. I had hiked an additional 2 miles looking for them. No wonder my poor feet were hurting.

JUNE 5, 1995 - at 6:30 A.M., just after daybreak, we hit a trail that was a lot more forgiving than we had been experiencing. Passing Tott's Gap, the trail bore right into more woods and communication towers. Signs of civilization are ever present along the A.T. in the form of pipeline right-of-ways, highline wires and other reminders that our planet is becoming ever more crowded.

At Mount Minsi, 1,480 feet, we had a break with a marvelous view of the water gap of Delaware River. Descending by switchbacks we came to a brook with a beautiful rhododendron growth, our first since we started this trip. Winona Cliff gave us more great views of the Delaware River. Across the river was the tilted strata of Mount Tammany, said to show the profile of an Indian called Chief Tammany.

From there we took a fork, at a Hemlock Grove, downhill to where Tweety Pie waited for us to come off the mountain. After a pleasant lunch with him, Wildflower and I hiked on to the Church of the Mountains Hostel. We found an interesting conglomeration of people there.

The Ridge Runners and their Boss, that we had met earlier, were a fun group They were receiving their campsite assignments along the trail. C.R. had shown we ladies how he could move ahead of us when he wanted. Being the gentleman he was, he didn't rub it in and helpfully suggested we make reservations at the Mohican Camp for the next day.

We met a husband and wife team, Fred, trail name (Stickflipper) and Dixie (Snapshot) who were thru-hikers. C.R. had been hiking with them, which probably accounted for his swiftness to the Delaware. Thru-hikers get along pretty efficiently anyway. We made reservations for all of us at Mohican, then set in for an interesting evening at the hostel.

Lonescout, a young thru-hiker came in later, all worn out and in need of rest much more than me, so I gave him my cot and slept on the divan in the main room. We had only hiked 6.6 miles today, even though the temperature was a comfortable 70° but this was an interesting place for a break, so to heck with it.

Sleep came slow for me as I realized I would be hiking over country with a history I had only heard about in old movies . . . the land of the Delaware River and the Mohicans.

JUNE 6, 1995 - Wildflower, Snapshot, Stickflipper, C.R. and me, Den Mama, started hiking out of the Delaware Water Gap at 350 feet elevation. Excitement was in the air when we crossed the Delaware River into the state of New Jersey. Looking west from the Delaware Bridge, I saw a doe and her twin baby deer frolicking in the river. What a sight! It's hard to explain how thrilled I am to be getting to New Jersey. There were times when I didn't really believe I would make it this far.

The trail followed I-80 and the Delaware River south to the Dunnfield Creek Natural Area where Tweety Pie was waiting. He could see that I was beside myself with excitement and I know he understood when I said a quick *"Hi"* and *"Bye"* and continued up the trail with the others. We doubled back north and then northeast, following Dunnfield Creek to Lord knows where. The A.T. was breath taking and there were other trails going every direction from it and across it. We were in Washington State Park on the northwest side of Kittatiny Mountain. At every clearing you got a different view of the fantastic Delaware River, which, at that time, was only 1 to 2 miles away.

At Camp Site #2, the man I call the Boss of the Ridge Runners met us. I guess he had seen us so much he took our picture. From there we looked down on a side trail worming its way to the Delaware River where it ended. In the middle of the river was two huge islands called Shawnee and Depue.

Other smaller islands in this area of the river are named, Labar 1, Poxono, and yes another DePew Island with different spelling. After the islands the river became narrow, forming a snake off to the north. I can only wonder who was given the responsibility of naming those islands as they are recorded today. Pennsylvania won't be out of sight for a while, since the state lines run right down the middle of the Delaware River.

On up the trail we passed next to Sunfish Pond, a glacial lake. A monument stated that it is a Natural Area and a registered national landmark. Geese swimming on the pond were unafraid as we passed. They didn't even act like we were intruding on their combination of wild, tame freedom. I hope they never have reason to fear humans. They are so beautiful. The area, including the trail, was quite rocky around the pond. Three deer were grazing a short distance off the trail.

Descending to a brook that we had to cross and further down the trail, we noticed some strange bodies of water. One was a big lake off to our right. There was no trail marking to tell us what it was named. About a half mile we saw another large body named Yards Creek Reservoir with three smaller ponds just to the north of it. As it turned out, these were storage ponds for the Yards Creek pumped-storage hydroelectric development.

We could have taken a trail down to this weird assembly of water but chose to remain curious. Later, we could see that Yard Creek did indeed run into the Reservoir. What looked like a spillway was on a finger of the body of water. It appeared to be too small to be an electric facility. To the left was a better view of Tocks Island.

The temperature was 78° and partly cloudy as we descended steeply to Mohican Road. We followed Tweety Pie in the jeep to the Mohican Camp. After making reservations for the night and a hot shower, we wandered to over Catfish Pond. It wasn't far and since we had hiked 10.3 miles today, I had no intention of walking anymore.

Lonescout came poking along later. He fixed his supper, then continued on down the trail. Turns out he really was a scoutmaster. The camp manager had food left over from a week-end group, so he kindly offered it to us. We graciously accepted. What a meal - potato casserole, lettuce salad, chicken patties and green beans. Hikers know how to devour food so don't offer, if you don't want to see it disappear. That night, we were happy and contented campers.

JUNE 7, 1995 - A heavy mist was with us when we left Mohican Camp at 6:45 a.m. Our plan was to slackpack to Millbrook-Blairstown Road where we would meet Tweety Pie carrying the heavier packs. For obvious reasons, we didn't take a side trail that circled off the A.T. then rejoined it later. The trail was called Rattlesnake Swamp. Would you have gone down there?

We passed up Catfish Tower. It stood 60 feet up and I am told there is a fantastic 360° view on top. Two miles up the trail, we came upon Lonescout, still in his tent. Hearing us passing, he popped his sleepy head out at us, greeting us a with a jolly, "Hello." On down the trail was a rhododendron thicket before we turned onto a gravel road.

Trusty Tweety Pie was waiting at Millbrook Road. We ate an early lunch, picked up the heavy packs and were on our way at 10:30 a.m. The sun, with its full face, drifted slowly from behind the clouds, raising the temperature to 85°. Two deer and a grouse with her chicks enjoyed the new day making me realize that I was in as good of hands as they. I smiled as we passed a murky swamp, ideal for the deer and grouse.

At a fork we climbed a steep hill, then a short walk revealed to our left a great view of Wallkill Valley and Pocono Plateau. We could also see the huge snake the Delaware River made as it twisted farther and farther from the trail. Emerging briefly from the woods, we looked down on Camp No-Be-Bo-Sco, Bergen Council, Boy Scouts of America. Whew, that was a mouthful! In short, it's a camp for the Boy Scouts, nestled around small Sand Pond.

About a mile and a half, we looked down ,on Fairview Lake. This area is covered with strange ponds and lakes. Some with roads all around them as if plotted for a housing district. There's just so many. It's impossible for me to describe them all. There was an awful lot of scenery I had to miss, such as the hike down to Buttermilk Falls.

It was a steep climb up Rattlesnake Mountain, 1,492 feet. By the time I reached the high point I was panting. Finding a rock outcropping where the view restored my desire to finish my dream hike and restored the air to my lungs quickly. There were sweeping views to my left of Wallpack Valley and through the trees to my right the landscape was plastered with more ponds and lakes.

Tweety Pie had given me a new Tracks Hiking Staff for Christmas and it was now revealing its purpose, especially getting over all the rocks that seemed to dominate the area all to often. Driving in on Brink Road as far as he could and hiking the short distance to the Brink Road Shelter just to spend the evening visiting with our crew, told a lot about my wiry husband. He does not like being alone. Thank goodness.

We were all making a well-organized group of hikers and the rapport between us was the way it should be. As a result, we hiked 14.2 miles and it was an inspiring day for me. After a marvelous evening of chatting about our adventures, sadly it was time to turn our minds over to the unconscious experience of quieted slumber. Three hundred and fifty feet behind the shelter you could hear the spring murmuring by.

JUNE 8, 1995 - our happy campers woke up pleasant and revitalized, as we each took our packs down to Brink Road where Tweety Pie had parked. He would take the packs to U. S. Hwy. 206, our next rendezvous. Rattlesnake Mountain was fading behind and we were now on the crest of Kittatinny Mountain. Everybody liked slackpacking. It was so much more enjoyable when you could spend more time observing the surroundings, such as the mile-long Lake Owassa from where Jacob's Ladder Trail led off to my left.

We entered the woods briefly, down a little, then the trail leveled out nicely. In a clearing, we could see U.S. 206 and Culver's Lake. It was a lot larger than other lakes we had seen. The temperature was cool and the hike was so enjoyable as we descended to U.S. 206 at 935 feet. Tweety Pie was there for us to pick up the heavier packs.

Snapshot, Stickflipper and C.R. could easily out hike Wildflower and me. They were always considerate though, in that they stopped often enough for us to catch up.

Snapshot worked for an outfitter of camping and hiking gear. Stickflipper worked for another company and they owned a farm like my husband and I. In their 50's, both were in the prime of health. They carried top-quality backpack and hiking gear that was the envy of any hiker!

Wildflower never mentioned her age, but I knew she was younger than me. She was a career nurse which was to come in mighty handy. About one quarter mile from the Mashipacong Shelter, I slipped on a rock. The fall caused my eye glasses to get cock-eyed, making a small puncture wound. She was able to make it stop hurting and determine its seriousness. Who would have thought I would have my own private nurse hiking with me? At 2:00 p.m. after 12.5 miles, we arrived at the shelter.

Taking care of all the chores, we began winding down for the night. Some milled around the area while others chatted about the next day. I was tired and turned in first. As I listened, talking became less and less before that veil, you never seem to predict will come, dropped and shut off all sound and thought.

JUNE 9, 1995, rocky road or, in this instance, rocky trail was the issue of the morning, after we left the shelter. To be honest, very little bothers me on the trail, but the rocks I could have done without. It was not to be, so I just kept apologizing to my poor feet. I was reminded that all things have a purpose, when the rocks helped us get across a swampy area.

Eventually the trees parted enough to allow a look to the east at some well-maintained farm country. For some reason, there was an awful lot of swampy sections that had to be crossed. Sounds strange, to be on a mountain ridge crossing swamps? Up and down, up and down, I was beginning to feel like a pilot for a commercial airline. Over a stream, we entered a bunch of large rocks in an open area.

At Dutch Shoe Rock there was a view of Lake Rutherford, the water supply for the town of Sussex NJ. The Rutherford Shelter would have been a nice place to camp because it was only a short distance from the lake. Camping was not on my mind. I was getting eager to get into New York State. When we arrived at the High Point State Park Office at Rt. 23 we signed the register and moved on.

After 6.7 miles we came to the High Point Monument. Yes, it marks the highest elevation in New Jersey at 1,803 feet. There are numerous side trails in this area, so we had to be careful to follow the white blazes. Tweety Pie met us at High Point State Park. After a short break we bid him good-bye and proceeded down a trail that went through swampy areas and pasture land.

There were a lot of old rock walls. At least someone had found something to do with all these rocks. We came upon a thru-hiker who called himself Beaver. Poor fellow was from Germany and told a strange tale of how he was hiking the A.T. in honor of his wife and baby. No, they weren't dead, so I could only ponder why they were not with him. He was getting homesick for his little family and hiking 28 to 30 miles per day, wearing himself down to a frazzle.

People hike the A.T. for some strange reasons. It seems his wife was originally from New York and relocated to Germany, where she now worked and lived with her husband and baby. I kind of think it is unusual for papa to leave mama and the baby to go hiking in another country. On his behalf, I did learn he was a house husband before he started his hike. His wife's family were still living in New York and she had plans to come to America at the end of July, 1995. In this day and time, that doesn't seem to be all that unusual. It was his dream, just as it was mine, so I am forced to understand.

Snapshot, Stickflipper, Beaver and C.R. had mail drops at Unionville, NY, a mile off the trail on State Highway 284. At this point, we are smack dab on the New Jersey-New York State Line. We were worn out completely when we arrived and like Mary and Joseph, there was no place to spend the night.

The only choice we had was for part of us to load into the jeep with the gear, forcing Tweety Pie to make two trips to haul us down to State Highway 284 at Sussex, NJ. There we found a motel with vacancies. By now, I am beginning to understand why I refer to hiking as a disease. We are all a little sick in the head.

Our weird group piled into a restaurant. Receiving our orders, Beaver snarfed his food down like he hadn't eaten for days. Conversation revealed that he was trying to hike so fast, he was overshooting his mail drops and running out of food and money. I tried to get him to layover and, at least this time, wait for his mail drop. It is beyond my understanding why he wouldn't do that. Instead, he told the Postmaster to mail it to the next post office. Go figure. He was a fellow hiker so we allowed him to spend the night in the motel with us. As weird as he was, I felt good about helping Beaver and getting to know him. After all, what hiker could judge another?

Wearily, we did our laundry while we had city utilities. It had gotten up to 75°, which is not too bad but we had hiked 14.4 miles, plus a mile into Unionville and out so our energy was at a low.

Since there were so many of us, we were forced to get two rooms. Snapshot, Stickflipper, Beaver and C.R. stayed in one of the rooms, since there were two beds. Wildflower, Tweety Pie, and me stayed in the second room. We all managed to sleep on beds, except Beaver, who was glad to sleep on the floor. I think he was feeling a little guilty for imposing on the group. As unpleasant as this situation may appear, it was still more comfortable than the tents on the trail.

JUNE 10, 1995 - Tweety Pie made two trips to get us all hauled back to the trail, at NJ 284. All and all we didn't mind helping Beaver. Even though he was going north in our direction, he frantically left us behind in his apparent desperation to finish the A.T. as quickly as possible. In my thoughts, I would liked to have told Beaver I understood, and if I could do it that way, I certainly would. Instead I watched him disappear up the trail. At 6:45 a.m., we began our hike north, actually southeast. It would be a while before the A.T. would head northeast into New York. The anticipation is hard to endure.

We started out crossing over another brook, then a swampy thicket. The trail followed a lot of road walking on the state line. Skirting around sod farms and cornfields, we took the opportunity to watch men and their farm machines at work. Getting over the Walkill River wasn't difficult and we began a climb up Pochuck Mountain, briefly leaving the New York state line back into New Jersey. Bluish gray sky prevailed as we reached the summit, exposing great views to the west of Wallkill Valley, High Point and a last good-bye to the Kittatinnies, on a gradual descent.

The trail was fairly level as we passed over stone walls then crossed a large, wet area on log boards or slabs that help hikers cross the swampy wet lands. We crossed over two more wet, boggy areas before the climb up Wawayanda Mountain through a grove of hemlock, then a field overgrown with red cedars.

It became so steep, switchbacks and several rock steps built into the trail were needed to make the climbing a whole lot easier. Wawayanda was the name of a creek. The Lenape Indians had given it this name because it means "water on the mountain."

As we drew near to the Wawayanda Shelter, a male hiker was coming toward us. It was a pleasant surprise for Wildflower. Her friend Ted, had come from Pennsylvania just to take her out to dinner. What a friend! It was a case of three's a crowd, so I hiked on ahead, leaving them private time together.

We were then in Wawayanda State Park and the shelter turned out to be close to the Visitor's Center. Tweety Pie had brought our packs to the center and I got all kinds of gentlemanly help as Stickflipper carried my pack from the jeep to the shelter and C. R. carried my water. Our water source was from the Park Headquarters. I was worn out and I don't get babied to often but its sure nice once in a while. We had hiked 17 miles. My feet were aching and I just wanted to rest.

There were bear boxes at the shelter to put food in. It was a large metal box away from the shelter with a heavy latch on it. That tells you something about what we could expect, bear visitors. True to his promise, Ted took Wildflower out to eat. It turned out to be a blessing for the rest of us. Upon their return they bore a delicious gift, blueberry pie. Bidding his farewell to Wildflower, Ted promptly returned to Pennsylvania. He seemed like a real fine person, of course anyone who brings blueberry pie is okay, in my book.

Full from supper, we put the pie in the bear box. Sure enough, during the night we heard a desperate bear trying to get at it. He used all his bear sense, but he couldn't succeed. Chalk one up for a well-constructed bear box. After the ruckus settled down I reached over to see that Tweety Pie was near me, then drifted into sleep.

JUNE 11, 1995 - I had never eaten blueberry pie for breakfast, but boy, did it taste good! After taking the packs back to the jeep, we decided to slackpack for awhile. Tweety Pie would meet us with the full packs down the trail.

The trail was fairly decent as we crossed the Warwick Turnpike which is a paved road. The scenery was made up of fields, Vernon Valley that used to be a glacial lake and log bridges such as the one over Long House Creek. Tiptoeing over rocks in one stream, in and out of wooded areas, we finally came to the New Jersey-New York State Line for the final time.

Leaving Wawayanda behind to ascend Bellvale Mountain we ran into some really huge rocks. At least they didn't roll under foot like little gremlins looking for the first opportunity to trip an unwary hiker. We headed straight northeast into New York so it was good-bye New Jersey. Entering another state meant I was one state closer to the end of my dream, so it was always a time for celebration for me.

Looking carefully you could see Long House Creek to the west winding its way down to the Upper Greenwood Lake and Tayler, as well as the Warwick Mountains, forming the western backdrop. As we twisted across Bellvale Mountain's crest to the east, there were vivid views through rocky ledges of huge Greenwood Lake, not to be confused with the much smaller Upper Greenwood Lake and Ramapo Hills. There were several views of Greenwood Lake but we also had some very steep climbing. You dared not look above your feet too often. Trees were mostly oak, hickory and pitch pine hanging on to a precarious life on ledges.

When we reached Prospect Rock, 1,433 feet, there were great views. It was a massive rock and presented a great deal of difficulty to climb, even though most of the rocks in New York seemed to be rounder, with a rougher texture than those in Jersey. As we descended to NY 17A, Tweety Pie was waiting. I was already one tired old hiker when we had to don the heavier packs the jeep had been carrying. Couple that, with the fact that I was keeping up with younger people and a trail was getting rougher and very steep at times, my conditioning was paying off. However, when we got to Cat Rocks, Wildflower and I took a blue-blazed trail that bypassed an extremely steep climb.

Another 0.3 mile we crossed a brook and found Wildcat Shelter. A hand pump poured forth such cold water I made iced tea . . . . without the ice. At 3:30 p.m. we called it quits. It had been 12.1 miles of very rough hiking, even though the altitude was not that great. I was one worn out Den Mama. That is one of the side affects of this hiking illness. Anyway, when your body machine has a lot of miles and years rippling across its surface and seeping into the bones, its time to say good night.

JUNE 12, 1995 - getting tougher for me to keep up with those young, experienced hikers but we were on our way at 6:30 a.m. anyway. Two miles down the trail, there was a site that rejuvenated me somewhat. A twenty-five foot waterfall was bursting out of a rocky cleft. It's called Fitzgerald Falls and I'll try to explain why I was in awe of its strange beauty. It is part of Trout Brook and typical of the falls where you see the gallant trout fighting to return home. There was an odor and a brownish color to the water that made beautiful unusual sprays, even on a cloudy day.

As we crossed over the brook, beneath the falls and ascended by rock steps alongside, there was no deafening roar but rather a peaceful, continual splash as the water met the pool below. The kind of sound I like to have lull me to sleep. That was the last thought I needed on my mind when the trail got dangerously rocky.

We were looking forward to seeing the New York City skyline on the horizon when we reached Mombasha High Point, 1,280 feet. On a clear day it can be seen, but that day was far from clear. In fact, we were getting concerned that it may rain, not something you need with a rocky trail.

We arrived at West Mombasha Road and went 0.6 mile to Pappy's Deli and treated ourselves to hamburgers. It hit the spot but It was a good thing we stopped because it started pouring rain and it was only 10:00 a.m. When we got back to the trail, it was exactly what I feared most, rocky, rough and wet. That day was rapidly becoming a difficult one. It rained off and on all day, just enough to block out all the scenery and keep the trail slippery and dangerous.

We hiked 8.8 miles to the Summit of Arden Mountain, 1,180 feet through scrub oak, then just as I thought this miserable day would never end, the trail dropped sharply over rough edged rocks to Hwy. 17, where my rescuer, Tweety Pie was parked. I was soaked to the bone and looking like an angry cat after a bath. He took my ragged self and the others to Southfield, NY, where we gladly checked into a motel.

Things were hung all over the place, drying. Have you ever been caught out in the rain, soaked to the gills then soon after find yourself in a dry, warm room? Feels good, huh? After a good meal in a real restaurant, this cat was ready to purr. Ten doggone hard miles. That's it, no more that day.

JUNE 13, 1995 - it was a pleasant breakfast at a restaurant where discussions were had about how things were going with all parties involved. It was decided that Tweety Pie would take Wildflower, Snapshot and me back to the trail to begin hiking. Then he went back to Southfield and picked up C.R. and Stickflipper.

It really didn't make much difference in our schedule, the two, more physical hikers, overtook us with little effort. At that time, I realized how much they had been restraining themselves. Believe me, it had been appreciated. In all fairness though and to preserve my pride a little, the trade off was the obvious convenience to them to have Tweety Pie as backup. It had worked out to the benefit of all.

The rain had stopped and the trail was not as rocky, so it looked like it would be a good day. Continuing over the Ramapo River and New York State Thruway we came to the former Harriman Family Estate where they had tried to start an Elk ranch before it was interfered with by the New York Thruway. So for the most part, it had failed. The trees had grass growing under them and were in full growth, contrary to the many scrub trees we had seen.

My Achilles tendon felt like it might be acting up again. The pain in my heel was hurting pretty bad. I had bought some new boots before this trip, so I decided to give them a try, especially since we would be leaving Tweety Pie after Arden Valley Road. I had him take them out of the carrier on the jeep. I had broke them in hiking 12 miles before we left Missouri. Tweety Pie said Half Beard's truck was parked in the Elk Pen Parking lot and he would have someone to spend the night with, if he stayed there.

The boots were helping my heel as we circled Island Pond and continued uphill through hemlocks and a rocky area, crossing a ridge of Green Pond Mountain. From here we looked back over Indian Hill and the many smaller mountains dotting the country side, such as South Buchanan and Arden Mountain, that we had hiked the day before.

It wasn't so bad descending slightly to cross an outlet of a swamp and passing through another grove of hemlocks and mountain laurel thickets. There are lots of hemlocks and we passed through groves of them often. Crossing a stream, a fern topped boulder caught my eye. It was held up by a small stone. As we crossed another brook and into the trees, I noticed Island Pond through the trees just below us .

Lemon Squeezer was a narrow, steep passage, like a crevice between two huge boulders. We passed through and it wasn't as rough as I had heard it might be. It is part of Island Pond Mountain, 1,303 ft., in a series of small mountains we were descending and ascending. The temperature was cooperating nicely at 68° as we hiked over Surebridge Mountain, descended, then up Fingerboard Mountain, 1,328 ft.

Except for the mountains, you would think we were in Minnesota. I have never seen so many lakes and ponds of all sizes. For instance, from the Fingerboard Shelter, we looked down to see that we are bordering the north side of a large lake named Lake Tiorati, with Seven Lakes Drive running next to it. Reaching the north end of the lake, we arrived at a junction of Arden Valley Road.

After a gradual ascent of Goshen Mountain, it was on to William Brien Memorial Shelter, a native stone shelter in a beautiful primitive woods setting. Forest fires had burned it in 1988 and the stones still had a lot of soot burned into them. Snapshot and Stickflipper pitched their tent, allowing the rest of us to stay in the shelter.

Later that evening, here came Half Beard trotting down the trail from behind the shelter. It was good to see him again. I tried to get him to hike with us, but we just couldn't work out any arrangement suitable for him. He decided to hike the strenuous way he had been, by hiking halfway out to a point and then back to his truck. Boy, twice the work! But whatever trips his trigger. Our group was covering the A.T. in the most efficient way, with the backup jeep hauling the extra supplies.

Four more thru-hikers calling themselves White Root, Big Al, Rhino and Wilber (father and son). came in as the sun faded over the mountains and lakes. They rolled their bags out and seemed contented to sleep outside on the grass. I was tired but satisfied at how things were going. Sleep came and ended all discussion.

JUNE 14, 1995 - 6:30 a.m. we left the shelter, while the four thru-hikers were still sleeping. We hiked to the crest of Black Mountain and on the south side I beheld the magnificent Hudson River. I was so excited I almost forgot an ever-present nemesis. The rocks, always waiting to relocate taking careless feet with them, if the owner should become unaware.

It had only been two miles to Palisades Interstate Parkway, but my, how things were changing. Cars were racing by like they were all late for some important appointment. We were like coyotes crossing the Parkway having to be careful not to get injured. That's how crowded our poor world is getting. It made me appreciate getting back into the wilderness.

Tweety Pie picked up our packs and we immediately reentered the woods. The hustle and bustle was temporarily out of sight but the rushing sounds would be with us for a while, after all this is New York. Reaching the concrete of Perkin's Drive, that seemed to have no other purpose than to circle Bear Mountain, we began to ascend, back into the woods.

The trail was nice to the summit, 1,305 feet. A different look of the Hudson River revealed a strange Island (strange, because it didn't look like an island), but only a shore line. Iona Island had a very small creek separating it from the shore. To the south, the Magnificent New York City skyline was supposed to be easily visible but the clouds or pollution blurred our vision.

Somewhat disappointed we descended, passing under a ski jump to the Bear Mountain State Park. School children were having a picnic with their teacher. They evidently were not used to seeing hikers and took a great deal of interest in our backpacks and stories of hiking. It added an unexpected ingredient to their picnic and we were rewarded with hot dogs and soda pop. If this is any example of New York kids and teachers; they're in good shape. We thanked them for their graciousness and moved on.

Hiking between the shore of Lake Hessian and the Hudson River on our right, we eventually came to where Tweety Pie was waiting. He informed us there was no place to spend the night. Snapshot and Stickflipper and Big Al, the thru-hiker, picked up their mail drops. Big Al was anxious and didn't tarry long before moving on down the trail. Tweety Pie took us to Beaver Pond Campground. For some reason I was feeling an old familiar stress, so we all decided we would lay over a day, mainly to stave off burnout. The campground, true to its name, was located on Bear Mountain and had showers and more-than-decent campsites. It was a good thing because this small town country girl just wanted to relax from a day of experiencing a little of what New York life must be like.

JUNE 15, 1995 - there was no hurry for anything, so we slept in. Call it intuition or whatever, but when Wildflower's nephew came by and picked her up to spend the day with his family, an old uneasiness crept in causing my nerves to twitch. Then again, maybe it was just the pesky coons that had visited our camp during the night. The stinking little rascals had raided our garbage, scattering trash all over the place, so we had a major clean up on our hands.

A peaceful tranquillity took over as a large family of Canadian geese waddled, without fear, around the camp. A deer calmly grazed near the trees, looking up occasionally as if to say, "Relax, human." That's exactly what I did for the rest of the day. While Snapshot, Stickflipper and C.R. walked down to the lake, I was satisfied to spend the day with Tweety Pie, who was also sensing my uneasiness. Paying attention to what I thought that lovely deer had told me, why was my brain in such a turmoil?

When Wildflower arrived back at camp, she gave me the bad news and the answer to my near psychic revelations. She was going home in one more week. Being prepared for something doesn't help disguise the disappointment. I wished, when they decide to quit, they would just do it. Being told, and knowing I would only be with her another week, just prolonged the sinking feeling, especially when you like someone and were getting along so well. Fervently, I prayed that night for the Good Lord to understand my self-imposed illness and give me someone to share it with. Just a good solid, tough, hiking partner would do, Lord.

JUNE 16, 1995 - Loyal Tweety Pie made two trips to haul everybody back to the trial. I sure hope my companions appreciated the valuable service he provided for them. A nice trail went through the Trailside Museum and Zoo but we were too early and it was closed, so we had to take the highway around it.

There were several things I would like to have seen in the museum and zoo. Maybe another time. It was 8:00 a.m. when we crossed the Hudson River on the Bear Mountain Bridge. This is the lowest point on the A.T., 124 feet. Walking a short distance along Route 9D made me appreciate getting back into the woods. Hikers are not dressed for public display and I'm sure we are a novelty emerging in and out of public places. Sometimes when I feel those stares, I am reminded of the lepers in the days of Jesus.

It was occasionally steep up Anthony's Nose. A little humor there. This is not a literal statement. So to stay on track, I must explain that there is some confusion as to which Anthony's Nose we were climbing. Some historians believe it was named as early as 1525 by a Portuguese sailor, Estevan Gomez who called the Hudson River Rio St. Antonio. The Village of Manitou north of Bear Mountain Bridge was once called St. Anthonysville. Washington Irving claimed it was named for Anthony Van Corlear or Anthony the Trumpeter. Others believe it was named after General "Mad" Anthony Wayne who led the successful march to capture the fort at Stony Point from the British in 1779. Two forts, Clinton and Montgomery, were built on either side of where the bridge now stands. I choose old Mad Anthony.

Either way when we reached the summit of Anthony's Nose, there were great views back at Bear Mountain, the bridge and Iona island, which is mostly all meadow. After a while, we gradually descended and then it got pretty steep before reaching a large hemlock grove. There was a campsite in the grove that was of no use to us, so I turned my attention to the old carriage trails used mostly for horse trails now-a-days.

Steadily climbing Canada Hills, I had a feeling of urgency. I was beginning to hate those feelings, but alas when we reached Hwy. 9, an unexpected, dejected Tweety Pie was waiting. He was not supposed to be there, so I knew something was wrong. Sure enough, he had hit a deer just as he crossed the Bear Mountain Bridge. The jeep radiator was damaged but he had done a patch job on it. Naturally, we were both worried about getting the jeep fixed before it could overheat and do serious damage to the engine.

He decided to risk driving it to Dennytown Road where he was scheduled to meet us. It was also where we would probably end today's hike. We had a lot of miles to cover walking, but hopefully, it would not be too far for him to drive. Re-entering the woods and crossing a swampy area by puncheon (wooden planks) the trail took us past the Mount Atonement or Graymore Monastery.

Steep sometimes, we passed over some of the most historical hills in our nation's history. Bitter fights were involved against the British in places such as Little Fort and Denning, the highest hill at 900 ft., dropping off to Ft. Defiance Hill. It was hard to Imagine what it must have been like as we crossed Old Albany Post Road.

This was the route used by the Continentals traveling from Fishkill, a military supply depot, to Continental Village, a troop encampment. There is still a small village there. The British moved north from Peekskill, routing the 2,000 Continentals camped there. The men scurried into the fortified hills we mentioned. As we ascended Canopus Hill and looked out over the countryside that included Old Albany Post Road, you could see why those hills made an excellent place to defend. The wild turkeys and their chicks, that crossed the trail occasionally, thought it was a pretty safe place too.

Soon we left the hills into Putnam Valley and the Clarence Fahnestock Memorial State Park to Dennytown Road. Tweety Pie and his wounded jeep hauled us to RPH Cabin (Ralph Peak Hikers) formerly a local hiking club, where we spent the night. A hand pump was the source of our mineral laden water. It was so bad, it turned our clothes orange. The caretaker, Joe, paid us a visit and ended up helping the troubled Tweety Pie find a mechanic to fix the radiator.

All things considered, it had been a pleasant day. Tweety Pie relaxed, so we made our plans for tomorrow. We would slackpack to the RPH Cabin meeting him at crossroads, if necessary, for supplies. It was an appreciated luxury to be able to hike light and depend on him always being ahead of us.

I found out that Tweety Pie was meeting some very interesting hikers on his separate jeep adventures, which would make a fascinating book within itself. He told us about a guy that we had as yet not met, called Ultralite. It seems he carried no more than twenty pounds, hiked in tennis shoes and stayed almost every night in a motel, eating out whenever possible. He had made it all the way from Georgia doing this. Unusual, to say the least. It had been a warm 85° and we chalked 14.4 miles off my quest. I was awfully tired and bid everyone goodnight.

JUNE 17, 1995 - 7:00 a.m., back to Dennytown Road, we started hiking on a trail that was steep in places before we came to an old narrow-gauge railroad bed built in 1862, another piece of history. It's purpose had been to deliver ore from Sunk Mine to Cold Spring Turnpike which is still fondly called by that name. In modern days it is Rt. 301.

The lighter packs made for some easy hiking and we soon reached NY 301 Highway at 930 feet. From there, we started ascending until we reached a hemlock grove, then following Canopus Lake around its west bank. It was pleasant hiking because it was a very pretty lake. Edging close to Taconic State Parkway meant we would soon be leaving Clarence Fahnestock Memorial State Park.

At one high point, we had a last gaze at Canopus Lake, a long body of water nestled between two mountains. On its eastern shore, there was what looked like, a pleasant sandy beach. Descending gradually to a steeper drop and a small stream, that it was necessary to cross, we ascended its other bank to an old wood road, bordered by stone walls. Ruins of an old building reminded us that this was once a thriving area. As we crossed another small stream and proceeded along the wall, I briefly reflected on what life must have been like before all the highways, turnpikes, fast cars and airplanes.

Before I knew it, we were ascending Shenandoah Mountain to its summit at 1,282 feet. It was the highest point in this section of the trail, so naturally we had great views to the east and the west. With a breeze gently caressing my face, I looked both directions at roads twisting and turning in the valleys seemingly making the many lakes and ponds their destinations. The Indians used to have a God for fire, wind and water. Their God of water seems to still hold a place in our modern times. Personally, I simply believe God put all those lakes and ponds here for us to enjoy.

Joe, the caretaker who had helped Tweety Pie find a mechanic back at the Ralph Peak Hiker's Cabin, had told us to stop at a new shelter up the trail that the A.T. Club had bought. After crawling over several stone walls, crossing a swampy area by puncheon and another hemlock grove, we entered a field and an old road that led to our left. To the right was the cabin and Joe busy mowing the yard. What a sight! The house was small but beautiful with the Shenandoah Mountain rising to the north and Hosner Mountain to the south, with its crest leading off in the distance to the east. There was a lovely patio for hikers to sit and gaze at scenery, that most will never see from their homes.

Joe didn't know when the cabin would be available for the hikers to spend the night inside. We had not expected to see him again so after thanking him for helping Tweety Pie we made the steep descent to the older R. P. H. Cabin where Tweety Pie had been waiting. Since it was noon, we had lunch with him. It was 85° and the sun was bearing down so we decided to call it a day.

Later in the evening as the sun sunk low in the sky and the beginning shadows of oncoming darkness crept over the camp, a couple, who called themselves Jingo and Ludo, came in. Jingo was a pleasant young lady and a thru-hiker. Ludo was her male companion, who hiked a short distance with her, before heading back home.

While they fixed their supper, I learned they planned to continue on down the trail afterwards. It didn't take too much convincing to get them to spend the night with us, since they had been putting on some miles. Even though I had only hiked 10.6 miles today, I felt pretty worn out myself. The evening drifted into night with good conversation, which is always fun. The human body demands rest in order to begin fresh each day, so sleep was the next order of business.

JUNE 18, 1995 - early to bed meant early to rise. We rose early that morning at 5:55 a.m. It was okay though, since it was supposed to get into the 90's and we wanted to get as many miles covered as early as possible. The plan was to slackpack to NY 55. The hike began crossing Hortontown Road, ascending rock steps and going over a stone wall to a path between two stone walls.

As we went uphill through hemlocks and crossed a brook, we entered Taconic State Parkway. From there it was a gradual climb to the ridge of Hosner Mountain, 1,040 feet. The views from Hosner was not as remarkable as they had been from Shenandoah Mountain. I was still overwhelmed and aware of the ponds of all sizes, especially to the south. However, the little roads were not visible.

Hosner Mountain was history when we reached the Mount Storm Ski area and descended to NY 52 at 800 feet. Traveling through woods shaded from the rapid rising sun was pleasant, until we had to skin over rock walls and cross more streams. The surroundings were lovely, but the temperature was rising and dampening our enthusiasm for scenery. We did cross an area that had to have been deliberately cleared to afford a fantastic view to the north and northwest of the Shawangunk and Catskill Mountains.

Over an overpass on I-84 we soon passed through a thicket of mountain laurel before ascending Mt. Egbert, to its summit at 1,329 feet. Again we looked to the south and west at a valley with creeks meandering across, interrupted occasionally by small ponds and roads. Always small roads, some seemingly going nowhere, one forking around a huge hill known as Depot Hill.

There was no need to stop at the Morgan Stewart Memorial Shelter, however, it was supposed to have a well with excellent water. Something to remember, should we pass this way again. Entering a rocky area we came to a cliff that afforded us a view to the north, disturbed by the Green Haven Correctional Facility, a bleak conflict with our freedom and those confined within.

The trail leveled when we crossed Depot Hill Road, then entered the extreme north side of the big hill with the same name. Descending and ascending, crossing more streams and passing through narrow crevices we felt like

187

we were on a slow motion roller coaster. We thought we had it made as we walked over a wooden bridge, that spanned a wide stream, until we came to a muddy area that we had to cross, tip toeing on rocks.

Time for a well-needed rest with Tweety Pie at NY 55. It was noon, so we ate lunch with him and picked up our backpacks, plus extra water. The A.T. Guide had informed me that in dry weather the stream at Telephone Pioneers Shelter could be dry. No use in taking any chances. Tweety Pie was going back to the R. P. H. Cabin to spend the night and put the final touch on repairing the jeep. Good old Joe, the caretaker, had found a mechanic to install a new radiator.

One of the disadvantages to slackpacking is the full pack feels heavier than normal. Such was the case as we started out. I felt like a camel when one stick too much is put on the load. It was four miles to the shelter but at this point it felt like it would be fourteen. Jumbled boulders were scattered on the left before a narrow passage between rocks. Shortly thereafter we passed between two swamps, on dry land no less.

We glimpsed a curious lake to our right occasionally and I wished I hadn't found out it's name, *Nuclear Lake*. There were also a couple of strange buildings, enough to strike my curiosity, so I took out the manual of this area and was startled to discover that this was formerly the property of the United Nuclear Corporation. Yes, it was used for nuclear fuel testing and research.

It ceased operating December, 1972, following an accident when two non-nuclear explosions released plutonium dust into the surrounding environment. They say the site was decontaminated by the Nuclear Regulatory Commission and the New York State

Department of Environmental Conservation, at least, for unrestricted use. However, they did additional extensive testing and found elevated levels of radiation in two of those weird little buildings. Since then, the National Park Service has proceeded to clean the site completely and raze the remaining buildings. I don't know if that has been done, or at what date that may have occurred, but my skin is beginning to tingle. Probably psychosomatic.

It was a beautiful area and all things considered, we enjoyed the walk through it. However, I was having second thoughts about the warning way back on the trail, that said we could take an alternate trail that took us further away from that site. After viewing the map, it would have taken us considerable distance out of our way. Huh! I hope curiosity really doesn't kill the cat. We got the heck out of here.

More swampy areas just before we ascended West Mountain and looked out over some farms. At long last we spotted our target shelter - 3:00 p.m. Contrary to what we expected, there was enough water in the stream to bathe and cool off. After a hot day of hiking it was a wonderful way to prepare for nightfall.

The view of the valley below from the Telephone Pioneer's Shelter was awesome, with Pawling Mountain as a backdrop and wetland surrounding the curling Swamp River. Two section hikers came in for the night. Having nothing in common with them, I cooked my supper and crawled into my sleeping bag. I had hiked 16.2 miles and Wildflower was going to be leaving soon. That was to torment me for some time and I was on a pity binge. Sleep is a marvelous thing. Once it has its way for a few hours, nothing seems to matter. Then daylight will again come as surely as night time and everything that was, will be there again, plus new complexities that always seem to be waiting. Take me away, Knight of the night.

JUNE 19, 1995 - a good example of why we often end a daily hike early is manifest by the fact that we left the Telephone Pioneer Shelter at 5:55 a.m. I hiked 16 miles yesterday. That was about all Den Mama would be able to average, especially over rough terrain. It did start out level that morning but immediately began a steep decline. After the steep descent, West Dover Road was reached, where we passed the largest white oak on the A.T. Known as the Dover Oak, with a circumference of 19 feet 5 inches, it was slightly larger than the Keffer Oak I saw in Virginia, with a girth of 18 feet 3 inches. What a sight to see!

Boy at one point, near Corbin Hill, I got another view of Swamp River to the north. It's west bank is swampy or wet land as far as the eye can see. It was definitely named appropriately and soon we had to cross some of those wet areas. The marshy areas had to be crossed on bog-boards, puncheon and even bridges.

That took awhile, until we reached more stone walls and a bridge over another stream. Reaching some railroad tracks that appeared to have been recently used, there was a large sign reminding us we were on the "APPALACHIAN TRAIL." There was a bench under the sign for the weary to rest. As it turned out, it is called the Appalachian Trail Railroad Station and still being used for hikers, who could take the train all the way to Grand Central Station in New York City and return back to the trail.

When we reached NY Highway 22, we hiked a half mile to a place called Tony's Deli, where I bought a $3.00 pint of Tom and Jerry's ice cream. The elevation here is only 450 feet. After that refreshment, we hiked back to the trail where we were welcomed with more stone walls and swampy areas to cross on rocks.

As we entered the Pauling Nature Preserve, owned by The Nature Conservancy, we found ourselves in heavy woods, mostly second growth, ranging from scrubs to mature. There were several large groves of hemlock with a mixture of a variety of hardwoods. Ascending to the Hammersly Ridge, highest point 1,053 feet, through more hemlocks and mixed hardwoods I noticed the large private estates.

There was evidence, in abundance, of the past, such as crumbling stone walls, foundations and dams. This area was heavily farmed during the revolution. Traces of orchards, fields and old roads are readily visible all along the trail. A mountain laurel thicket and more swampy areas were crossed on puncheon and logs, signaling the end of the Pauling Nature Preserve.

Leaving the Preserve, we crossed more streams on logs and rocks, grassy fields and stone walls. It was compounding the 95° temperature so we reached the Wiley Shelter just in time, 12:00 High Noon. Ten miles was enough with all that swamp stuff. Not a bad place to stop. The shelter had a thoughtful caretaker. He had hung clothes lines, put tarps over the picnic tables for shade and good supply of magazines for hikers.

Tweety Pie arrived around 3:30 p.m. with a brand new radiator installed in the jeep. Thank goodness, now we can go back to slackpacking. Joe arrived shortly thereafter and we listened as the two told about *the adventure of the new radiator* and all the problems it entailed. They had parked the vehicles a short distance from the shelter on Duell Hollow Road. Tweety Pie brought his sleeping bag up with him and spent the night with us at the shelter. It was good having him with me. I can't explain how secure I feel in his presence. Dark, dreamless sleep ended that day.

JUNE 20, 1995 - 6:30 a.m., the temperature was already 70° and climbing so it didn't take a prophet to see that it was probably going to be another sweltering one. It made the fact that we were slackpacking, an item to be grateful for, as we crossed a wooden bridge over the gurgling Duell Hollow Brook. Just 1.1 miles brought us to a long-awaited goal, the New York-Connecticut State Line. A shout of joy rose in unison from our entire group. Another state completed on the A.T. is like a victory in a football game.

My first miles in Connecticut were easy with an ascent of 0.8 miles up Ten Mile Hill to an elevation of 1,000 feet. Views were limited until we descended to Ten Mile River, turned right and continued along its bank. There was then some nice scenery and well-kept campsites all the way to the Ned Anderson Memorial Bridge. Named in memory of the man who had laid out the original A.T. route in Connecticut, maintaining it for twenty years.

Crossing the bridge, it was only 0.5 miles to the bank of the Housatonic River. Just southeast of the bridge, Ten Mile River empties into the Housatonic. The river, at this point, was wide but shallow. We walked its bank for a while, then reached Bulls Bridge Road. We didn't go down the road but I understand one of the last of two covered bridges in Connecticut that allows traffic, was there. That puzzles me. I had always heard that covered bridges abounded in this state and were used for people who lived in rural areas.

Bulls Bridge is historical, along with this whole area. It was once the route from Hartford, Connecticut and Poughkeepsie, New York and was named after an early settler who had an inn near the present location of Bulls Bridge Inn. The inn catered to such people as George Washington and others equally as famous. The climb up Schaghticoke Mountain by switchbacks was steep. We had one more hello and good-bye to New York as we passed briefly in and out on the crest of Schaghticoke Mountain. After re-entering Connecticut, we came to Indian Rocks on the Schaghticoke Indian Reservation. We had a great view from there of the reservation, Housatonic River and U.S. 7 snaking along the river below.

Entering Dry Gulch involved a steep descent into a narrow and rocky ravine. It was steep climbing out onto a ridge. More scenery welcomed us at an open ledge. Housatonic Valley sprawled out below with hills, swampland and Segar and Bull Mountain ending the southeast border. After that reward, we descended again into Rattle Den, a ravine with a mixture of large hemlocks and jumbled boulders.

After crossing a brook, that supposedly had reliable drinking water, we again ascended steeply to the east ridge. In the valley below, we looked over Kent, Connecticut, where the river skirted its northwest city limit. On the other side of the river was remains of an old blast furnace. Kent, in the 1800's, was second only to Salisbury, Connecticut, in iron ore production within the state. Mt. Algo Lean-To looked like a nice place to camp, but we were eager to get on down Mt. Algo to Conn. 341.

The chance was greater that a surprise meeting was possible each time I met with Tweety Pie, especially since we had met so many hikers. Sure enough Lonescout was with Tweety Pie, chatting over their life's experiences.

My visit with Lonescout was brief but pleasant. C.R. was leaving to visit his sister in Connecticut for a few days.

I was already missing him, as he and Lonescout disappeared from sight moving swiftly down the trail. Tweety Pie took the rest of us to Housatonic State Park. After pitching the tents, I had a welcomed hot shower before settling down for the night. It had been a hot, 93°, with a 12.6 mile hike and the shade and inevitable sunset was welcomed.

JUNE 21, 1995 - we left our tents standing in the park in anticipation of coming back after the day's hike. The reason for that was we knew there were no camping sites close by where Tweety Pie could reach us with the jeep. It didn't hurt that we would be guaranteed hot showers again. Tweety Pie delivered us back to Conn. Hwy. 341. at 6:30 a.m. The city of Kent was only 0.8 mile south and would have been an interesting place to visit but I was there to hike. Macedonia Brook was crossed on a log bridge before we began a steep climb. I understand that brook floods quite often.

There were a lot of rock outcroppings along the ledges. Two major formations farther off the trail are Glacier Rock and Numeral Rock. Passing around the southeast base of Fuller and Pond Mountains, we reached Caleb's Peak, 1,160 feet. The Housatonic River flowed far below with the Penn Central tracks and U.S. 7 Highway keeping it company. All visited Kent before the river made a sharp bend, following its gorge, separating temporarily from the highway and railroad. Highway 7 again snuggled close to the river and the Penn Central bid them both farewell, joining Conn. 341 on its way south.

The trail zig-zagged steeply down well-designed rock steps for the first part of the descent, then leveled off gradually. Five miles later, we emerged from a mature forest and reached the top of St. John's Ledges. It took my breath away to look at the beauty we discovered. What a site of the Housatonic River and valley just below. Off in the distance, the valley rolls up Kent Mountain with St. John's Peak, 1300 ft. and Mauwee Peak, 1406 ft. peeking up behind. Off to my left was Flanders Mountain, 1385 ft.

There is so much to describe that I was to see later on. For the time being I had to drop 500 ft. through huge rocks and steep cliffs. Fortunately, there were steps built into the cliffs by an A.M.C trail crew from New Hampshire. It helped, but was still strenuous. The cliffs are so steep they are frequently used by rock climbers for practice. After reaching the bottom, we looked up at a wall of solid rock. At the base of these ledges, there used to be a group of houses called "Alder City" where seventeen children had been ferried daily across the river to attend school in Kent Village. St. Johns Ledges was named after an 18th Century owner, Timothy St. Johns.

Turning left under the cliffs was a well-cut trail to a river road with the largest big tooth aspen tree in Connecticut, standing guard. A short distance further was the site of Swift's Bridge, the last of three bridges that used to be there but had succumbed to a flood in 1936. The remaining bridge had been named after an early settler.

Passing through a forest of red pines that were planted in the early 1930's. It was one of the most photographed areas on the A.T. I was saddened by the fact that they were all dying from a blight. Some of these beautiful pines had been cut and the logs used to build four of the shelters on the Connecticut A.T. What an exciting experience that must have been.

It was almost flat hiking for the next five miles on an old road along the Housatonic River. It is one of the longest river hikes on the A.T. Crossing the Sharon-Kent town line was a gate and another casualty of the 1936 flood, the North Kent Bridge ruins. The trail used to cross the river there.

It was time for a well-needed break at the Stewart Hollow Shelter located on the river where Stewart Hollow Brook empties. A short ways up from this site was Stony Brook Campsite and Group Campsite. We were making good time now so we stopped for another break along the river when we saw a sea gull and a lot of geese taking their leisurely time also.

The ascent over Silver Hill was steep and the descent to Conn. Hwy. 4 equally so, where Tweety Pie was waiting. It was a good time for lunch. He was hungry too, after keeping himself busy cleaning the trail heads and cutting brush so we and other hikers can see the trail signs. That's just the way he is. An unsung hero.

Den Mama was weary but still full of spunk when she crossed beautiful Guinea Brook, then climbed to the summit of Breadloaf Mountain, 1,000 ft. Two more miles to Pine Knob Loop, a side trail to our right, appropriately named since it loops off the A.T. and joins it again shortly up the trail. The view from here, looking over Housatonic Valley, included a welcome sight, the campground where we were staying.

Carse Brook was crossed on a log bridge. It is one of the many brooks or creeks, as we call them in Missouri, that flow south into the Housatonic River, which we will be leaving for a while tomorrow. Tweety Pie waited at West Cornwall Road. After a rest, we drove down to the Old Cornwall Covered Bridge, then back to Housatonic State Park where we had left out tents.

I was melancholy after getting back to the campground. I walked alone down to that pretty river and reflected on why I was so determined to endure this hardship I had put myself and my husband into. Maybe I needed to meet people in this unusual environment. At our ages, it is a strange experience.

Snapshot and Stickflipper were going to start hiking on their own again. I will miss them. We had one more day for all of us to be together. How do you say good-bye to people who share such unusual and emotional experiences with you, in such intimate and close circumstances? They become like sisters, brothers or even my own children. Then in a period much shorter than a lifetime, they disappear like vapor. Oh well, I was feeling today's 16.4 miles in 84° temperature and I need the tranquilizer called sleep.

JUNE 22, 1995 - 6:30 a.m., Tweety Pie drove the group back to West Cornwall Road. Clouds hid the hot sun on an overcast day, making the temperature easier to bear. Ascending through two huge boulders on a path called Roger's Ramp, we soon reached the steeper climb up Mt. Easter, 1,350 feet. Climbing mountains is a major part of the game, so getting conditioned for that type of exertion is imperative. It is not for those who have heart conditions. Views west included wet lands or swamps and a better display of Carse Brook and its beginning. A swampy area appears to be its origination as it formed a pond on its lazy path to the river.

A five-mile hike led us past the Sharon Mountain Campsite to an unusual spot called Hang-Glider View. It was built and named for hang-glider enthusiasts. It is a sloped runway for hang-gliders to launch themselves. In addition to that, it is one of the better views on the trail.

Starting with the Housatonic Valley below, your eyes rise to the Taconic Range including Bear Mountain and Mt. Everet in the distance. In the right foreground, I could hear automobiles racing on the Lime Rock Automobile Race Track. Evidently, the wind was blowing in our direction and the roar was deafening.

For a brief moment, I envisioned what it must be like to take off and soar like an eagle on those man-made wings. Then I saw myself crashing head over heels and that was enough to motivate the hike down the mountain. On another ridge, we had one more barely visible look at Kaaterskill High Peak in the Catskills.

Actually, we were now in a section called Sharon Mountain but it is named more to designate an area, than a mountain. It led us past Belter's Campsite and Belter's Bump, a scenic outlook named after the former owner, Willie Belter. When we reached U.S. 7, it was no surprise to see Tweety Pie had company. He is a very friendly guy with a Jack Nicholson smile that goes from ear to ear, so it is normal for him to attract people. Fortunately for the less outgoing me, because I often get hiking partners as a result.

In this case it was a lovely couple, Darwin and his wife Betty, two retired school teachers from North Carolina. In all fairness, I had talked with them by phone about hiking with me before, so I can't give all the credit to "Smilin Jack" Tweety Pie.

They had been looking for us and the search paid off. Betty was going to run backup for Darwin in the same way Tweety Pie worked with me, so it was ideal for us to stick together. Unfortunately, Darwin could only hike two or three days. Betty would follow Tweety Pie with their car. The arrangement was made to meet them again in three days, because they were going south to finish hiking another portion of the trail. I could certainly understand that!

Tweety Pie couldn't resist a strawberry patch nearby and picked two liters of strawberries. Then our group hiked across the Housatonic River that we had left behind for awhile. It whispered its welcome back. After a zig and a zag, there was a school. It was the Housatonic Valley Regional High School, the first regional high school in New England and opened in 1939.

From there we went up a hill into the woods and followed close to some railroad tracks. They seemed out of place here. Further on we drew close to a bend in the river and an immense stand of pine trees. A gentle breeze whispered through the tops of those huge pines and I felt a foreboding feeling that caused me to quiver, then shake, until it left my mind, at least for the moment.

The trail followed a road between a power plant and an old canal built in 1851, then Iron Bridge at Falls Village. The bridge was built in 1870 to replace a 127-year-old wooden one. A bridge, much like the old wooden one, had been taken apart and reassembled in order to carry the Appalachian Trail across Swatara Creek.

As we entered Falls Village, I was reminded of a song. I'm not much for singing anything but church songs but the lyrics of *"It's Over"* echoed in my head. *"Setting sunsets in the sky. Falling stars that seem to cry. You won't be seeing sunsets anymore, it's over".* *

Wildflower decided to stay there, since she was leaving for home the next day, anyway. Snapshot and Stickflipper picked up their heavy backpacks to go on down the trail. Like a stray puppy I hiked with them, knowing full well it was time to part. Nevertheless, we chatted as if nothing was about to happen. My mind was briefly dimmed of sadness as we walked a short distance along the east side of the river. Then we came to a dam where we crossed to the west side of the Housatonic. Before the dam was built, a railroad bridge spanned the river there.

Just north of the dam the foundations of the famous Ames Iron Works can still be seen. The factory was founded in 1833 and employed as many as 800 men in three shifts. It produced the Ames "super cannons" for the Civil War, made of the hard Salisbury iron. It was a case of not enough eggs in one basket, since the factory went bankrupt when their contract with the army ended soon after the war. Later, another company manufactured railroad wheels in the same plant.

The falls are supposed to be spectacular during high water but it was pretty dry now. You could see the ruins of a blast furnace that had still been operating in the middle of the nineteenth century. Reentering the woods and curving north away from the river again, we began the ascent to the summit of Prospect Mountain, 2,690 feet. From there my spirit was lifted, as we looked out over the valley, Canaan Mountain and the limestone quarries for which Canaan is noted.

Then we reached the point I had been dreading. Snapshot and Stickflipper were taking a very steep, blue-blazed trail to the left that led to the Limestone Springs Lean-To. I could understand why they had decided to leave me. There were just some places I could not follow.

I had carried the strawberries that Tweety Pie had picked and gave them to my devoted companions as a feeble gesture of my appreciation. Tears don't come easy to me and it has been said that I keep too much emotion stored inside, but a torrent was building behind my eyes as I said good-bye and chokingly told them I would like to hike with them again someday. Eyes moist, they turned away and quickly stumbled down the hill. Their hearts were breaking too.

Like a lonely zombie I walked 0.5 miles to a huge rock formation called "Giant's Thumb", once called "Tomsteen Rock". There are some interesting theories as to its origin and why the name change, but they escape me. I was thinking of the story of Lot's wife in the Bible, who had turned to a pillar of salt when she looked back at the cities of Soddam and Gommorah. Weird, huh?. I felt if I looked back toward Limestone Spring Shelter, the memory of Snapshot and Stickflipper would turn sour or salty. Perhaps it was the taste of the tears that trickled down my cheeks now that I was all alone again. My thoughts were going wild. Hiking was bringing out emotions I had been hiding for years. Being dependent on my husband was one thing, but that was all I had allowed.

The trail was nice enough but this area was as full of confusion as was my mind. I was approaching a place called Barrack Matiff. The origin of the name is not really known. Like Giant's Thumb, there are theories, such as the name is a corruption of some obsolete Dutch words, whatever the heck that means. However the earliest settlers in the city, Salisbury, now lying far below me, were actually Dutch.

The modern topographical maps refer to the mountain as Wetawanchu. There are Indian caves on its western base, so probably, the Indian word is accurate. Edgar Heermance, who wrote the first guidebook, and many guidebook editors after him, misnamed it Barkmeteth Ridge. The people of Salisbury only accept Barrack Matiff, always have and always will. Go figure, I thought, as I descended steeply to U.S. 44.

Tweety Pie and, to my delight, Wildflower were waiting for me. I didn't know if her relative would pick her up while I was gone or not. Returning to Housatonic State Park for another night, our group was now down to three. I dread the thought of hiking that rough trail alone and Tweety Pie was beside himself. He rarely ever tells me what to do, but he was nearing that point. The Wildflower and I had hiked 230 miles. All said, she had made a great hiking partner and yes, I will truly miss her.

JUNE 23, 1995 - Wildflower watched as I packed my tent. She was leaving hers standing in anticipation of her nephew picking her up later in the day. For a person who doesn't take good-byes and emotions very well, I was sure getting a steady dose. With dismay and a hug of farewell from both us, Tweety Pie and I left Wildflower and drove to U.S. 44 where I would again started hiking single.

It was only a mile across the fork where Connecticut 41 had headed east, leaving U.S. 44 to its southeast course. Actually, it allowed the trail to by-pass the historical city of Salisbury where the two highways separated. In a parking lot, just north of a big white house, Tweety Pie was waiting with a concerned look in his eyes. In his own way he was forced to suffer my hiking. I think either one of us would be like a duck without water if something serious happened to the other.

Like a concerned father watching his child taking the first bicycle ride, he said he would stay in the parking lot for a couple of hours in case I decided to turn back. I gave him a peck on the cheek and told him to just be at Jug End Road in Massachusetts. He waited anyway because I couldn't disguise my fear of heading into that rugged country.

Like a gypsy vagabond, I headed up the old wood road on a gradual ascent. That wouldn't last long. I knew there would be some steep climbs in the next 20 plus miles I was to try to cover that day. The weather was nice and the trail actually leveled off in a short distance to Plateau Campsite where I crossed a rutted motorcycle trail. Briefly, I turned and looked back at the lot and white house. For a moment, I yearned to be in my house in Missouri.

The city of Salisbury was visible from here and I pondered its uniqueness. Founded in 1741, it became known as the arsenal of the Revolution. One of the most famous blast furnaces built after the war was located at Forge Pond (now called South Pond) a little more than a mile west of Lion's Head, where I was headed. A village had grown up around the furnace and there had been enough children to support a seventy-one pupil school. Also, there had been a four-clerk department store and a ballroom, no less! Be that as it may, there are only a few campsites now and a dirt road that is never plowed in the winter.

The climb through a birch tree forest heavily undergrown with fern was steep to the summit of Lion's Head, 1,738 feet. A blue-blazed Lion's Head Trail leads to the left to Bunker Hill Road where cars of weekend pleasure seekers can park. I suppose they enjoy looking down on the large Twin Lakes of Salisbury. Washinee is the north cucumber-shaped lake and its sister, Washining is round with an island in it. Caanan and Prospect Mountains can also be seen in the distance. Great views. When I reached the north outlook, I could see Bear Mountain and way off, Mount Greylock looming above the horizon. I could see why the locals would like it up there.

Soon I bypassed the Riga and Bond Lean-To's. No time to rest though. Birch trees were mixed with hardwoods now. Crossing Ball Brook on a log bridge, I could see a lovely campsite. I was tempted to stop but I had a long hike ahead.

There are old charcoal roads that used to lead to the big furnace on Forge Pond. Occasionally on high mounds, I would see circles about twenty feet in diameter where piles of logs were placed and converted into charcoal by controlled burning. The charcoal was used to feed the furnace where iron implements and weapons were forged. There is a legend that one of the anchors for the ship, U.S. Constitution ("Old Ironsides") was forged there.

Climbing Bear Mountain, there are rock gardens with stone ledges in some places. There were views too numerous to mention. Finally, I reached the summit of Bear Mountain, 2,316 feet, once thought to be the highest point in Connecticut. It is still the highest mountain completely in Connecticut on the trail.

There was a stone monument built in 1885 by Robbins Battell of Norfolk VA, to mark the highest peak in Connecticut. It was once 22 ft. high and remained undamaged for 80 years but has since been vandalized and rebuilt three times. It is now only one half its original height and shaped like a pyramid with its top knocked off. Nevertheless it was easy to climb, affording some great views. It just dawned on me, that was the highest elevation I had been on that year.

It was an appropriate place to take a break. My steep descent was over exposed rock and I was grateful an unpredictable rain had not caught me off guard. This could have been miserable. Sages Ravine was ahead and somewhere in between the Connecticut-Massachusetts state lines.

Funny how that invisible line, crossing grass, undergrowth and even through the middle of trees can be so important in a given circumstance. Otherwise it is completely unnoticed by we mortals. For that matter, the fact that God has had his earth devided into nations, states, cities and even our little private domains should be insignificant, but is it?. I wonder if He really cares what is claimed by whom. Anyway, I was happy to have another state out of the way on my obsessive quest. An A.M.C sign welcomed me just before I went down into the ravine. Hello, Massachusetts!

Sages Ravine Brook led me to the right 0.7 miles. Large trees, gentle waterfalls with quiet pools and a cool breeze drifting through my hair was a luring temptation to sit down and ponder the conflicting beauty I had experienced. I fought the temptation, with my sometimes too cold and calculating mind, and crossed the brook.

There was a trail register on the other side that I signed. I was startled out of my solitude by a hiker that appeared out of the trees and came toward me. His trail name was Ultralite and young enough to be my son. Typical of hikers, we struck a friendship that could last a moment or a lifetime. The likelihood of a moment was discarded as we hiked together for awhile.

It was obvious he wasn't feeling well. He had seen Tweety Pie in the parking lot back at Conn. Hwy. 41 and had discussed his illness with him. He had Giardia, a lower intestinal disease that was slowing his pace and causing him more than a little concern and discomfort.

After crossing Bear Rock Stream, we found ourselves on a gradual climb through hemlocks. We both appreciated the easy walking as we left the woods and emerged onto open cliffs where a panoramic view, sweeping from southeast to northeast, met our eyes. I was able to see a geographical history of Bear Rock Stream. It came out of a dammed up pond called Plaintain Pond, then drifted through a gully into a swamp area with brooks running from every direction.

Again, I am amazed at the marsh and swamps in the northern states. The whole valley to the northeast is brooks, small swamps and roads, lots of roads. These people up here live in rural areas, wherever they can get a little solitude from their hustle, bustle life styles in the big cities.

The trail followed the cliff a little closer than I cared. The summit of Race Mountain was within reach. Its elevation was 2,365 feet. The scenery below was spectacular but similar to what I described earlier. Being so far above everything is always fantastic. Ponds, brooks and roads. I bet there were some weird adventures going on down there as we passed above the many people and their homes dotted all over the scenic beauty.

The trail sagged between Race Mountain and Mt. Everett Summit. The sag had a fascinating environment at the top end of Race Brook Cascade, a short distance down Race Track Falls Trail. Five falls combine into an outstanding cascade several hundred feet deep. I would like to spend time exploring the beauty here, but I have a long way to go and the trail was steep and rocky up to the summit of Mt. Everett, 2,602 feet. Probably one of the most astounding things about those mountains is how far you can see on a clear day. For instance, from there I saw Mt. Greylock, 40 miles away. Peaks are everywhere. Barely visible are the Catskills and I had no idea how far away they were.

People do not realize that these mountains are as high from sea level as some mountains in the Rocky Mountain Range. When you drive to Denver, Colorado, and look at some of the awesome peaks surrounding you, we tend to forget that you're looking at them from 5,000 ft. plus elevation. We ascend these 2, 3, 4 and even 5 thousand foot peaks from only a few hundred feet above sea level. It's not how high the mountain, but what elevation you start from. I was told that some of the mountain roads in the eastern ranges cause the deaths of as many truck drivers as do those in the west. So these babies are often steep and dangerous.

A gravel road led off to the left and circled around Guilder Pond and its popular picnic area that can be reached by automobile. It is the second highest pond in Massachusetts, at 2,042 feet. We heard a lot of people laughing and playing and I think it prompted Ultralite to stop at Glen Brook Shelter, a short distance up the trail. I felt sorry for him and wished him luck, but I had to plug on.

Gradually I began lowering into valleys between mountains and around Mt. Undine, then an easy ascent up Mt. Bushnell, 1,834 ft. Up and down some minor peaks until Jug End Summit became a welcomed sight. Down some rock outcroppings, I looked to the north and saw big old Mt. Greylock a lot clearer. As if to test my stamina, it became very steep down to Jug End Road to good old Tweety Pie.

Tweety Pie had two backpacks with him and I wondered what poor souls he was helping now? To my delight, agony and ecstasy, they belonged to Snapshot and Stickflipper. They had caught up with him and were going to hike with me again. This was as good as it gets. Should I have to explain my emotions? Well, if you have ever watched a movie that causes you to gulp and sob with sadness, then you have it. It's a tremendous emotional outlet until you realize your eyes are red, you're embarrassed and if you're like me you get a doggone good headache. You don't want to watch that movie over and over again, no matter how good it was. So it was with those two. I had said good-bye. I had cried my tears inside and out and now I would probably have to do it again. Yes, I was ecstatically happy.

Our buddy, Lonescout, also stopped by and was visiting with Tweety Pie. His boots came apart so he had left the trail to get new ones, which put him behind. He was keeping Tweety Pie company while he waited for Snapshot and Stickflipper to come off the mountain. When they arrived, he took off up the trail.

It was 3:30 p.m. and I was worn out and finished for the day, so I withheld my feelings at seeing those two again. Tweety Pie took us over to New York State where we found a campground to spend the night. There was a platform to set up free standing tents. My tent isn't free standing, so it was necessary to tie it down on the board deck. I hoped no one interpreted my withdrawn attitude as anger, it's just that I am not a person that deals well with emotion. Some might even say I am an introvert, but Den Mama was a changin'. Casual conversation, a good meal and my good old sleeping bag was all I needed.

JUNE 24, 1995 - a cool day greeted us when we arrived back at Jug End Road. Tweety Pie was relaxed, knowing I had company again. Crossing a stone wall, we were swallowed by white pines, then another wall into a hundred yards of wetland pasture. A series of bog bridges led us to higher ground on a hemlock ridge. The next swamp we went through was on high ground, thank goodness.

In a couple of miles we crossed over Hubbard Brook. Just beyond, we found a monument of Shay's

Rebellion in the field where it had ended in 1787. Poor Ultralite was there after leaving a motel where he spent the night. He was not ready to continue so we left him.

Arriving at U.S. 7, just south of the city of Great Barrington, MA, we passed through a pasture to reach the Housatonic River. As we crossed the river, I became aware that this would be the last time I would see it. It had inspired a special romance and emotions within me that I had no idea was lying beneath the surface of my being. There is a lot of history along that old river's banks and now mine is deeply intermingled with them.

In and out of woods and up a ridge, we soon came to a glacier boulder where we crossed through a cleft in the boulder itself, with a little spring at the bottom. Passing another glacial boulder that had been split, we climbed moderate to steep, for over three miles to the ridge top of East Mountain.

When we stopped there to eat lunch, Ultralite came straggling in behind us. He opened up raw ramen noodles and began to eat, giving me the seasoning packet. He said he ate this way real often because it kept him from carrying a stove. No wonder he has lower intestinal problems. I have no idea what eating like that would do to me and I'm not about to find out.

The next 0.4 miles offered some good views from ledges and rock outcroppings. To the south and west, the magnificent Catskills loom in the distance. The Taconic Range with Mt. Everett sticking its 2,602 ft. derby above like a 6 ft. 7 inch Englishman in a crowd, was easily visible to the west. The weekend hikers were out in numbers, taking away the feeling of being in the wilderness. That is part of the trail today. It was enough to inspire passing up the Tom Leonard Shelter, even had we wanted to stay there.

Down the mountain between a finger lake to the northwest and a larger one to the southeast, we began to see devastating damage that a tornado had created as it passed through the area of Great Barrington, in May of 1995. Trees broken in half and stripped of their branches lay all over the place. Trail crews had done a quick job clearing the path so we made good time to Massachusetts 23.

Meeting Tweety Pie, we tried to get a motel, a sometimes difficult task especially on the weekends, and so it was. Back to the trail that had been relocated because of the tornado, we pitched our tents in the best place we could find. Tweety Pie elected to stay with his jeep by the highway.

Something about all this made me sleepless. I was trying hard to put the day out of my mind when I could have sworn I heard Tweety Pie screaming. I got up in a nervous state and went over to Stickflipper's tent. He was awake and said he thought he had heard something unusual. I told him it sounded like Tweety Pie and would he go with me to check on him.

Arriving at the jeep, Tweety Pie was sleeping like a baby. It was a relief, but I knew I had heard screaming. We checked the area up and down the highway for a while, before returning to our tents. Strange things had happened to me during my many hours of hiking so I was not surprised at anything. Laying in my tent with my mind skip jumping all over the place, I remembered someone saying that during the tornado, three young people had been killed in their car just up the road from where we were. Could it have been their ghosts crying out one last time as their memories of the tragic incident faded? Quivering at the thought, my eyes began to get that in and out amnesia. I thanked the Lord that Tweety Pie had been all right.

JUNE 25, 1995 - as we took the tents down and prepared to go back to the jeep, I was in deep thought about last night. It was a renewed relief to see my husband and I am sure he wondered why I looked at him so much during breakfast.

The trail was relocated to the old A.T. because of the tornado. It presented a climb of 1.5 miles to the junction of the new A.T. Gradually descending to Red Maple Swamp, ushered in the crossing of several marsh areas. Using old bog bridges and very carefully, over stepping stones put there for that purpose, we got out of the mess at Blue Hill Road.

A steep climb through a boulder field brought us to the top of a cliff where we looked back at East Mountain and the lakes we had passed between. After passing by another old semi-circle, level charcoal pit we soon came to an outhouse, telephone and picnic area associated with Benedict Pond. It is possible to camp there for a fee. We continued around the south end of the pond on our merry way.

A convenient bridge over the outlet stream from the pond allowed us passage over the last gurgling life of Stony Brook which turned into no more than a wet area. Sad, in a way. The brook led an active life before feeding Benedictine Pond. Steep terraced ledges loomed on the right and I was thinking how rough it would be to climb those rascals when, sure enough, we began the ascent to the ledges.

Crossing the outlet to a beaver dam, we found ourselves on the edge of the ledges. We again looked back on East and Warner Mountains with the Catskills hovering in the distance. After turning left, away from the ledges, we began a moderately steep descent and crossed a series of brooks. A spring on our right signaled a walk up to the Mt. Wilcox South Shelter. We descended steadily to swampy Swann Brook below Beaver Pond.

Wending our way through Beartown State Park, we passed the trail that led to the Mt. Wilcox North Shelter. Both shelters slept 8 to 10 people but it was early and we had trail to cover. There were more ponds, not to be confused with the ones I had just passed, which were probably built by beavers also. They're all over that area with swampy places prevalent everywhere. We passed another one where a brook forms a fork with both ends ending in a field.

A hemlock grove preceded a sharp left and incline to a winding trail passing Sky Hill, then leveling off to three stone walls. Crossing the walls took us out of Beartown State Forest. When we reached another hemlock stand, we peered through at the lower Tyringham Valley. This led us into a cool, shaded gulch with mysterious caves and boulders. The trail rose to a white-pine ridge paralleling the valley. Zig-zagging down a steep log road we came to Fernside Road, then continued down on switchbacks.

There was a brook with a gentle scenic waterfall. Then fences, some barbed wire, hedge rows, hemlock groves and bog bridges over wet fields, finally led us to a bridge over Hop Brook that brought us to the main road to Tyringham. Tweety Pie waited patiently with two more surprises. They were Darwin and Betty.

Boy, from loneliness to friends everywhere. I was glad to see them and Darwin joined us on the trail as my growing group decided to hike on to Pond Road. It didn't take us long to clear Baldy Mountain, about 1,800 ft. tall with Merry, Merry Brook bubbling its way into some swampy mess. As we neared Knee Deep Pond, we went between two wet areas and the one to our south was, indeed, the final goal of Merry, Merry Brook.

We were ready for a good rest and a hot shower when we reached Pond Road, where Tweety Pie and Betty had driven around to meet us. There was no inn in the village, so we drove to Lee, Massachusetts, to the motel where Darwin and Betty were staying. Some ate heartily at the restaurant but I was sick of the heat outside with a sprinkle that was compounding the humidity, so I pecked at my food in anticipation of a hot shower and air conditioned room. The motel wasn't bad and the bed even better. While the others talked, I laid down to allow rest to remove the toll 17.4 miles had taken on my body.

JUNE 26, 1995 - back to the trail at Pond Road. It was 7:00 a.m. and Darwin was feeling poorly, so he decided to stay behind. A gentle breeze was tugging at the hair behind my ear. I hoped it would continue blowing the humidity around and keep things cooler. Entering a cool pine woods helped us master the climb to Upper Goose Pond. A stone fence separated us from a house on the right, then another marsh and small pond.

Entering a hemlock forest, we crossed over the outlet to upper Goose Pond on a bridge made out of telephone poles. It was really quite pretty through here, especially if you like a lot of inland water. Actually we were circling the pond until we reached the trail to Upper Goose Pond Cabin. Snapshot and Stickflipper hiked down to the cabin to take a peek.

I continued on a level trail and looked back at the pond which was more visible from where I was. It was finger shaped and sort of like a big drop of rain that had fallen and tried to dribble off to the south, stopped, then remained in that configuration. Really, the Upper Goose Pond is to the south of a much larger pond called, you guessed it, Goose Pond. If it confuses you as to why they didn't call the smaller pond Lower Goose Pond, join the crowd.

It was only 1.3 miles where I crossed Massachusetts Turnpike (I-90) on twin bridges. From the last bridge I could see yet another large pond lying between the Interstate and U.S. 20. I crossed the outlet stream which strangely enough was on the north side of Greenwater Pond. This always throws me. I keep thinking that running water should always go toward the Gulf of Mexico. That's why it's so wet up here. Water could look like it is really going somewhere, then spread out and stop at the flattest area, no matter the direction. It's all based on a down hill principle.

In 0.4 miles I reached U.S. 20 and met Tweety Pie. I took a break with him while I waited for Snapshot and Stickflipper. When they arrived they were bubbling with excitement. They had met the caretaker of Upper Goose Pond Cabin. It must have been quite a meeting and the cabin impressive. So much so, it made a fairly dramatic change in our plans.

Snapshot and Stickflipper had made arrangements with the caretaker to meet us at Pittsfield Road in order to lead us back to the cabin, where we were, obviously, going to spend the night. Well, we had done stranger things, so we all agreed. As many cabins as those two had seen, it had to be something out of a fairy tale. After the break, we continued the hike, which after all, is our main objective. Starting out on an old logging road, the trail was quite level and pleasant hiking as the excited twosome continued to babble about their discovery. Surprisingly, we went from below 1,500 feet elevation to the summit of Beckett Mountain, 2,100 ft., with only a slight notice of incline. Perhaps it was because of the increase in the two-way conversation between Snapshot and Stickflipper.

I looked back at the two Goose Ponds and discovered why they were so hard to see from below. Hills surrounded them, for that matter there were a lot of hills in the whole area within my view. Walling Mountain was easily reached with little change in altitude. It's summit was only 2,230 feet but it was so overgrown with trees and underbrush that all scenery was hidden from view. The trail downhill was rocky, which really appealed to me and my poor abused feet.

Circling Finnerty Pond, it was apparent that this little body of water owed its existence to rain and snow, however it had an active outlet creating a wetland between the hills below. We're now in October Mountain State Forest and for some reason that name still sounds appealing and poetic to me. After skirting Finnerty Pond on stepping stones, we crossed that outlet I spoke of and some tributaries of Washington Mountain Brook. I don't know where Washington Mountain was but it must have been somewhere to the northwest.

Anyway, we had a pretty steep incline through a gully to the heavily overgrown summit of Bald Top Mountain, 2040 feet. Crossing a brook, we passed the little trail to October Mountain Lean-to. It was a level and wet trail through woods, due to a nearby swamp, and perhaps because it had begun to sprinkle on us when we barely reached Pittsfield Road.

Talk about luck. It started raining cats and dogs as we climbed into the jeep and the caretaker's vehicle. True to her words, she had come to lead us back to a small two-track road that ended 0.5 miles from Upper Goose

Pond Cabin. We all hiked to the cabin as the rain slowed to barely a sprinkle.

Stickflipper and Tweety Pie, like two little boys, canoed around Upper Goose Pond Lake with the caretaker. Her drinking water supply for the cabin was across the lake so the canoe was a part of her everyday life that she seemed to enjoy immensely. The bigger Goose Pond, separated by a small stream from its little sister, Upper Goose Pond, is a reservoir supplying water to the surrounding communities and is equipped with a spillway.

It was easy to see why Snapshot and Stickflipper wanted to go back there. Comfortable cots waited for us upstairs in the quaint cabin. It was great as the evening cooled off with a brisk breeze off the lake. The smell of fried potatoes and onions filled the cabin as Snapshot fixed supper. Lucky me, the lady loved to cook. It was one of those adventures you don't want to end.

The caretaker was in her thirties and presented herself as a rustic, outdoor type person. As much as she meant to us, I am ashamed to say I never learned her name. We spent the evening with her telling interesting stories and legends about the area. It seems there had been history we had overlooked back at Tyringham. Stone walls and cellar holes we had passed were all that remained of a Shaker community that thrived back in the 1792-1875 period. The Shaker's leader had merged his church with the Mormons and their leader, Joseph Smith Jr.

Back at Webster Road there had been another thriving community in the early 1800's. They actually had two schools and a legend about a self-taught bone setter called Widow Sweets. The first Chiropractors were called bone setters and bone crackers. It was amazing how much this lady knew about this area's history. I listened until I began to nod. Rather than appear ill mannered, I excused myself and wearily climbed the stairs to my cot. Life was good, I thought, as my friend, sleep, nestled into my mind to prepare my body for another day.

JUNE 27, 1995 - I carried good memories with me from this cabin by the ponds. It was 7:00 a.m. when we arrived back at Pittsfield Road. A cool breeze was blowing across the soaked land keeping the ever-present bugs settled down. A gentle trail started out over a stream by a wooden bridge, then up and beside a 30 ft. overhanging cliff. Left to the ridge, it wasn't long before we reached the top of Warner Hill at a surprising elevation of 2,050 ft. I knew, because a sign told us we were at its summit.

Descending gradually through fern trees, I was puzzled at that elevation until I realized that I had become disoriented. When we went back to the Goose Pond Lakes, we went down by jeep, then back up the same way. The elevation had changed very little if we had continued on the trail without going back. For that matter, we only went down gradually and back up slightly higher to Tulley Mountain. Warner Hill and Tulley Mountain were probably no more than 25 ft. difference in height. You might say we had been hiking on one up-and-down ridge since we left Becket Mountain.

It was muddy in places but, in general, a forgiving trail all the way to Dalton, a distance of 9.6 miles. Tweety Pie was talking to a thru-hiker in his late fifties who called himself, simply, Scallion. This was his third time to thru-hike the A.T. Not all that great a chore, when you discover he had been a marathon runner in his young days. Nonetheless, I envied him because I would do good to hike it once, but then I'm getting a much later start. He told us about a lovely little cafe, so we ate lunch there. I had a hamburger, fries and a Coke. That may not sound too glamorous, but for me was a welcomed feast. I was honored when he decided to wait, and of all things, hike to Cheshire, Massachusetts, with us.

The best way to describe this section of the trail was up and down, mostly all pine trees, oak and hemlock. The land was acquired through the generosity of the Crane family of Dalton. U.S. currency and other eloquent papers are still manufactured in their mills. It is pretty country with hemlock woods and other varieties. At the "Cobbles" (huge rocks), we had a superb view of the valley below. The big rocks are almost 2,000 ft. above the city of Cheshire that is only slightly below 1,000 ft. It was, however, enough difference to allow some great views of the city and its unique reservoir. Consequently the Cheshire Reservoir resembled very closely, the two Goose Ponds we left behind, except much larger.

Well, it was time to start the fairly steep descent into the city. It was about 4:30 p.m. when we entered Chesire. Snapshot and Stickflipper barely made it in time to pick up their mail at the post office. We walked to the St. Mary of the Assumption Church Hostel. It was set up to allow wayfaring hikers to spend the night in their parish hall. A picnic table outside was there for the hikers to cook and eat their meals. 18.9 miles had passed beneath our feet today and I was amazed that I was only a little tired. Maybe it was the fact that Scallion was so skillful at telling his hiking stories, which I always loved to hear.

As the sun faded over Cheshire Reservoir, even Scallion could not keep his voice from becoming a blur. Rather than cheapen this master story teller's adventures with a nodding head, I excused myself and made my way into the parish hall.

JUNE 28, 1995 - leaving the church hostel at 6:05 a.m., I was excited at finally getting to ascend this 3,491 ft. monster, Mount Greylock. We had been seeing this peak for some time now from quite a distance. The views should be absolutely amazing, since it is the highest point in Massachusetts.

Snapshot and Stickflipper decided to give me a thirty-minute head start for two reasons. They would be able to hike at a faster pace for a while and it would take that long before I got into too much hazardous climbing. A sharp climb eased off to gradual, before I reached a field and looked back at Cheshire, its reservoir and the cobbles above. Cheshire circles around its reservoir and I find that unusual since most of us rarely see the source of our city's water.

Cliffs on my right reminded me of how rugged this hike would be. Passing by a brook running below in a gully, I had a steep climb to reach a hemlock ridge. From there, a sudden drop revealed Kitchen Brook flowing through a valley into Cheshire from its source tributaries in Mt. Greylock State Reservation.

It was breezy up there as I left the ridge and entered some high ground between two swamps. I crossed a brook flowing east in a gully with rocks scattered about indicating some swift runoff water ran through here at times. On a small open ledge, I got a peek to the southeast, at some large wet area around the Hoosit River at the east end of Cheshire.

Descending to the boundary of Mt. Greylock State Reservation, I entered a red spruce grove. It was pleasant in those trees for at least a mile, then I wove my way through huge boulders. What a variety!

I don't know if it's a compliment to my hiking or not, but I caught up with a hiker who called himself Beach

219

Bum. We hiked together for a while before I discovered we had something very precious in common. He had hiked with my previous companion, Wildflower, in 1991. We were having a good visit, but I became overwhelmed with a loneliness for Wildflower. After all, it had not been that long since she had quit and returned home.

My mind was cleared of emotional thinking as we went down a pitch of stone steps only to find ourselves in the midst of a steep, narrow ridge. I got a couple of more views between rocks to the south, similar to what I had just described. We passed up the Mark Noepel Shelter, 0.2 miles off the trail. We reached another ridge that was dominated by another type tree that Beach Bum said were balsam fir.

As we hiked the Saddle Ball Mountain Ridge, the trail veered to the east around a large balsam swamp. There was a view from a knoll to the east of some side trails and off in the distance of the many populated areas surrounding this tourist area. It's not a sight that hikers enjoy describing since we are romantics and like to think we are escaping into the wild. It's probably only an illusion we do not wish to face.

Crossing a sphagum-moss bog brought us within easy reach of Rockwell Road where I found a missing Tweety Pie. That was all right, since I had decided to wait for Snapshot and Stickflipper to catch up anyway. As if on cue a few minutes later, they all arrived about the same time.

Tweety Pie continued in the jeep to the summit of Mt. Greylock. The rest of us hiked. It was a steep climb to the 3,491 feet elevation. On the way up, we passed a small pond used for water supply. Stunted spruce and fir were trying their best to reach a dignified height. The final hike to the base of War Memorial Tower was by steps. I was huffing and puffing and my ears were popping like marimbas.

I still had enough energy to join the rest in climbing to the top of the stone tower. This was, indeed, the highest point in Massachusetts. As the breeze pulled at my hair, I felt a chill. I understand the climate up there is identical to northern Canada. They will get no argument from me. As I looked into parts of New York and Vermont, I was overwhelmed at how very small we are. Yes, I could see that there was a large population, but closer view revealed the streams on the mountain side, the beginnings of well-known brooks in the valleys below. Rockwell Road could be seen on a fairly straight course until it reached the base of this huge mountain, then it took one large switchback, so the cars would not have such a steep climb. They overheat here the same as they do on steep mountains in Colorado.

After descending the tower, we took a break before parting with Tweety Pie. It was a sharp decline off the peak itself, then leveled as we crossed where the Thunderbolt and Bellows Pipe ski trails go off to the east. I mean it when I say "go off". I can only imagine what it must be like, when this mountain is covered with several feet of snow, to sail off into seemingly empty space to the roads below.

There was an unusual milky quartz near the dome shaped, tree-covered Mt. Fitch, elevation 3,110 ft. A fairly steep short drop and an equally short rise put us on Mt. Williams. Actually, it's all the same mountain as far as I'm concerned. It seems that if there are three peaks on a mountain, each peak is considered another mountain. I will say this, we went up a steep Mt. Greylock to almost 3,500 ft and eventually reached 200 ft., almost sea level before we arrived at MA 2 in North Adams.

As I looked back, I was amazed at how high in the sky we had been. I reflected on how exhilarating this section had been, as Tweety Pie drove us to the Mountain Goat Outfitters in Williamstown. They were a good group who permitted hikers to camp in their backyard by a beautiful stream. I was tired after 14.4 miles today. Thank you Mt. Greylock for your lofty heights.

JUNE 29, 1995 - Williamstown was formerly West Hoosac. The name was changed because of a last will and testament by Colonel Ephraim William. I don't know the details but he must have had a lot of influence. At any rate, the city was a pleasant place.

It was 6:00 a.m. when we crossed over the B & M Railroad and the Hoosic River by way of a steel and concrete foot bridge. Two more foot bridges were crossed before we walked beside an old spillway releasing water from a circular dam, then it was steadily up again through hemlock and patches of laurel.

The temptation was great to keep looking back at the changing view of the city, Mt. Greylock and the snaking Hoosic River flowing through it, but the trail was steep, forcing us to climb over a slippery, dangerous footing of jumbled boulders, of granite, marble and quartz. After a couple of steep narrow switchbacks, we ended up on a east-facing bluff with a campsite that overlooked the Hoosac Range.

Passing a mossy pond, hanging on for dear life, we came to an open area of quartzite cobble. A short distance further was the Pine Cobble Trail leading off to the left and a generous view including the marble top Of East Mountain. A dip in the ridge took us through azalea, sheep laurel and pretty pink lady's-slippers.

Emerging from the woods brought us to Eph's Lookout, yes, named for old Ephraim Williams. We were at 2,254 feet elevation, carefully looking back at Williamstown, the Berkshires and magnificent Mt. Greylock, up close for the last time. Any sadness was quelled when I spotted the boulders on the Massachusetts-Vermont State Line. I had actually crossed another major section of the A.T. Good-bye Massachusetts. Hello Vermont. Another major trail called The Long Trail joins the A.T. here and they coincide for 101.9 miles, then the Long Trail turns north for 165 miles to the Canadian border.

The Green Mountains of Vermont are properly named. It was definitely green along the trail. There were beaver ponds and a lot of logging roads in that area. We reached Harmon Hill, 2,325 feet, with a view north. Descending was very steep on rock steps they had built into the mountain and they helped a lot. When we reached VT 9, 1,360 feet, Tweety Pie was there along with Lonescout, Scallion and his wife and their grandson, plus two other hikers. We all had a nice visit before going our different ways. Tweety Pie brought us to a private campground. It was good to have a hot shower. We pitched our tent by a pond, where the bugs were on the war path. It was 3:00 p.m. after hiking 18.3 miles. I would rest.

JUNE 30, 1995 - taking a day, we slept in. It was 7:00 a.m. before we crawled out of the tents. After a relaxed breakfast, we went shopping for groceries, then checked the trail north of us. Since we have the whole day to ourselves without having to reach a "goal", we used some time to find a place to spend tomorrow night.

Ice cream had been on the grocery list and, of course, potatoes and onions.

When we got back to the campground, Snapshot performed her usual feat with potatoes and onions. The fragrance of frying onions and potatoes wafted in the air. Preparing and eating a meal at a campsite is a wondrous experience, enhancing all five senses: touch, sound, smell, taste, and sight. What a meal!

It was time for Tweety Pie's barber appointment. I gave him a haircut with his rechargeable razor and it worked pretty good. I'm not a professionally trained barber, however, when it comes to sheep and Tweety Pie, I get by without too much complaint. If I do get too much moaning and groaning, I remind my subject that I am probably the only *Clipper-Campsite Hair Styling Salon* on the trail, that I know of. Perhaps I'll start one, full time when I finish my dream hike. Let it be known, that Den Mama will never turn down a new adventure.

The bugs were so bad by the pond, I had to put my bug shirt on. Mother Nature is usually pretty nice to hikers and campers alike. Lest I offend her, I want her to know we really do enjoy and appreciate her governing authority. We all agree there are some nuisances we must endure, but endure we will.

The day off was enjoyable and relaxing, however, everyone was ready to call it a day. Tomorrow would bring new hiking adventures and we had to rest up for it.

JULY 1, 1995 - 5:55 A.M., arriving back to the trail with Tweety Pie, I found myself still half asleep. I thought I had slept pretty good but found myself manifesting some reluctance to begin a hike with a groggy head. The trail ahead had little access for motorized vehicles, so it was a hesitant good-bye to my husband.

What the heck, it's a beautiful morning so onward and upward. My enthusiasm was dampened somewhat when we entered a dark woods with trees that looked less than friendly. That intersection of VT 9 and the A.T is notorious for vandalism and theft, so don't leave your vehicle there overnight.

Crossing a bridge named in the memory of William A. MacArthur, we followed the stream's bank briefly before turning left uphill. Actually, it was steep enough to give a sick mountain goat a challenge to get home. The effort brought us panting to an old woods road and a lookout. At 5:00 to 6:00 A.M. you don't see anything but hardwood trees and fading darkness. Shortly we passed through a fissure between Split Rock. I uttered to myself a complaint, "Oh my aching back," and it had only been 0.6 of a mile.

Passing a trail that led 300 feet to the Melville Nauheim Shelter, we again ascended across Black Brook to the southern side of Maple Hill, 2,620 feet. From there I could see the outline of Snow and Haystack Mountains. The rising sun provided a shimmering backdrop. It was dark to the west. Circling Maple Hill we reached its high point before descending to twin brooks below.

A bridge over Hell Hollow Brook led us into balsam and spruce trees which only meant one thing, swamp. It had a wood puncheon to cross over. From swamp to a steady climb to Porcupine Ridge, 2,815 feet, following a ridge that led more up than down, we found ourselves at the summit of Little Pond Mountain, 3,100 feet.

Another narrow ridge led us over a peak with no name. That peak was a prelude to the summit of Glastenbury Mountain, 3,748 feet, with its beautiful, stately tall spruce. The whole mountain was covered with them. Something about tall pine trees makes the temperature feel several degrees cooler and so it was up there. It was a beautiful setting for Goddard Shelter, that we passed before reaching the summit.

There was a restored fire tower. Without climbing it, my view was limited to the tall spruce from ground level. It would have been too much effort to climb the tower and expend energy needed for hiking. Descending, in a northward direction past a big rock and a variety of oak trees, the walking was pleasant. Arriving at the Caughnawaga Shelter, we determined it was a good place for a break. A brook with potable water passed only 30 feet in front of the log cabin style building. It was a welcome break, but we managed to keep it brief.

Climbing to a small ridge and then steeply down, the trail was very rocky. My walking staff became caught between two rocks causing me to loose its rubber tip in that never-never land of lost objects. I searched for it, but it was a lost cause. At first it wasn't that important until I kept hearing the metal clang on the rocks. Talk about irritating! In that environment it absolutely interfered with my peace and quiet.

Oh well, we crossed two small streams and ascended to below another nameless peak. I guess when you have so many peaks you get tired of trying to name them all. I would gladly let them name it Den Mama Peak since that sucker was 3,412 feet tall. Maybe, after finishing that adventure and writing about the wonder of the A.T., I might be considered .

I can't believe things like that were flashing through my mind as we circled an old beaver pond and crossed two branches of South Alder Brook. That kind of thinking ceased, when we started a steep climb, eventually leading us to Story Spring Shelter. It was tempting to quit there, but a lot of hikers had the same idea. Regardless, we were getting awfully tired.

No one was disappointed to begin a gradual descent over a heavily logged area to USFS 71 where good old Tweety Pie waited. Before I could get my pack off, he told us to hike on to Kelly Stand Road. Another two miles was difficult, but we all grunted what could have been considered approval and like trail mules in a row, proceeded forth. He would have been facing a rebellion if he had said go another two miles when we reached Kelly Stand Road. Instead, he took us up the road to a campsite he had found the day before.

A large monument said that Daniel Webster spoke to a Wigg Political Party Convention on the spot, July 7th and 8th, 1890. Fascinating, but all I could think was, "I have hiked 22.6 miles today, the most I had ever hiked in one day. Show me food, drink and a place to lay my weary head and the heck with the Wiggs."

Tweety Pie and Stickflipper were busy propping up a broken down makeshift table someone had left there, which made a nice place to prepare our supper. All things considered, my eyelids were sending a message through my mind to my aching legs, that a bed had better be made ready soon.

JULY 2, 1995 - was I ready at 6:00 a.m. for the climb up Stratton Mountain, 3,036 feet? No! It had been a long hike and getting more difficult by the day. I was grateful for my companions who kept prodding me on. With eyes half open, we worked our way to the bridge over Deerfield River into an old logging camp in the middle of some oak woods.

The route was fairly level but I knew that was temporary at best, as we passed a beaver pond. Signs of what was a prosperous population in the mid-nineteenth century, on and around Stratton Mountain abounded here and there. Holes of cellars used to store winter canning and shelter from the occasional storm were still there. Some remnants of apple orchards manifesting that they did not have to have the farmers caring hands to survive over long harsh years. Lilac bushes, that some pioneer wife planted to give scent for her dream home, still crept into my nostrils. Silently, I thanked her for the sweetness still present.

Crossing a well-graded dirt road signaled the climb toward switchbacks hidden in the woods. A bench cliff took us below and into a gully between Little Stratton and the rest of the Stratton Mountain Range. Wandering by a spring, more switchbacks lay ahead. The almost 4,000 ft. peak was finally reached. On top of that was a fire tower that Stickflipper climbed. He described his view to we landlubbers below. It went something like this. Somerset Reservoir and Mt. Pisgah to the south, tall Glastenbury Mountain to the southwest and the Taconics with Mt. Equinox, the highest peak in this range, directly west. Mt. Ascutney was to the northeast and Mt. Monadnock, southeast. To our north was the Stratton's north peak with the upper station to a chair lift.

His description tempted me to dare the climb, but Den Mama needed her energy. A chill went up my spine and I realized it was the chill of the early morning hours. The sun's rays peeked over the mountains to the east, as if to see if all was well to start a new day. It was cold on that mountain and dumb me had started out in shorts. All I could do to try to keep warm was to wear my poncho. It gave some warmth due to its rubbery insulation.

A caretaker was camped on the summit for the purpose of assisting hikers and maintaining the ski lift that lay off to the right. A wide trail followed the ridge to the northern summit. Down more switchbacks beside a swift running stream, we were privileged to a western view of Stratton Pond, the 14,300 acre Lye Brook Wilderness and Equinox Mountain. I looked for only a short time since it was time to begin the descent by switchbacks. Switchbacks are valuable, and they help eliminate some of the drop by snaking you up or down a mountain, rather than going straight up.

When we crossed a dirt road the drop leveled off as we passed into the woods and over a brook. Another small beaver pond welcomed us to the Stratton Pond Junction. The pond's well-traveled trail led off to the northwest to a vehicle access road. Stratton Pond is the most visited spot on the Vermont A.T. Its ecology is being threatened by all the traffic and special care is encouraged. Nestled 2,555 ft. between two mountains, it was uniquely beautiful. There was an island in the pond connected to the mainland by a wooden bridge. A charming place to visit.

It was warmer around the pond and because of its popularity, there are five shelters. Slightly uphill, with little elevation changes, we crossed a ridge and stream to reach a footbridge over the Winhall River. Following the river upstream for a ways, we crossed several wet areas before ascending away from the river.

Normally the bugs were pretty rough in these areas, but the merciful wind blowing briskly most of the day, kept the bugs at home. We were in the Lye Brook Wilderness and old Vermont woods prevailed with a mixture of hardwoods and a sprinkling of spruce groves here and there. It was nice to see an area where the lumbering industry had been held at bay. I suppose the difficulty of access, because of the many streams, has kept this primitive wilderness in tact.

Crossing a brook into an open area, ended the protected wilderness. Old Rootville Road took us 200 ft. down to Prospect Rock, still pretty high at 2,079 ft. elevation. A couple of miles brought us to VT 11 and 30 highways, 2 miles from Manchester Center.

An excited Tweety Pie waited with a story that made us all envious. Shortly after we began hiking this morning, a large bull moose crossed the parking lot at the trail head. Would you believe, with all the wild country we humble hikers crossed, he was the first of our group to see a moose? From a parking lot, no less. We had hiked 17.5 miles today (in the wild) and with mixed emotions we listened to his description of the huge antlered beast.

Really, I was happy for him, but he continued the description as he drove all the way to the Zion Episcopal Church Hostel. Those antlers were as big as the jeep by the time we arrived. The Hostel allowed hikers to use the floor of the congregational hall for their sleeping bags. Shower and kitchen privileges were allowed. All that for a small donation and believe me it was well worth it. Must I say my last words before blessed sleep? "Yes Tweety Pie, that must have been quite a moose!"

JULY 3, 1995 - the peace and calm of the church hostel made it a good place to sleep in, so we got a late start. Tweety Pie took us back out to VT. 11 & 30. Beginning at 1,840 feet, we all felt like saying in unison, "Yes, Tweety Pie it must have been one heck of a moose, good-bye."

We had only minor elevation changes when we crossed a brook in a gully. Spruce Peak was only 2,060 ft. high, so you can see we had pretty level walking. The ascent was more steady to Bromley Mountain, 3,260 feet. A couple hiking the Long Trail had their dog with them. As he sniffed along the trail, I was filled with longing for my little dog that had been so good to hike with. It was a beautiful ski area so we went into the warming lodge. Though it was a very small building, it was nice. Naturally the ski lift was not in operation for one obvious reason. There was no snow, thank goodness.

Ending our brief visit, we descended steeply to the north summit of Bromley Mountain, a little over a hundred feet down. We continued our descent to Mad Tom Notch, 2,446 feet. The late start today limited us to only 5.3 miles but allowed us to return back with the waiting Tweety Pie to the Zion Church Hostel for another sheltered night.

Later in the afternoon, Beach Bum came straggling in with another hiker who had a different trail handle, Nurse Without A Purse. He was a male nurse, get it? I thought it was cute and we enjoyed talking about the difference in the Long Trail, which both men were hiking. It was a long and relaxing afternoon. Occasionally it was a good idea to break the rigid routine, which was so demanding.

JULY 4, 1995 - 6:55 a.m., back to the trail and the schedule with a steep climb to Styles Peak, 3,394 feet. From there we had a south and east view in the direction of Bromley, from whence we had come. It's nice to see the landscape from an aerial glimpse on occasion in order to get an idea of what really surrounds you while you are immersed in hardwoods, spruce and wetlands. You could see how VT 11 slanted below Bromley Mountain and Peru Village, less than two miles off in the distance. However, it was still early in the morning and visibility was limited.

We had as steep a drop down as we had climbed, then up and down over several knobs eventually to the forested summit of Peru Peak, 3,429 feet. Zigging and zagging, down we went to Griffith Lake with Peru Peak Shelter and the lake's campsite in the same proximity. The lake was lovely but not as large as some of the bodies of water they call ponds. That leaves me to wonder what or who decides what is a lake or pond. In Missouri a pond is very small and a lake is usually much larger.

Oh well, the mixture of hardwood trees and spruce made an interesting combination. We hiked through both hardwood and spruce forests for a while over an easy trail, until we reached a swampy woods road and began climbing to Baker Peak, 2,850 feet.

The last scramble to the top was on some of the prettiest white rocks I have ever seen. They were in the form of a solid mass and I might add, rough edges. Dangerous if wet or windy, there is a by-pass trail, but I believe I would have risked passing the by-pass trail regardless. As the sun reflected off the rocks, they shined and glistened like diamonds. The view at the top was so terrific, we decided to take a break.

The Green Mountain Forest is breathtaking. The area around there is a very popular ski resort with the Bromley Ski Trails and a huge alpine slide. It was an easy hike down the mountain past Lost Pond Shelter. If there was a pond nearby it was indeed lost, because I sure couldn't find it. Not that I looked very hard. Only a short distance further was the Big Branch Shelter and down the trail, Big Black Branch beside USFS Road 10 at an elevation of 1,500 feet.

A lot of day hikers were out and not all of them were admiring one of the fanciest pit toilets I had certainly ever seen. It was a six-sided toilet that looked like redwood and supplied the necessities for the Little Rock Pond Campsite. For those with a technical mind, it is called a Clivus Multrum Composting Toilet. Boy, I hope that is self-explanatory. Tent platforms are also supplied, but you have to pay a fee.

It was not difficult to determine the length of this hike was taking its toll on all of us. Twelve miles later at 2:00 p.m., we were ready to quit for the day. None of us was sad at seeing Tweety Pie who drove us back to the Zion Church Hostel to spend the night. We showered and, in general, let our bodies rest while we visited with the other hikers. We were envied when Snapshot fixed another meal of fried potatoes and onions for us.

JULY 5, 1995 - An already weary group arose at 6:45 a.m. to eat a normal breakfast of instant oatmeal, tea and pop tarts. Back on the A.T., it was easy hiking to Lula Tye Shelter and Little Rock Pond. Hardwood trees dominated the forest around the pond. Their wide forked branches were eerie with the morning's mist clinging to each leaf in a desperate attempt to keep the inevitable evaporation from taking place.

It is interesting to note that there are two shelters and a campsite located at that little remote pond, nestled among those large, beautiful trees. A further testament that we humans are forever attracted to water equally as much as precious diamonds or emeralds. As we skirted the eastern shore of the small body of water, it was shimmering that early in the morning and reflecting the least amount of light.

To further substantiate the popularity of our water love affair, Little Rock Pond Shelter was crowded and there were a lot of people camped throughout the area. Leaving the crowded area, we reached a clearing where we crossed Homer Stone Brook. It was a steady climb to the west of the summit of White Rocks Mountain, 2,680 feet. The rest of this area involved crossing a pasture and another brook to Greenwall Shelter, built in 1962 to provide sleeping accommodations for eight people.

It was two miles to Wallingford Gulf Road, VT. 140, where we planned to meet Tweety Pie for our lunch break. He was talking to the young couple who had the dog. There was always soda pop in our ice chest so we shared with them. I have noticed that a lot of people go out on these trails with very little preparation. Tweety Pie always liked to share his sodas with other hikers. They really appreciated it.

We only took a short break and left Tweety Pie telling his stories of our adventures. A mile up the trail, we passed the site of Buffum Lodge that had been destroyed by fire in 1966. It was steep up Button Hill and disappointing as well. I had come to expect anything on this trail and since we had found buttons on a previous hill where the button factory had been, I expected to find keepsakes here. Outrageous, there were no buttons there! Just a 2,010 foot climb. There are plenty of shelters in that section of the trail.

We passed our fourth shelter that had been named the Minerva Hinchey Shelter. Those shelters were built in honor of corporate moguls who used to have luxurious cabin sights in the New England Mountains. This particular one is an open frame structure, built in 1969 by GMC. Descending to Spring Lake Clearing, 1,620 feet, with some pretty good views of the Coolidge and Taconic Range in New York, wasn't too difficult.

Controlled burning is used to manage the views and provide clearings for wildlife in the area. Suddenly we dropped steeply to Clarendon Gorge. Its craggy gorge was cut by the Mill River. The sculpture artist ran deep below, cutting wrinkles deeper and deeper into Mother Earth. It was a surprise to see Tweety Pie. He had hiked up from the highway to meet us. I really wished he hadn't done that so often because of his wooden leg, but the reason for his motivation on this occasion, was soon made obvious.

We came to a very high suspension bridge that spanned the gorge. Too much for my adventurous husband to resist. As it swayed precariously, I had some difficulty with balance. I can only wonder at how he manages as well as he does. The view was awesome. The river looked like a thread below, and an ingredient of awe was added looking down from that swinging perch.

The bridge is dedicated to the memory of Bob Brugman, a young hiker who drowned here during a flood in 1969. When we reached VT 103, we had descended to 869 feet. The jeep was parked there so after 14.4 miles, we decided to end today's hike and drive to a motel for the night. We were all extremely drug out, due to the fact that the church had a fellowship in the congregational hall and we didn't get to sleep until after 11:00 p.m. The otherwise quiet hostel was not a wise place to stay, this night.

The lady who operated the motel was friendly and since she was going to town anyway, Snapshot risked imposing on her to bring back some ice cream. At home this would not qualify as a special event but out there we are like little children, when an opportunity presents itself for the delicious frozen delicacy.

While we were chatting and slurping lazily, Ultralite came strolling in. He hitched a ride to the motel. It was nice to see he was okay. He settled in like the old friend he had become to all of us.

JULY 6, 1995 - back at the trail I glanced at my watch, 6:30 a.m. This section had the Coolidge Range of the Green Mountains, the highest in Vermont. After stepping over the Green Mountain Railroad Tracks, I was under no allusion that it would not be rocky and steep as we climbed through a steep notch onto a high projecting rock.

Descending slightly we crossed an old military road, built during the French and Indian War. Hardwoods and spruce forest kept us company past Clarendon Shelter to the ascent of 1.760 ft. Beacon Hill, with its airplane beacon. A pleasant change in terrain met us in the form of a sugar maple grove, followed by pasture land. After a few ups and downs and a brook to cross, we reentered the woods.

Their is something tranquil about walking in the woods along a friendly brook and that's what I got to experience as we reached the west bank of Northam Brook. It was brief, but we reached the waiting Tweety Pie not long thereafter at Upper Cold River Road. It was always a relief for both of us to see each other and reaffirm that we were okay.

It was far from the end of the day, so we picked up our backpacks just in case the rugged trail ahead wore us out too much to reach Tweety Pie. In that event, we could be comfortable spending the night in one of the shelters. Over a bridge and back into the woods where, with a little breeze, the wide- branched hardwood trees kept the temperature decent.

Leaving the hardwoods and entering the spruce trees, I knew it was a signal that the trail would get rough soon, and it did. The spruce can survive at higher altitude than the big branched trees. It was rugged, steep and rocky to the southern flank of Little Killington. Equally as rough to Consultation Peak where the spruce fought valiantly to compete with barren rock. At 3,760 feet, it was a tough battle. The wind and cold, coupled with the deep snows building to snow slide proportion in the winters, even made the rocks struggle to keep some form, other than smooth and flat.

Crossing the Juggernaut Ski Trail, I was glad I was hiking in the summer and not climbing a slippery, icy mountain in the dead of winter. There are actually some people who get their kicks doing exactly that. Fortunately, my disease only drove me to cover miles. Granted, over rough country, but the threat to my life was minimal.

Topping Shrewsbury Peak, Killington Peak loomed ahead. Crossing the Juggernaut Ski Trail one more time, surprisingly, it was a gentle trail through an evergreen forest along the southern and western slopes of humongus Killington. Passing the spur trail that led 0.2 miles to Killington Peak, 4,235 feet, second highest peak in Vermont, we arrived at Cooper Lodge, 3,900 feet above the sea. Just beyond the spur that led to the peak, it was a stone and frame structure with 16 bunks, built in 1969 by the Vermont Forest Service. A good spot to take a well-earned break.

Snapshot and Stickflipper went back to the steep spur trail to climb up to the high Killington Peak. I stayed with our packs at the shelter where the view was limited. I wasn't alone since there were plenty of hikers there and a group of young people, who were learning trail maintenance. When my two eager beavers returned, they were in total awe of what they had viewed from their eagle's perch. I listened to their description during the 2.9 miles to Pico Camp, an enclosed shelter, as I had listened to Tweety Pie's moose tail.

They had been able to see the Green Mountain Range from Glastenbury to Mt. Mansfield. They even saw the Adirondack and Taconic Ranges as far away as New York. In short, they viewed all the peaks we had traveled and much more. I was left a little empty but that trail was rough up there and I had to keep my body in tact to the end of the Appalachian Trail. That was my goal and dream.

There were many hikers at the Pico Shelter which is at the beginning of a long 2.5 mile drop. Another steep trail led up to Pico Peak, 3,957 feet. A summit station was at the top most section of a chair lift for the Pico Peak Ski Resort.

Following the ski trail for about 300 ft., we then turned into the woods where a path zig-zagged down the mountain. On the way I saw a brook, at least for a few minutes, before it dove into a deep sink hole. I watched that until I stumbled and woke up to the fact that I was still walking down a steep trail with a full pack. I couldn't help wondering where that mysterious brook would end up. Maybe supplying some farmer with a well that never runs dry.

I was to pooped to pop when we finally reached the last descent to Sherburne Pass on U.S. 4 Highway but ol' Den Mama made it.. Tweety Pie was happy to see me and that was all that mattered. If I was a little jealous, as Snapshot and Stickflipper told about their sights from the magnificent Mount Killington, I did my best not to show it.

The lodge at Sherburne Pass was a pleasant sight but I knew it was too expensive for we poor wayward hikers. However, it was a good meeting place. I was surprised, that of all people to meet inside, Nurse Without A Purse would be the last I expected. He had caught a bus to get there and was debating whether to take the Long Trail or hike the A.T. with Rhino and Wilber. I was awfully tired after 16.9 miles of rugged, high country, but thrilled to see those guys.

Tweety Pie drove us to Giffords Woods State Park where we rented lean-to's. It was more reasonable for our budget. Snapshot and Stickflipper phoned two hikers they knew who lived in Vermont. It seems, they had met them in Pennsylvania. Their trail names were Alpo and Quilter. Must have been pretty good friends because they came in around 7:00 p.m. and spent the night with us.

I was having some mixed emotions as I watched the sun set with a pleasant 85° temperature. There is another song that explained the old, recurring feeling. It goes something like this, "It's crying time again, you're going to leave me, I can see that far away look in your eyes." Boy! I knew I was tired when I start getting that emotional, even before something had happened. It was very definitely time to hit the sack.

JULY 7, 1995 - that old feeling that I was getting ready to be abandoned did not go away after sleep. Alpo and Quilter took Snapshot and Stickflipper out for breakfast. They were not back when it was time for me to begin hiking so I was ready to expect the worst. A concerned Tweety Pie drove me back to Sherburne Pass. We were silent on the way because we had been through this before. My goal was so close and I dreaded the thought of having to finish all alone.

Tweety Pie finally brought the subject up when he realized that I was actually taking off by myself. He started planning the closest places he could meet me. Telling me I could slackpack for a little while to someplace not too far away. In a dream state I uttered

"Okay." I kept thinking, hoping, my concerns were all about nothing as the trail climbed steeply for 0.6 miles.

Deer Leap Cliffs were only 2,500 ft. but it was obvious that even though the elevation was all right, the trail could be a lot rougher. It was a correct assumption. In only a short distance I was climbing over big boulders on a very rocky trail. Then, just that quick, I was at the Maine Junction where the A.T. and the Long Trail separate. I wondered which way Nurse Without A Purse had decided to go. I tried to pretend it didn't matter as I turned on the A.T., climbed a spur and descended passed a spur trail to Ben's Balcony, 2,100 ft.

It was downhill to the boundary of Gifford Woods State Park. The deeper I got into the park the more I kept waiting for Stickflipper or Snapshot to turn and comment about the undisturbed hardwoods. A little further was twelve acres of predominant virgin sugar maples, (Vermont's State Tree), with a spattering of more species of alders. Scattered among all that was an ancient hemlock that I was to learn later was over 400 years old. I listened to the many species of migratory birds that visit there. The birds I heard reminded me of dear Wildflower. Also, there was no Stickflipper or Snapshot eagerly saying, "Look Den Mama, isn't that beautiful?"

There was an inviting campsite called Tent Platform No. 11, where a neat, stone building housed toilets and showers. A little further was a caretaker's house with shelters and tent sites including fireplaces that could be rented. A good place to rest but VT 100 was just ahead and it was still too early for me to call it quits. I am a very stubborn lady and I would finish the A.T., make book on it!

I couldn't hide the redness in my eyes when I met Tweety Pie. He knew what was troubling me so he only stated that those two should be along shortly. I said "sure", picked up my full backpack and continued on the trail, hoping that he was correct..

The purpose for all the campsites was soon manifested. The trail took me around the lovely Kent Pond. It even had a boat ramp. There are so many people crowding the big cities in this area, I am glad they have places like that to get away from it all. Bearing to my right, I crossed an overgrown meadow and then a bridge over an inlet to the pond. I then had a pleasant walk along the brook and pond shore. It was wooded so it was cool and for a while at least, I was tranquilized.

Maybe *too* anesthetized by the beauty and atmosphere, because when I reached Thundering Brook road, I became disoriented. I had to find white blazes indicating where the A.T. leaves the road. I rarely got that confused and wandered up and down the road for thirty minutes before telling myself, "Mary Twitty, Get a grip on yourself." Finally I calmed down and just followed the Thunderbrook Road to wherever it would lead me.

After several hundred feet, I found white blazes leading me on to an old dirt road, used as a ski trail in the winter. I passed a house which made me feel a little secure. Then crossing several bridges I left the old woods road to climb up a steep boulder-strewn rise of land only to descend slightly. I then came to Thunderbrook Road again and after going down by switchbacks I crossed a bridge over the Ottauquechee River. It felt like I was climbing a mountain as the trail went up by switchbacks and an old logging road.

Several brooks had to be crossed before I came to a sharp bend that exposed a spectacular view of the Ottauquechee River Valley with the Coolidge Range in the background. Actually, I realized that this whole section was, in reality, between two mountain ranges, the White Mountains of New Hampshire and the Green Mountains of Vermont. Between or not, I was doing some steep climbing up switchbacks. The hill I was on was 2,600 ft. but it was a gradual descent to a logging road, before another steep climb to the north shoulder of Quimby Mountain.

Finally, two day hikers came by. One man's trail name was Old Ridge Runner. To be honest with you, I was glad to see someone but in no mood to talk. They were impressed with ol' Den Mama out there hiking the A.T. all by herself. So much so, they took my picture on the switchbacks. After a good luck and good-bye, I again began huffing and puffing down steep descents and equally steep ascents.

All in all, it was quite pretty through there. At one place, there was a drop-off over a rock bluff that I had to literally climb down a ladder built of logs. At last, I crossed Mink Brook where I found a blue-blazed trail that led me to the log Stony Brook Shelter. All I have described was only 8.3 miles, not including my frustrated walk up and down Stony Brook Road looking for those white blazes. I was extremely tired.

Two scruffy day hikers were there eating lunch when I came in at 12:00 p.m. They asked me why I was all alone, so for safety reasons I told them I was waiting for my friends to catch up. It put them on the alert but quite honestly, I really didn't worry about the other hikers as being a threat. Most are good people.

While eating my lunch, in came Snapshot and Stickflipper. I hid my joy in order to pretend that I knew they were coming. It was 1:00 p.m. by then and trying hard to rain, so, thank goodness my two lost friends agreed that we should spend the night where we were.

Water from a bubbling Stony Brook was only ten yards from the shelter, so it was a pleasant place to rest.

Later in the evening, Ultralite came sauntering in, and decided to spend the night at the shelter with us. Snapshot built a crackling bonfire that helped keep the bugs away. I was alone no more. One day I shall tell all my hiking friends how very important they were to me. I closed my eyes with pride in tact.

JULY 8, 1995 - began hiking at 6:15 a.m. and I was a lot more relaxed. It was good to have my companions back with me. Leaving Ultralite in his solitude, it became apparent that we were between two mountain ranges, the New Hampshire White Mountains and the Vermont Green Mountains. That was steep and rugged country, but oh so beautiful.

By switchbacks, we reached a narrow ridge and easier climbing over several knolls. After passing a pond, we did what hillbillies would call, using one short leg and one long to struggle along the north side of a ridge, until we reached a narrow sag, the locals referred to as Continental Divide. More switchbacks led us down into a magnificent open hardwood forest.

Crossing Chateauguay Road and Locust Creek we went up a small knoll and down to a brook that had, what looked like, clean water. However, we had no need for water and we saw more switchbacks waiting ahead. When it leveled off somewhat, we entered a stand of stately birch trees then it cleared briefly and allowed us a view to the southwest of Bridgewater Valley. I cannot elaborate enough on how beautiful these northeast states are.

When we reached Lakota Lake Lookout, 2,439 feet, I couldn't believe the last view could be surpassed. It was my kind of scenery. A small lake below and the marvelous

243

New Hampshire White Mountains way off in the distance. It couldn't have been too far away though, because it was rapidly becoming overcast and they were still visible. The trail got easier after we climbed Sawyer Hill and descended through pasture land that really needed the water the clouds were carrying. It was so dry the dirt puffed up under our feet like fine powder.

I was feeling a degree of urgency as the clouds took on an ominous darkness. We were going around the western side of what they call the Pinnacle and I knew it could get slippery. Climbing past Don's Rock, we were able to see the Coolidge Range of Mountains. As we reached a rise in the land called Sawyer Hill, we descended down the center of a long ridge where a side trail led to the Winturri Shelter. It was tempting but our goal was not far away.

Back to short leg, long leg, following the slope of a long ridge, then down a shorter ridge. An old chimney and cellar hole told us a happy family once lived there, probably wondering on a day like this long ago, if the clouds would shed precious rain on their garden.

Then, just like that the city of West Bridgewater spread out in the west and Mt. Ascutney rose in the south in a panorama of civilization and rustic beauty. It got more civilized as we descended steadily into old fields and woods. We continued down into a shallow sag, small ridge and more woods. Talk about civilization, there was a field with an electric fence that we had to crawl over on a wooden stile. As I went over the fence, I can remember thinking, "No rain now, Lord. Please no rain now."

Several more non-electric fence rows brought us to a bridge over a small creek. Soon after that, the epitome of civilization greeted us, Vermont Highway 12 and a parking area where Tweety Pie waited patiently. We really didn't mind getting off the hills, rocks and woods. The deluge arrived and rain was pouring down from buckets. I imagine we looked rather ridiculous, running with our packs bouncing on our backs the last few yards to the jeep. After 13 miles of hiking, who cared? We were more like wet rats than intelligent human beings when we dumped the packs in the rear of the jeep and scurried into the seats for shelter.

As we sat there, Tweety Pie told us he had found a friendly farmer who liked hikers and would allow us to camp in his hayfield by a creek. The rain quit in a little while, allowing us to set up the tents. I was itching after we beat down the wet weeds in order to make a path to the creek. Sounds awfully crude but that old creek felt like a Jacuzzi in the Waldorf Astoria as we jumped in for a wonderful, welcomed bath.

There's a difference in an altitude of 882 feet. The air is heavier than at 2 to 3 thousand feet above the, not to far away, ocean. Perhaps it was the humidity after the rain. Perhaps it was the heaviness of our supper. Perhaps I really didn't care and it was only me, that all of a sudden, felt like I weighed 500 pounds. My eyelids were heavier than I thought, as it became impossible for me to hold them open any longer. The last thing I saw through the half open tent flap was the fading sun's rays glistening off the wet field. The last conscious thought I had was of that dry field. I hoped the dust was settled down and I love my Tweety Pie and friends. "Please, Lord, don't ever let them leave me again."

JULY 9, 1995 - ushered in an early sunrise, peeking between Dana Hill to the north and Hurricane Hill to the south. The first rays affected the warmth of our campsite in the open field. It felt good as we packed the tents to begin the day's hike. At 6:00 a.m. we had everything ready to go. It wasn't a long climb up Dana Hill, but it was steep. It was enough to get the old heart pumping before we descended to Woodstock Stage Road.

Most of this section was to be wooded and cleared hills, ridges, and valleys. We would go from approximately 700 ft. to slightly less than 2,000 ft. elevation frequently. Old farming land with rock fences and cellar holes are prevalent in the area. It was populated decades ago and continues to attract people escaping from city work and the struggle of everyday life.

A group of Dartmouth College runners passed us with their muscular legs churning like powerful pistons. What I wouldn't give to be in that physical condition. But then I thought, "Will they keep those bodies in shape when they are my age?" They glanced at me as they passed and I wanted to shout, "Hey, I'm Den Mama and I have hiked this trail all the way from Georgia and I'm not stopping until I cross Maine. What do you think about that?" I just nodded and moved on.

Dartmouth Outing Club maintains that section of the A.T. to the New Hampshire State Line. As I viewed the continual signs of civilization moving in on the old A.T., I wondered how long the trail could retain its rugged beauty. Passing through a notch in Breakneck Hill, it was easy to see the farmhouses dotting the countryside. It is the beauty of the land with babbling brooks that is the financial attraction for eager real estate salespeople.

Miles were passing rapidly, when we topped Thistle Hill at 1,800 feet, not too bad for a hill. Soon the trail made a sharp right turn. The old A.T. went straight ahead and the new route went to our right. Someone had piled brush across the old trail but it was still confusing. Stickflipper noticed the change, so we followed the correct path. After swinging around to a slight ascent over Bunker Hill, it was a steady drop to Joe Ranger Road.

The elusive Ultralite and Tweety Pie were shooting the breeze when we arrived. Ultralite had taken the wrong trail and got lost on top of the hill. Wandering around, he finally found the correct A.T. When he got to White River in West Hartford, he ran into Tweety Pie. After telling him about the confusion on the hill, he advised him to go back and check on us, in the event we had made his mistake. It was thoughtful of Ultralite and, had I been hiking alone, would have helped me a lot. The alert eyes of Stickflipper and Snapshot rarely made a mistake.

They made a makeshift sign telling hikers how to find the new A.T and put it on the old trail by the brush. We put the heavy packs in the jeep with Tweety Pie and slackpacked on down to West Hartford, VT, a very small village. We crossed the White River on a 400 ft. iron bridge. Tweety Pie was at a little grocery store, inquiring where we could camp. Lucky us! We were allowed to camp by the river. Swimming was even permitted in the river and like gleeful children, we took full advantage. It was almost like washing away the 14.6 miles of hiking.

JULY 10, 1995 - sleeping in was anything past 6:00 a.m. Snapshot and Stickflipper needed to go to the local post office to pick up their mail drop. It only took them a few hours but it made a world of difference. We had been away from home for quite awhile and all things were becoming a little more stressful and would increase from there on, to the end.

Around 8:00 a.m. we finally started hiking. Ascending up to a shoulder of Griggs Mountain, 1,570 feet was a combination of steep, but tolerable, hiking. Another 3.8 miles further brought us to Happy Hill Cabin, a closed in shelter and the oldest on the Appalachian Trail. There were a lot of the familiar hardwood and tall pine trees. It had been a short section so it wasn't long before we arrived at U.S. 5 in Norwich, Connecticut, where Tweety Pie met us.

The New Hampshire State Line was just across the Connecticut River so Tweety Pie asked us to hike on into Hanover, New Hampshire, crossing the Connecticut River. The citizens of Hanover probably never appreciated their little ice cream stand as much as we did. Cones of our favorite ice cream were purchased and we continued on, past historical Dartmouth College.

Hanover is not a large city, actually less than 7,000 population. The college charter was started and approved by King George III, December 3, 1769. New Hampshire Governor Wentworth prepared the charter. It was established to basically teach reading and writing English to the youth of the pagan Indians. It was also used to convert them to the Christian Faith. Actually, it was Rev. Eleazar Wheelock who went into wilderness and built a log cabin that was the beginning of the great Ivy League College. The first class of four students graduated in 1771.

We found Tweety Pie at a service station and discovered we had all been invited by Alpo and Quilter to their home in West Fairlee, Vermont, for the night. They had built a shelter by a lovely stream flowing through their land. It was nice, with a patio and picnic tables.

Since Alpo was gone on a business trip, Quilter became our hostess and did a fine job of keeping us entertained. In all fairness, it didn't take much, just home cooked food and rest was sufficient. It turned out that Quilter had a hiking staff just like mine. She didn't use her rubber tip so Tweety Pie bought it for me. Now, I wouldn't have to hear my stick making that annoying clanging on the rocks! The temperature was pleasantly cool that day and made the 10.4 miles go by fairly easy.

JULY 11, 1995 - refreshed after the visit at Alpo and Quilter's shelter, at 7:00 a.m. we returned to the service station in Hanover, at the edge of town. There we entered a field and began a rocky climb up the mountain to the loop trail that took us to the Velvet Rocks Shelter. The river we crossed was at 400 ft. elevation. Nothing on this trail would even be that low again.

We chose not to hike out to the shelter because a strange man was supposed to be camped there. Having been warned about Crazy Ward from southbound hikers, he didn't sound like anyone we needed to know. Quietly we bypassed Crazy Ward with a silent farewell and proceeded to some slab ledges, using switchbacks through other ledges.

After crossing a dam on a large beaver pond, it was obvious we were on a steady upward trend with very little descending. Up and up we climbed to the South Peak of Moose Mountain, 2,290 feet. That was no place to be hiking in the rain but it sure looked like it was on its way. Coming upon another jutting rock ledge, we crawled under it, made ourselves comfy, using the time to eat lunch. It wasn't a long wait for nature to drop her wet gift, one and one-half hours worth. We really didn't need that and proceeded cautiously in the cold between the south and north peaks of Moose Mountain. After topping the North Peak at 2,300 feet, we had to be careful because it was a steep slippery 1,380 ft. descent to Goose Pond Road.

Tweety Pie had a nice surprise for me. While he was cleaning up the parking area, which he usually does especially when he gets bored or worried, he had found a nice hiking stick. We were all ready for a break after 13.4 miles. It was only 2:30 p.m. so we drove back to Quilter's place for another night. Quilter told Stickflipper about a neighbor who had a pair of huge pulling oxen. He was going to give them a workout and Tweety Pie and Stickflipper were not about to miss that. Two eager little boys trailed after the man just to see two big oxen pull something.

Meanwhile, Quilter showed Snapshot and me her quilting room. Wow, was she an artistic person! Her quilts took a lot of effort and were absolutely beautiful. Of course, now we know where her trail name originated. Snapshot was busy fixing fried potatoes, onions and grilled hamburgers. The kids came back and were excited about how those big oxen could pull big things. It was a great supper with excellent company and dulled our loneliness for home, considerably.

It was great to be in New Hampshire, if for no other reason, it meant I only had two more states to go. Straight across New Hampshire wouldn't have taken too long but we would be angling the long way to the northeast. But, as the sign said when we crossed the state line from Vermont, *"You have hiked 80% of the Trail, but have only done 50% of the work!"* As I drifted into sleep, I wondered about that, but my motivation was rekindled.

JULY 12, 1995 - good-byes do not come easy for me. I hoped it would only be a short *aloha* for Quilter. She had provided us a very important and timely break. My thoughts were on her as we drove back over this beautiful country to Goose Pond Road.

Back on the trail, crossing another beaver dam, the climb started out gradually and then got very steep all the way to Holt's Ledge. From the ledge viewpoint, we could see why man and bird found that perch appealing. It was the top most part of the Dartmouth Skyway and a sign cautioned everyone to respect and protect the nesting site of peregrine falcons. We spent a few minutes looking for these courageous little predators but unfortunately this was not the day for them to be hanging around. They could have been someplace but we were pretty well engulfed in fog, so our vision was severely impaired. I doubt very seriously that theirs were affected.

The misty over- and undercast was keeping the temperature around 60°, just right for hiking. It would have been nice if, after the fog burned off, it could have stayed that way but I was under no such illusions that it would. We watched our steps as we descended rather steeply, at first over several ridges then after a small brook, it became much easier to a blue-blazed trail that led to the Trapper John Shelter.

A south bound hiker was on the climb up the ledge. We had a short visit before continuing to Dorchester Road. Glancing around we didn't see Tweety Pie so we went the other 2 miles down to Lyme-Dorchester Road. The usually punctual Tweety Pie wasn't there either. A day hiker took Stickflipper back to Dorchester Road and found him as confused as we were. It was an honest mistake and we had simply missed him. They should name one of those roads something else.

Anyway, it didn't take the Tweety Pie long to come back for us. We went to one of the many ski lodges in the area named, Robert Peter Brundage Lodge and Ski Lift. The caretaker allowed us to spend the night in the yard. It was convenient and even had an outside water faucet with good water, and we took full advantage of it. A group of young rock climbers were camped a short distance from us. They had been practicing on the rock ledges and eagerly chatting about their accomplishments.

It was only 5.6 miles that day. Due to the wait for Tweety Pie back at Lyme Dorchester Road, I was pretty rested. With the lengthy, relaxing afternoon ahead, I spent some time walking for pure fun, around the ski lodge. I was imagining what it must be like with several inches of snow and more falling like a winter white blanket. Then I saw myself sailing off one of those steep hills into white space and the daydreaming was over. It is July and barren except for the forests and I was satisfied with that scene.

JULY 13, 1995 - it was warm as we crawled out of the tents, sometime around 5:00 a.m. That could only mean one thing, it was going to get much hotter when that New Hampshire sun clawed its burning fingers higher in the sky. With that warning, it didn't take us long to break camp and drive back to the trail at Lyme-Dorchester Road. It was only 6:00 a.m. when we hastily hit the trail.

The ascent was gradual at first, as we left an overgrown field and began slabbing up the west side of Winslow Ledge. Over a minor ridge and across a stream we actually went down a bit, then level. If I kept my eyes looking at the ground, I could convince myself it was not going so bad, until I looked up at Lambert Ridge looming steeply above.

Turning left across a bridge and parking lot signaled the time for digging in. We started ascending immediately to the first of a series of ledges on that rocky spine. That's just what it looked like, the back of some prehistoric monster. Among the panting and now sweating bodies, there was beauty. Glistening, white quartz sparkled out of the many rocks with its own strange beauty. Finally, after one long steep hump I thought we were there, but one more shorter hump had to be defeated before we peaked over the huge ledge.

It wasn't enough of a decline to take my breath but we made a right turn, only to face the ascent of Smarts Mountain, 3,240 feet. No humps, just up, steeper than any of the humps on Holt's Ledge or Lambert Ridge. Firewarden's Cabin was once exactly what the name inferred, before it was converted and maintained as a shelter. What a place for a shelter, not far from the long decline down to South Jacob's Brook. We went from over 3,000 ft. to 1,500 ft. in 4.5 miles to the valley below. It would have been a relief to have a bobsled with wheels to ride down.

A wooden bridge took us over the brook and we again climbed a steep hill, then a slight decline to North Jacob's Brook. Actually, the two branches were once part of the main brook before they went their separate ways. The north branch gave birth to Pickeral Pond just south east of there and the south branch just headed out into the valleys and gullies like a confused young child lost in the elements of the world.

I was grateful to slab around the side of a hill, rather than straight over each one. We reached a side trail to the Hexacuba Shelter before ascending again to South Cube Summit, 2,911 ft. high. The spine of the ridge up there was rocky and narrow for a short distance before a left turn dove us back into the woods, wonderful woods, of beautiful, tall, maple trees.

Another sharp right turn took us steeply down by switchbacks. Two thirds of the way down, we crossed Brackett Brook and I knew NH 25A was not far ahead. When we arrived, Tweety Pie was talking with our good friend Quilter. She had been working in the area and stopped by to bring us a blackberry pie. Mmm . . . nice surprise. That lady was definitely not hard to like.

Tweety Pie drove us to the Mt. Cube Sugar House. He had arranged for us to pitch our tents in their yard. You learn to appreciate all the good people who cater to hikers along the trail. There was a pond nearby we could swim in. You can't beat that, Shangri-La! One beat Den Mama was ready for that day to end. Fourteen miles on one big roller coaster in 90° heat is all any kid needs to make a blanket feel awfully good.

JULY 14, 1995 - we have been winding down the last few days. I hoped it wasn't a sign that everyone, including me, was burning out. After packing the tents and the rest of the gear, it wasn't long before Sugar House opened. We had heard their breakfast was excellent, so we decided to wait. It wasn't a bad decision. The hiker's special was pancakes and maple syrup. The pancakes were just right, not too doughy and the syrup, what can I say? it was maple country. The hot tea washed them down like maple ice cream.

It was after 9:00 a.m. when everybody was full and we got back to the trail. The sun was already sending a message, "You get up late, you're gonna pay the price." It had all the ingredients for another short day. I knew I was going to have to break that pattern somehow.

Crossing highways always made me more than eager to get back into trees. Two swampy areas were unpleasant since along with the swamp you must invariably battle the bugs. Atwell Hill was fairly steep before it eased off. From there I looked back on 25A and Gillman's Corner.

There was another one of those upper-lower pond deals. Upper Baker Pond was the larger and northwest of

Gillman's Corner. It looked like a huge raindrop that had run as far as it could, then remained in that form. The other Lower Baker Pond was smaller and shaped like a bullet that had already hit a target and slightly deformed, as a result. It lay to the southeast of the corner. I expect those ponds play a major roll for flood control.

From Atwell Hill we curved north over more roller coaster terrain. We had to put up with another swampy area before an easy climb up Ore Hill. The hike was less strenuous today. Once we got up Atwell Hill there was little elevation change. Even the ascent to the summit of Mt. Mist, 2,220 feet, was only a few hundred feet above the little valley we had started in. What goes up must come down is always true with mountains, unless you choose to remain a hermit and live off the mountain. It was a steep descent to a saddle between Mt. Mist and Webster Slide Mountain.

Fortunately, a side trail went up Webster's Slide Mountain and the A.T. continued to go down to the east of its base, past a pitiful little spring called Hairy Root. It was trying to keep the sun and mother earth from draining its life blood and very existence. Having never thought of pools of water in that way before I decided, as we circled Wachipauka Pond, that I was getting weirdly philosophical. . . . or it was time to go home.

Wachipauka Pond was a little bird-shaped pond that looked like it was loosing some of its waistline. Me and that pond had a lot in common. The only thing was, it can dry up and when rain or snow comes, live again. Ol' Den Mama will dry up, go back to Mother Earth and that will be that. When you get down to it, water and blood are not that different.

When we got to NH 25 where Tweety Pie was waiting, we were near the melting point. The postmaster in

Glencliff informed Tweety Pie that he could drive within a short distance of the Jeffer's Brook Shelter that where we were hoping to camp. That was good news. Since it was only 1.1 miles further up the trail, we put our packs in the jeep, took a deep breath and headed into the woods. Crossing Oliverian Brook over a foot bridge, it took a lot of restraint to keep from jumping in. The urge was quelled when, just at the right moment, we found the trail to our shelter.

Tweety Pie drove south to USFS 19 which, true to the postmaster's word, put him only a short distance away. We walked to the road and carried our ice chest and backpacks back to the shelter. It was always nice when a shelter is close by a road so Tweety Pie could spend the night with us. He got lonesome all by himself sometimes, however he has an uncanny ability to find companions.

A lot of time was spent taking turns going to the brook to wash and soak in the cool water. The sun was bearing down at 95° and there was not a breeze to be found. Two male southbound thru-hikers came panting into the shelter carrying their food drop that they had picked up at the post office. Talk about hot. We made fans out of their cardboard boxes. Everyone was waving arms until they got too weary, then it was back to the brook. Our left over pie and pizza from the ice chest provided a tasty meal, especially since no one wanted to heat up or cook anything.

The ice cream I had the other day was taunting my mind until I finally cooled down enough to figure our day's mileage; 11.3 miles in the heat of the day was not to shabby. The only problem is this turned out to be the hottest night we had to endure on the trail. Heck, if it had gotten too bad the state sanitarium was only a little way up the trail. I could have spent some time in those beautiful surroundings with a cool, padded room. Now I knew I was slipping. I never claimed I was not a little sick in the head.

This section of the trail had been a baby compared to what we would face the next day. No one talked about it much, but it was on all our minds. Sleep did not come easy.

JULY 15, 1995 - carrying our ice chest and backpacks back to the jeep didn't seem like much of an effort. We were still thinking about the White Mountain Range, knowing full well it was going to be some of the toughest mountains we had or would encounter. Tweety Pie could not hide the worry in his eyes, even though he knew why I was there. He waited around until we passed the property of the State Sanitarium, crossed some fields and disappeared into a crop of trees.

I was more than happy to pass the trail to Hurricane Mountain and move on to a brook crossing. Uphill began on an old woods road through conifer pines, shrubs and old hardwoods. As we passed a stream, we made a steep climb and I thought, "this is it". A side road led to the south peak of the dreaded Mt. Mooselauke, the subject of everyone's thoughts.

The expectation turned out to be premature when the A.T. turned left and took us to an old carriage road that actually descended to a place called Breezy Point. About 2.5 miles further we contacted NH 118. Leaving the road behind and sticking to the carriage road, we made another left and entered heavy woods. All of a sudden we had a glimpse of a ravine we had heard about. It was beautiful and had its own lodge called, naturally, Ravine Lodge. What a place to spend a weekend. The road continued on up to some outstanding rock protrusions.

Even though we were weaving up the mountain, it was getting awfully steep. The trees bent and the wind began to blow. Soon after that I realized *this was really it!* We were climbing the mysterious mountain called Mooselauke. Mooselauke means "high bald place" to the Pemigewasset Indians. It used to be part of their hunting grounds. In the 1800's the European settlers farmed the area and the Indians retreated from the wave that was descending upon them.

When the region was opened for land grants, much of the virgin forests fell prey to the good old white man. True to form in 1850 when agriculture fell off, the logging industry moved in and wealthy resorts were built for the rich to hide away from the angry poor folks. Two trails for horses were built clear up to the summit in 1860. There was even a summit hotel built called Prospect House.

Tourist trade boomed due to man's strange desire to either be near the rolling, unpredictable oceans or high in the equally unpredictable mountains. I guess they also felt closer to God in the mountains and we were 4,802 feet closer on that monster. Due to the huge hordes of people swarming to the summit, the Mooselauke Road Company had to build a five mile carriage road. Only parts of that still exist and we were hiking on some of it.

In 1899 to 1914, the paper companies moved in and stripped all, but the hardest to reach, timber from the western slope. Finally in approximately 1920, the USFS purchased most of the land. The Dartmouth Outing Club ended up with Prospect House, maintaining it as a summer hostel. More about that later.

The mysterious mountain was beginning to live up to the many stories told about it. It was hot out and looked like rain. That was no place to be in rain so we stepped up our pace on the steep road that was actually still in pretty good condition for hiking, at least. About three-fourths of the way up, I learned why people are cautioned about this summit. Its elevation and barren summit causes some weird weather.

A first class thunderstorm hit us, rumbling its anger. We found shelter in a cluster of trees and put on our rain gear. Lightning, like silver spears and golden arrows, made war on the mountain and I was beginning to believe it might send that anger in our direction. We debated about the danger of the lightening versus the soaking rain. I said a little prayer and soon after that, the storm quit in about the same way it had started. Move over Medicine Men, Den Mama had arrived.

We were only a little way from a section of the Carriage Road that would make easier walking, but take us above the tree line to the awesome summit. To show how Mother Nature can come full course, the wind howled as if to say, "Look around wanderers and behold my lofty throne." I looked, believe me, I looked, at a burned and charred foundation of what was once the glorious Prospect House. Yes, it burned to the ground in 1942 and I will bet the arsonist had been those burning, scorching bolts of fire that had frightened me, only a short while ago.

Not only was that the vengeance that should have reminded man not to invade sacred places, but the carriage road, that had once hauled the rich and pompous to those heights, fell into serious disrepair. It is now only fit to bless we lowly hikers on our wandering quest to satisfy our terrible restlessness.

Meanwhile, the blowing wind puffed its pure breath and the clouds began to part. As we followed rock cairns across the summit of this mountain that was becoming so endearing to me, there were breathtaking views all around. I looked down on clouds floating in the valley below. From this thirty square miles of balded

259

earth, towering in its majesty above the White Mountains, I felt my smallness in sharing a part of this place where violent storms are a natural part of its being.

I looked upon the deep ravines with puffy white gondolas floating below over the wonderful forests. As the pilot-less white boats drifted up the sides of the other mountains, they splintered into brilliant waterfalls of mist. The other mountains seemed lowly and bowing to my lofty perch.

I could have sworn the wind puffed a message in my ear. "Go and write of what you have seen and felt." Even though it is beyond my abilities, the seed for this book was planted and in my feeble way I try to make a beautiful flower or tree of knowledge grow and testify to the wonder of this planet, our home, our spaceship, if you will, through time and eternity

I had to use my hiking staff to brace myself against the powerful wind until we descended from the summit to below tree line. As though the wind had only been a part of the mysterious heights, it ceased at a certain level. I stopped and looked back, not realizing at the time, I had made a strange vow.

Back to reality, whatever that is, we decided it was time for our bodies to be nourished, so we stopped for lunch. The sun came out making my experience on the mountain seem like a dream, a dream that has lingered in my waking hours until this very moment . . . . you are now a part of my insanity.

For once we were grateful to the sun as it warmed our chilled bones. Into the packs went our rainwear. Finishing our food we were off again. Following Beaver Brook down through scrubby evergreens we passed through a swampy area and ascended slightly, skirting around Mt. Blue. Mt. Blue is only a few hundred feet lower than Mt. Mooselauke and I was glad to bypass its summit, lest it dull my previous, precious experience.

We ended up on the right side of a swift spring. While passing between Mt. Blue, 4,530 ft. and Mt. Jim, 4,180 ft., Jobildunk Ravine was exposed to the south with Baker River plunging through. I looked as far as I could through the pines and hardwoods until the river was no more. I understand it splinters down near the Ravine Lodge.

The A.T. descended gradually and quickly became dangerously steep. At one point it dropped so steep I feared for my safety. After the rains, it was an ideal spot for a serious mishap. I hardly noticed the series of cascading water to my left. At the lowest cascade the trail descended a little more gradually. Crossing the brook, we were ready for a break at the New Beaver Brook Shelter, 250 ft. to the right.

Inside, two southbound thru-hikers were still sleeping peacefully in their bags. Turned out they had been hiking with the two young men who spent last night with us. We all wrote in the trail registry, then it was back to the A.T. I thought the hard part was over until we began to descend so steep that it was necessary to use ladders and rocks to get to a safer place. Following Beaver Brook was a little easier, especially when it eased my pain somewhat with lovely cascades, spewing cooling mist on my brow.

In spite of that, my poor knees were hurting. The steep descent had taken its toll. It was especially good to see Tweety Pie waiting at NH 112. We had come from nearly 5,000 ft. to 1,870 ft. there at Kinsman Notch. Leaving the parking lot we went 0.5 miles east to Lost River Reservation, where we found a phone. Snapshot called Alpo and Quilter to arrange for them to come to our location and pick them up. Alpo came and took the two back to their place in Vermont.

That was good for them to get away for a day and allowed my husband and I some time alone. Tweety Pie and I went to the Wildwood Campground not too far from the A.T. and got a beautiful tent site, nestled among tall sweet smelling pines. I truly kept waiting for my husband to make a statement about a strange, new glow surrounding me, after the experience on Mooselauke. If anyone would see it, he would. Nothing was said, so I guess it is an inner, spiritual thing. But it was there, believe me, it was there.

Pine cones were everywhere so we decided to clean the tent site. It turned out to be quite a chore since they had sticky sap clinging to the little fins, inside and out. We did the best we could and ended up transferring the sap from the cones to us. Everything in the forest ended up stuck to our shoes from the goo they had on them.

We had only hiked 8 miles today and even though I was very tired, I was still concerned that the short hiking was becoming a habit. Any day I expected something would make the decision for us all to just throw up our hands and go home. It had happened before but I wanted so badly to finish the A.T. Haunting Mooselauke was with me all night and to this day.

JULY 16, 1995 - no reason to rush, so Tweety Pie and I got up late, fixed instant oatmeal, pop tarts and tea and drove into North Woodstock. We did our laundry, bought a few necessities, just like normal people. Well, not exactly like normal people. At the hardware store we got Coleman fuel for our stoves and, oh yes, glue to stick that doggone rubber tip on my hiking staff so I wouldn't lose another one.

The grocery store had all the things most people like and buy. As for me, it was my ice cream. It was a good opportunity to phone the kids. We did try to phone home at least once a week. If you think my husband and I were footloose and fancy free, that was not the case.

Sometimes I forget to mention the family you leave behind to accomplish dreams, but then again until writing this book, I never talked to people much about my life. It had been a great therapy for me and I have begun to unload things I had been keeping suppressed. I might add, my self- esteem has been skyrocketing and I feel like a very important person. For you folks out there who feel lost and don't know who you are, make a date with Mooselauke, you may find a dynamo sleeping inside of you.

Slowpoke, our oldest son started this adventure with us and had to drop out because of his health, mainly. Bless his heart, he had problems staying in shape, which is important if you are going to walk as far as hikers do. Next is daughter, Janet, who is married to a nice guy, Jack. They have blessed us with three grandchildren; Tammy, 21; Ross, 19; and Carrie, 16. They own a farm and even though they stay physically fit, mentally they are unable to leave their responsibilities to hike.

Our youngest son, Clyde, married a sweet girl named Debbie. They have two children; Katrina, 18 and Lance, 16. Our children and grandchildren turned out to be as independent as my husband and me. Yes, we are proud they did. We wouldn't have been out there if they hadn't. But, independent people need to be apart once in awhile. That's just proof that they are independent. Clyde, Debbie and their children live in Arkansas so they don't miss us as much as the rest, who reside in Missouri.

While doing the laundry, a couple on a bicycle built-for-two came in. They left the bicycle outside, of course. They were biking through New Hampshire and Vermont. I think I will stick to hiking but it sure sounded like fun. They expressed some interest in taking up hiking when they finish their biking adventure.

Back at the campground, I went through our gear in 75° temperature. It was a great day for just laying back. In the back of my mind I couldn't help thinking it would also have been a great day for hiking. Meanwhile, Tweety Pie was using the glue to attach the new tip firmly to my walking staff. I told him to say a prayer for the glue to hold the tip firmly to the rod. Strangely, a scripture came to mind, "Thy rod and Thy staff shall comfort you." It will even do a better job with a good rubber tip.

JULY 17, 1995 - Tweety Pie and I are just naturally early risers. I guess it is the nature of farm folks, even though it was pouring down rain. We ate a cold breakfast in the Jeep and tried to keep as dry as possible. 7:30 a.m., Alpo brought Snapshot and Stickflipper back to camp. We hadn't seen Alpo for a while so we said our hello's and good-bye's and told him to give Quilter our blessings. After that it was planning time and we all decided it would be too wet and dangerous to hike. This section in the White Mountains of New Hampshire is pretty moist anyway, due to the many waterfalls and swift streams.

With that settled, we drove over to where the trail met U.S. Highway 3. Tweety Pie would meet us there the next day. It was a beautiful drive, but the planned meeting place was a little hard to find. There are a lot of tourist and recreational interests, due to all the tall mountains surrounding the area.

Arriving back to North Woodstock, our stomachs were sending mixed messages that it was time for fuel. Our fuel station of choice was the local Burger King. The burgers were excellent with lettuce piled high. After that, we decided to work off the meal by shopping the outfitting stores, primarily to look at day packs. Tweety Pie was concerned that my 25° sleeping bag might not keep me warm in the White Mountains. At his prompting, I bought a 10° rated sleeping bag and a day pack. Snapshot and Stickflipper bought day packs and gloves.

We wanted to be rested tomorrow, so we called the Plume Hostel and reserved a room with two beds for $18.00. Then it was back to the Campground, to take down my water soaked tent, pick up our ice chest and get back to the hostel. It was so nice, we decided to reserve two nights. At 18 bucks for the four of us, it was a good deal. The manager permitted me to dry my tent out in the laundry room to get it ready for the next day.

While cooking our supper, a very strange character walked in. He was a section hiker who called himself, Saltie. Proudly he told his slogan, "Saltie is my name, hiking is my game." I'll bet he had said that a hundred times to hikers. Saltie was a spry old fellow to be in his sixties, tall and lanky with graying hair, probably caused by years of stress.

Tweety Pie hit it off with Old' Saltie from the git-go. It's astounding how almost anyone can identify with him. He should have been a psychologist or someone in the human relations field. They spent quite a while shooting the breeze before we decided it was time to turn in.

JULY 18, 1995 - 6:50 a.m. and time to leave the Lost River area. It would have been a lot of fun spending

265

time on the many side trails, exploring that phenomenal area. It's actually a brook that drains the southern part of Kinsman Notch.

What makes it unusual is, it disappears below ground into a narrow subterranean gorge. There are many caverns as a result of the swift water's patient sculpturing for thousands of years. It actually emerges into swirling potholes, making spectacular waterfalls.

Some of the caves can be reached by trails, boardwalks and even ladders. Hikers can ill afford to spend time at every popular tourist attraction such as that. It does take some restraint to resist the temptation. Hikers would make excellent tour guides. Most of them could select some wonderful places to visit and explore for people on *non-hiking* vacation time. I certainly accumulated a long list.

A lot of exciting hiking was ahead and we eagerly followed a ridge and then a very steep climb to Kinsmen Notch. The new day packs proved to be a good investment and already were making hiking easier. We passed on the east side of the ridges highest point, 3,009 ft. It was obvious right off the bat, that we were going to be in some high elevation. I had no idea how hairy it was going to get. Within 5.2 miles we passed the trail to Gordon Pond. It is the source of Gordon Brook that plummets down 4.8 miles to Highway 112 creating Gordon Falls 1.3 miles down the trail.

Passing over a knob on the southern ridge of Mt. Wolf at 3,360 ft. we were afforded a nice view of Gordon Pond. It was disappointing in size and amazing how much water proceeded forth from it. Finally, we reached the summit of East Peak of Mt. Wolf, 3,478 feet. Not much of an ascent and as we descended gradually to the Eliza

Brook Shelter, I was beginning to think the trail might not be so bad after all.

The Shelter was a good place for a break. We had been hearing two hikers closing in on us and when they caught up, they decided to take a break also. After leaving the shelter, we crossed Eliza Brook, then turned upstream on an old logging road. Leaving the road, the trail got rough and steep taking our attention off the falls and cascades to our left in Eliza Brook.

Yesterday's rain had made the rocks and tree roots, that jutted up in the trail, very slippery making me cautious with every step I took. Crossing the headwater of the brook, the climbing continued to be steep with the same slippery conditions. *"It can't get much worse than this,"* I thought. At Harrington Pond, it was a little easier, but still ascending. I finally faced the realization that we were heading upward to South Kinsman Mountain, 4,358 feet tall. It got worse, to the point that we were actually climbing hand-over-hand in the steepest sections. If it had not been for Stickflipper pulling me up on occasion, I would have been in a world of hurt.

That was why my husband and I got so rattled when I had to hike alone. Even with the help, both my arms were bleeding from the jabbing, bushes and scrubby evergreen trees along the trail. It was some of the worst punishment I had endured and it wasn't because of my age either. We met a group of young people and one young boy around 13 years old, was literally frightened out of his wits. His eyes were wide with fear as he clung to the inside rocks. A leader was staying close to him to prevent a potential disaster.

No one was disappointed when we all reached the summit of South Kinsman. The group of young people finally had all their people up, along with the frightened boy. I honestly felt sorry for him because, at that age, pride is at its highest peak, so it doesn't take much to blow their ego right out of the saddle. It doesn't get much better with age. Everyone rested, to get ready for the descent.

Descending wasn't too bad because there wasn't too much drop into the valley between South Kinsman and the summit of North Kinsman Mountain, 4,293 feet. At the open summit of North Kinsman, a short trail led to a cliff, giving us a view overlooking Kinsman Pond. Descending to the pond we circled it and the Kinsman Pond Shelter, continuing on an eastward heading. As I have said before, those high ponds are a special attraction to hikers and locals.

The descent was sometimes steep to the Lonesome Lake Hut, the first hut on the A.T. going north. The Appalachian Mountain Club (A.M.C.) maintains the A.T. from Kinsman Notch, NH to Grafton Notch in Maine. The A.M.C. Huts are closed-in structures and vary in size. They are operated by a hut "croo." There are no showers, but they have bunk beds and serve dinner and breakfast. They charge $50.00 for overnight and two meals. Not bad for day hikers and people who want to spend a couple of days in a wonderfully rustic atmosphere, at an altitude of around 3,000 ft. Our group of hikers only stopped for a cup of hot chocolate. Lonesome Lake was near by and was such a beautiful, high altitude lake.

The trail gave us a break as it almost leveled out, more like a gradual descent because we were still dropping. It was almost fun passing the lovely lake, crossing its outlet called Cascade Brook. We hiked beside the brook for a ways among the evergreens, before crossing it again on a quaint wooden bridge. Crossing on rocks over Whitehouse Brook became a comical, but challenging event. Stickflipper turned out to be the best rock hopper and we told him he should change his trail name. He took the dig like a gentleman and even helped me cross the rocks.

Tired but in a good mood, we met Tweety Pie at U.S. 3. We had gone from about 2,000 ft. to 4,358 ft. to our present altitude of 1,450 feet., and all that in 16.1 miles. Not bad, however I doubt that my poor arms and elbows would agree. I complain a little but the truth be known, hikers become very familiar with the quote, "No pain, No gain." Like Mountain climbers, if there was little or no risk, it would be much like walking around a block or in your city park. Of all people I never thought I would be one to say, "I love it!"

A worn out group of hikers dragged themselves back into the Burger King for one big heaping of fuel in the form of cheese burgers piled high with tomatoes and lettuce. At the Hostel, we did our laundry, took a hot shower and engaged in a lot of discussion with Tweety Pie about that unusual section of trail. I played down the rough climbs but scraped arms betrayed me. Tweety Pie hid his concerns as he helped get my pack ready for the next day. After that, the blanket was wrapped around me and consoled my aching body into deep sleep.

JULY 19, 1995 - back at the junction of U.S. 3 at 6:30 a.m., it was determined that meeting places for Tweety Pie were few and far between in the White Mountains, therefore we would not see him for three days. He would go back to the Plume Hostel for a couple more nights. We, on the other hand, would carry full packs, spending our nights at trail campsites.

Those mountains are extremely rugged and I don't know if I would rather be the hiker or the one who leaves his wife, wondering what may happen to her in three days. It's something that must be considered when you follow a dream. Most have risks of one kind or another.

Tweety Pie learned a long time ago that hiking was important enough for me to take the risks. He also is aware that I am very stubborn and bull headed. I'm not sure you would choose hiking for a dream if you weren't a little self-centered. At that point, Stickflipper and Snapshot had become awfully important in my script of life, if for no other reason than the fact that they were not a heck of a lot different that me. They had their reasons for being out there and I was fulfilling something in their script.

A paved bike path bore left over a modern steel bridge. It was deceiving as we followed it a ways, then crossed two brooks and entered the woods. Swallowed by those woods, made me wonder if I was being swallowed by my ambitions also.

Was I being fair to my husband and children? Should I have been sitting in my home waiting to hear the many problems that young adults have? Should I be a life long parent, interfering in the affairs of two people merging, to learn the lessons of cohabitation as my husband and I have had to learn? We are still learning, I might add and do not want, nor need, any interference.

It seems to me that people grow older and much more dissatisfied with life, when they do that. No, I am satisfied that I am doing what I feel makes me a special human being. Tweety Pie doesn't seem to be manifesting any harm, as a result. For that matter, he and I seem to enjoy each other now, more than ever.

For a while, the trail was a gradual climb, heading into high country, that created a false security. Crossing a few more gentle brooks, the climb revealed the true nature of that section. With the heavy packs, the steep climb to Liberty Spring Campsite was a good training session. It was then I realized my condition was pretty doggone good. Just like that, we were above 4,000 ft. Wow!

Can you imagine the thrill of knowing you can walk and walk over terrible terrain and feel energy in your lungs and legs surging? If you can't, go out and walk around your block once, then do it again and again until you know you have walked twenty miles. If you make it, then you will know a smidgen of how I felt.

A lot of hikers were camped there for a well-needed rest. It was tempting, but we had a long way to go and talking to them about what was ahead would not help. Franconia Ridge was reached by climbing over rough and steep cliffs. Well, I knew the elevation in that section was above 4,000 ft. How much worse could it get? Scrambling up Little Haystack Mountain, the elevation became 4,706 ft.

I was taken back to my experience on Mt. Mooselauke as the cold air begin to bite. We had left the tree line 500 feet ago and were following a narrow, almost barren ridge, except for a stunted spruce and a few alpine species. It was like an alpine tundra and it did not take an expert to tell you that life up here was extremely fragile. Even the hiking traffic could affect the delicate ecology. With rock steps and small walls hastily built to keep the foot traffic away from the more threatened areas, the tundra was eroding.

While Mooselauke echoes in my brain I'm compelled to reason, if the mountain tops loose their lofty peaks, it will be disastrous for the lower lands. Many things have their beginnings there and are absolutely necessary to the mortals below. Those swift and sometimes calm brooks that cascade out of those royal peaks are like blood vessels filling the ponds and lakes. They fill those wells that the farmers brag about never going dry.

The cold was magnified as the wind blew harder and harder. It can get above 80 miles per hour and freezing temperatures up there, without any notice or reason, even in the middle of summer. As we stopped to put on our jackets, we got a small taste of what it must be like to climb the frozen mountains; the ones where even the professional mountain climbers loose their lives frequently.

When we reached the steep and rocky cone of Mt. Lafayette, we were at 5,249 feet. I knew, as barren as it was, it was the highest peak in that section. There would be many more climbs as we descended, but height was becoming an exhilarating thrill to me so I wanted to cling to it for a while. Slightly below was another feeble reminder of man's loosing battle to Mother Nature. The remains of another summit house was evident by its worn foundation. But this was a good place and time for us to eat our lunch.

A young lady, calling herself Water Witch, appeared on the knob of Mt. Lafayette and came down to the foundation. She decided to take her break with us and an enjoyable conversation ensued. It was her first day on the trail and she was going to finish the A.T. all the way to Katahdin, Maine.

It amazed me, how, in that environment, so many people knew how to say hello and engage in conversation before saying good-bye. We pass hundreds of people in our shopping malls and rarely does anyone say hello to a stranger, what alone, enter into a conversation about their future plans.

The Greenleaf Hut was 1.1 miles down the Mountain. It was easily visible from Mt. Lafayette as was the Franconia Notch and Profile Lake, further in the distance. It was a planned location for the hut due to the unpredictable weather up on the ridge. Hikers are advised that if a severe storm should arise, they are to get off the ridge as soon as possible.

The trail was rough and steep, descending from the North Peak of Mt. Lafayette. It was a relief when we entered the tree line that afforded some protection from the wind and cold. Strangely though, when you get to the elevation where the trees survive in forests, the weather becomes calmer. No wonder the Indians considered these high places sacred.

Proceeding along Garfield Ridge, there was a water source under the moss in a stream bed which we did not use. I suppose it would be fairly pure, that high up. Water under green moss, well yuck, it just turns me off. We had to cross a swampy area just before Garfield Pond, another high altitude small body of water and one of the sources of a brook, that trailed off down the ridge into the trees.

It was a steep climb around the summit of Mt. Garfield whose barren cone stands 4,488 feet, slightly above the forest line. The climb difficulty was compounded by the fact that we had to skirt the peak on the northeast, down hill. Soon we began the descent, so actually the climb was just a prelude to the steep, rocky downhill drop to the Garfield Ridge Shelter and Campsite.

A caretaker was on duty and we had to pay $5.00 to camp there. There were no complaints, as we all had our strength challenged by that awesome high ridge with the bitter cold and relentless winds. We had become spoiled by not having to carry these full backpacks and they were now sapping our energy. All in all, 11 miles under those conditions was nothing to be ashamed of. The young Water Witch finally made it into the shelter. She was feeling the pains of beginning a rigorous hike, but had a cheerful personality that we all appreciated.

I snuggled up in my new sleeping bag that night. Tweety Pie had been right. The extra padding and warmth was comforting at that higher altitude. I had one more day out of the way before I would see him again. There was a spring running nearby and after all was quiet, if you listened very carefully, you could hear Hawthorne Falls dripping and spraying below. With that and the bristling wind blowing on Mt. Garfield just above, the mother of all hypnotists took me into a strange, deep sleep.

JULY 20, 1995 - climbing out of the sleeping bag to enter the chilled mountain air was invigorating, to say the least. A quick breakfast in the early morning hour and we were ready to leave the shelter. A short distance down was another trail called the Franconia Trail that led to an off the ridge campsite named 13 Falls Tentsite. The trail became extremely steep and rocky again as we dropped off the ridge for 0.5 miles, then it was only a slight incline to Galehead Hut. That was a short distance from another steep climb to South Twin Mountain. For that reason, we decided to stop for a glass of lemonade before climbing to the summit at 4,902 ft., to be exact.

It was a wonderful surprise to find the trail had been well maintained, which made the extremely steep climb much easier. I shudder to think what it would have been like. otherwise. It was one of those summits that you couldn't help huffing and puffing to reach, creating the necessity for another break.

We viewed the Pemigewasset Wilderness all the way down the rocky descent down to the junction of

Gayot Shelter. The wilderness encompassed 18,560 acres of undeveloped mountain land. Need I say more? It is marvelous to see. Even though the logging companies had stripped it once, it had recovered and was reclaimed by nature. The reforesting by man in 1986 and the protection as a wilderness, gave Mother Nature some help. Let's hope it will stay that way.

At first we had planned on spending the night there at Gayot Shelter but since it was off the trail we changed our plans. Besides the Zealand Falls Hut appeared to be in a more beautiful setting, farther down the ridge and we were feeling our vinegar.

Down the mountain a little further we came to a ledge. A very unique ledge. We had heard of a bird called Canadian Gray Jays that occupied the cliffs and ridges in that area and we had our first encounter. They are like our Blue Jays in Missouri but lacking the little peaked crown on their heads. It was an experience to see them, but what happened next just blew my mind. If you have ever tried to get close to a blue jay you know that is an absolute no, no. I had a cookie in my hand and the little suckers came right down and took it. Needless to say, we all lessened our cookie snacks by holding out our hands and feeding those wonderful birds.

Is that wrong? Are we interfering with nature or is nature trying to soften us up just a little, by allowing these creatures to interact with us? Well, it was their boldness that motivated me and I will never forget the experience, no matter what.

The barren summit of Mt. Gayot was really a knob on the way down but still 4,506 ft. altitude above the tree line. The trail was easy along the Zealand Ridge, of course everything seemed easy after the worst was over but in reality it got pretty doggone steep on a woods trail that led

275

to Whitewall Brook. We crossed the brook just before reaching the Zealand Falls Hut.

Snapshot surprised the dickens out of me when she asked the Hut Master if we could work for our night's stay. I was even more surprised when she said yes. It was a humbling experience until somebody said jokingly, "We're working our way over the A.T." It's not unusual for the huts to let thru-hikers work their night's stay, especially if they need help. Hiking, on the level that we were, is expensive and you have no income. All three of us felt lucky and grateful for the consideration.

We had made a good decision to stop there. The waterfalls by the Hut were beautiful and after last night, I was hoping I would be able to let them lull me to sleep. But first we used the clear pure water to wash the trail dust off, before assuming our duties, helping in the kitchen.

The Hut began filling up with hikers in the afternoon. A lot of young kids came in. The Hut wasn't far from a road and other trails merged there. So much for listening to the water falls, it was a noisy night. Since we were part of the croo, we had to eat after all the guests finished. Then it was work, work, work. We helped clean up the kitchen before we could go to bed. It wasn't all that bad, since we had quit hiking at only 6.9 miles.

JULY 21, 1995 - the Hut Master woke the guests up at 6:30 a.m. Normally, we were on the trail by then, but I yawned and went back to sleep while the guests were eating breakfast. Finally when things were clearing out and winding down, I got up, stretched and popped my bones, then folded up the blankets on the bunks. Each bunk had three wool blankets and there were about 36 bunks. Hey, that was over a hundred blankets! After they fed us a delicious breakfast, the Hut Master had us sweep all the floors and mop the bathrooms and dining room. At 9:00 a.m. we left the Zealand Falls Hut, shining like a silver dollar. I'll tell you the truth, we didn't mind a bit. We were proud they had that system that allowed us to help out.

The day was one where the sky was leaving little misunderstanding that it was going to bless or curse us with rain, depending on your point of view. At any rate, we put the rain covers on our packs and began the day's hike. The trail was about as level as could be, as we were gradually working our way out of the elevation, only to begin again in another section.

Skirting Whitewall Mountain was done for the most part on an old railroad bed of the former Zealand Valley Railroad. It was used primarily to transport timber out of the Zealand Notch before the 1900's. Actually there were as many as 17 such railroads back then and many of the side trails are remnants of those.

Relics laying here and there testified to the hustle and bustle of the day and time. In 1903 the Zealand Notch area was inundated by fire. 1907 followed suit in the Pemi area ravaging the Zealand and Garfield Ridges. Mt. Gayot and Mt. Garfield were once wooded all the way to their lofty peaks. Today they are open summits and will probably remain so.

So what did we gain by going to the extreme, taking the trees that are like bristling hair on the forearms of Mother Earth's high peaks and forests? Some made meager livings for a few years and others made fortunes. I wonder what is left of the moneys earned and if it is still benefiting anyone at all.

Regardless, I enjoyed my hiking that day. It was so much easier than the last three days and allowed my mind to wonder into the why and wherefore of my existence. Passing the trail to Thoreau Falls, I tried to see a view from there but forest and the ridge blocked it. It was only a slight incline to Ethan Pond to our left with its campsite on its east end, easily visible.

Not much further we reached the high point of the incline and began the steeper drop to slightly above 1,000 ft. One more steeper decline, cross the railroad tracks and we were at our days destination. We had made good time hiking the 7.6 miles to Crawford Notch and U.S. 302. Tweety Pie was waiting eagerly and had a relieved look on his face when he spotted me.

There are those who may feel sorry for Tweety Pie and think he misses out on all the fun. Let me dispel your concerns. He and a friend called Saltie had driven over to Mt. Washington and took the Shuttle bus to the summit. He described the views as being great, however, the clouds kept fogging the poor things in. Pity, pity, pity. Don't get me wrong, I am glad he can always amuse himself and believe me . . . . he always can. His whole life is one adventure after another, so I hope you join me in the relief that Tweety Pie is content most of the time.

I have been mentioning a notch and perhaps you may be wondering what the differences are from a ridge, gully or valley. There is very little, except a notch is like a steeper gap between two mountains. As you will see, they can sometimes get extremely rough.

It was only 12:15 p.m., so we ate a light lunch and drove to the A.M.C.'s Crawford Notch Hostel. It had nice bunks, showers and a kitchen. I felt guilty that we had been getting so many short hikes in and could not help but wonder if it wasn't taking too much time off that year. I suppose it was natural that being away from family and home that long, took a psychological toll. Couple that with the fact that it had been a long and strenuous journey, I suppose we were getting into a rut. Tomorrow we would start hiking the Presidential Range. It was going to be rough and full of high mountains again and I had to renew my dedication to accomplish my goal, finish the A.T. that year and not later.

The Caretaker tried to help Snapshot get reservations at the Mizpah Spring Hut, but nothing could alter the fact that they only had room for two people. It wasn't difficult to see that this was very important to her and it was causing her to be upset. I told her not to worry and take the reservations for her and Stickflipper. Lord only knows, I would sacrifice a little luxury to have the two of them hike with me. After all, it was only one section and a relatively short one at that. I would carry my tent, if need be, and camp in the Nauman Tentsite only a little way before the hut.

She was able to get reservations at Lake of the Clouds Hut for all three of us for July 23, 1995, so the issue was resolved. What worried me was it rattled her cage so much, I feared the pressure might be getting to her.

As with the previous section, camping above tree line which is 4,200 ft. is prohibited. The weather is uncertain and can turn violent with very little notice. Hurricane-force winds and freezing conditions do happen - even in the summer. The Presidential Range will be a challenge to our stamina and mental attitudes.

JULY 22, 1995 - as Tweety Pie drove us to Crawford Notch, it was obvious that we all knew this historical section was more or less a culmination of any hiker's dream. The elevation of 1,277 feet, where we started was a blessing. It was just less that we would have to go up, to that frightening ridge. We started by crossing the Saco River Bridge then disappeared into hardwood forest. It didn't take long before we began a steep and winding climb. As we climbed over a mile it didn't take a genius to see this was not going to be an easy short hike. I was already getting awfully tired when we reached the Webster Cliffs. From there we looked down on the valley below, with the river running through and the Crawford Notch rising steeply behind. Directly below was the parking lot we had just left.

Tweety Pie was still visible sitting by his Jeep. I could only wonder what was going through his mind as he watched his fanatical companion enter those woods to fulfill a dream, that at her age should never be more than just that. It was awesome looking out over that beautiful backdrop to my worried husband. Tenderly I blew him a kiss in thanks for being so patient with me and my terribly exhilarating infection. A kiss, he may never know, was sent into the air with total gratitude.

We followed the cliffs for a little over a mile before reaching the summit of Mt. Webster, 3,910 feet. A slight descent was only an illusion but what I was feeling was no imaginary problem. We stopped for a break before continuing on an up and down trail, over three small humps. My stomach was doing somersaults and I felt an abnormal chill. I made it to the summit of Mt. Jackson 4,052 ft, before one of the worst symptoms for a hiker was manifest. My stomach problem worked its way lower and the humiliating event occurred. It's called diarrhea and I hope everyone can sympathize with me. I was weak and humbled. Finding a little puddle of water on the trail, this proud lady cleaned up the best she could with a prayer that no one would come along.

Fortunately Snapshot and Stickflipper had gone on ahead and were waiting for me up the trail. I said a prayer to the Lord that if he wanted me to experience humility, His will was done. I asked that, as a result, he would respect me and not let this interfere with the hike and if I truly deserved mercy, let me make it to the hut where a bunk would be made available.

As we descended over ledges through woods and several meadows another problem, that is a result of diarrhea, took its toll on me. I was sore as a boil. I can look back and let a smile cross my face but oh was I miserable at the time! I was one drug out lady that arrived at the Mizpah Spring Hut.

Longingly I watched Snapshot and Stickflipper check in for their reservations. When the attendant informed us that there had been some cancellations and I would have a bunk also, only me and my favorite Father knew how really wonderful an event was occurring. All I wanted to do was rest, but first I washed my clothes in the bathroom sink and hung them out the back door to dry. I went to bed before dinner with the satisfaction that the worst of my degradation was now my secret and, of course, you know who. He doesn't seem to embarrass me as do these equal mortals. I dozed off hoping that the rest of my prayer would be answered..

It costs us $44.00 a piece, since we were Appalachian Trail members and boy was I grateful that we didn't have to work. The Hut Croo served us a marvelous dinner that I ate cautiously. They make all their own bread and delicious finger foods for dessert. It went well and I was even able to enjoy the jolly group while they entertained us the rest of the evening.

There was one tired and weak Den Mama that evening, but my stomach was okay and after treating my rawness with ointment, the soreness was going away. Thanks old friend, I thought as the memory of this horrible day faded away into peaceful amnesia.

JULY 23, 1995 - it was one unusual hut was my first waking thought. The Hut Master woke me with the most pleasant alarm I have ever experienced. He was walking up and down the halls singing an Irish Melody. His voice was not that of an amateur and it was such a unique way of treating the patrons. I dressed, feeling refreshed as *"You take the High r-r-r-road and I'll take the low r-r-r-road, and I'll get there afor-r-r-r ye,"* echoed in my mind.

It was nice to be served my breakfast in a dining room, but this bright eyed Croo was not finished yet. They continued entertaining us with a delightful little skit, after breakfast, no less. A church group was there as guests and unbeknownst to me were having a church service outside. Sunday morning had slipped up on me, would you believe? Rarely do you have an outdoor church service on the trail, so it was an innocent oversight. Snapshot and Stickflipper had joined them, I was to learn later. Since I was unaware of all that, I continued getting my backpack ready to go. It is a wonderful thought that people can hold a worship service in the greatest chapel anywhere, the great outdoors. Did I feel guilty that I had missed this happening? Not really. I had my religious experience yesterday and it turned out about as good as you can expect. I think my Lord knew how very much I appreciated him. Mizpah Spring Hut will be a place I will recommend to anyone for a rewarding experience.

All this did cause a late start and it was 8:45 a.m. when we got back to the serious business of hiking. In about a mile, we reached the Alpine Summit of Mt.

Pierce, 4,310 feet. We should have been looking down on the tree line for the next 12.7 miles, but fog was coming in on us making an eerie glow with rays from the sun lacing the dense mist, like chocolate swirl in vanilla ice cream.

The temperature wasn't cold so we kept moving until we arrived at the Lake of the Clouds Hut. The fog closed off the sun and became so thick you couldn't even see the Hut until you were right in front of it. I realized we had reservations but what we had all overlooked was the short distance between the two huts. Snapshot tried to resolve the expense issue by checking with the Hut Master to see if we could work for our night's stay. To be honest, I was still feeling a little weak and that Hut was so large and rather cold after Mizpah I just didn't really want to stay, let alone, work.

I'm not a very outspoken person and was confused as to how to tell them my true feelings. My mind wasn't working well, but I managed to say, I thought we should hike on up Mt. Washington where we could catch the shuttle bus down and spend the night with Tweety Pie. Snapshot wasn't too happy and hastily canceled everything. I knew I was in a little bit of trouble again as we hiked up the rugged trail to Mt. Washington, 6,288 feet. The wind began to blow, but not enough to get rid of the dense fog, just enough to sock us in solid.

Not surprising, Snapshot and Stickflipper moved out ahead of me. Talk about a lonely feeling. I could barely see the trail in front of my feet but the terrible fog suddenly turned into a warm, comforting blanket and I soon caught up to my companions waiting at the summit. I got there at 2:00 p.m. and the shuttle bus was to leave at 3:00 p.m. Our tickets cost us $15.00 a piece and, at least for me, it was a timely investment. I needed to feel my husband's arms around me for at least a few minutes. The tension eased and we had a good ride down to Pinkham Notch.

Needless to say, Tweety Pie was surprised at the unscheduled meeting. He was really not looking for us, but for some strange reason had hung around, as he said, "just in case." Yes, I think this weird adventure my husband and I started several years ago has made us a little connected, in a psychic sort of way.

I was full of mixed emotions during the drive into Gorham, NH. We made arrangements to stay at the Hostel. It was an unusual place, in that we had to climb outside stairs to get to our rooms. Fortunately, there was also a motel there with a laundry. It was a good time to wash dirty clothes and for me to reflect on my present circumstance.

We had only hiked 7 miles, so the rut we were in, continued. Maybe I was expecting too much in that hostile environment. There was very little talk except when I took the opportunity, in a private moment, to tell Tweety Pie about my humbling experience up on that ridge. Something was gnawing at me. I was certain I was not going to get by unscathed because of the forthrightness I had used with my hiking buddies. What will be will be. I need rest.

JULY 24, 1995 - Tweety Pie drove us back to the Pinkham Notch shuttle bus office. I knew it was coming. I just didn't know how soon. While we were waiting, Snapshot was staying by herself in an unusual way. Stickflipper was talking with Tweety Pie. As I meandered over to listen, my legs were quivering. Stickflipper was telling my husband they were going to start hiking by themselves again in four days.

I broke down like a little child and tears wouldn't stay inside. I tried to tell him in the best way I could, that I was sorry for whatever I had done to hurt his feelings. I really did not understand why those things had to happen. I realized that they had been a great deal of help and comfort to me on the trail, but it was an even trade in my opinion, which I never brought up. My husband and I had been supplying the jeep and backup for getting us to decent campsites, mail pickups and the occasional luxury in a motel. Well, I had dealt with this before and somehow it worked out. I believed it would again.

The shuttle was ready to leave. This event ended some of the tension, at least temporarily, as we loaded our packs on the bus. It was a very quiet trip back up Mt. Washington and the mountain was not in the mood to make the situation any better. The wind was gusting as high as 45 to 55 miles per hour and the fog was dense. It was blowing, like heavy rain, and making puddles of water on the pavement.

We waited inside the observatory until the wind died down to at least 35 to 40 miles per hour, according to the special instruments on the wall, that helped keep track of the unpredictable winds. Meanwhile, I put on my long handles and rain gear in an attempt to stay warm. At 10:30 a.m. we finally emerged from the observatory to begin hiking. The fog made it more than a little difficult to find the A.T. When we did, the trail was rocky and dangerous.

As we made our way to a lower elevation, hiking became much easier and it got a little warmer. In the fog it was hard to see Snapshot and Stickflipper, but I soon realized they were some distance ahead of me. It stayed that way the next six miles to Madison Hut. They had quite often hiked ahead of me when the hiking was fairly easy and safe, but it was obvious this was deliberate.

The clouds finally broke away and allowed me to at least get a glimpse of the Hut on the way down to it. We didn't have reservations so I assumed Snapshot and Stickflipper would try to work for their night's stay. When I arrived, I went straight to the Hut Master and asked if I could work. He agreed and as I suspected my two hostile companions were going to work also. I had made up my mind to do everything I could to improve our relationship and then let the cards fall where they may.

The Hut Croo was a friendly group. They must have a fine training program to get these guys to be so consistent in their personal relationships. After locating my bunk, I was relieved to get my long handles and wet rain gear off and hung up to dry. When I went to the kitchen it was clean as a pin. I began sterilizing the silverware by dipping them in Clorox water.

A thru-hiker, who called himself Mr. Misserable, had arrived and the Hut Master allowed him to work his way with the rest of us. His intentions had been to work for the A.M.C. doing trail maintenance. I told him I could sympathize with his trail handle. The guests began pouring in, as the sun was fading into the horizon. I think it was the most beautiful sunset I had ever seen. I guess it must have been the clouds and the remnants of the thick humidity of the fog that created the reds and yellows that melted into the deep, deep purple. It made me feel awfully lonely until I began mingling with the more-than-friendly guests. Unknowingly, they had made turning in for the night much easier for a confused Den Mama. Snapshot and Stickflipper did not go out of their way to talk to me and I procrastinated, doing very little to promote conversation. Boy! I'm not an extrovert anyway, so eating crow doesn't come easy for me. Maybe tomorrow.

JULY 25, 1995 - Mr. Misserable turned out to be a nice guy. He even volunteered to do the work this morning for me and my companions. The Croo agreed to the arrangement and bid us a pleasant farewell. Mr. Misserable may be miserable himself but he sure isn't passing it on to others. I decided to take a lesson from that as we were able to start hiking early due to his kindness. Thanks, Mr. Misserable for being such a nice person.

I started ahead of Snapshot and Stickflipper simply because I wanted to keep them behind me as long as possible. At least that way, they would see or hear me if I needed help. They would catch me anyway but we had a very steep climb ahead to the summit of Mt. Madison. For 0.4 miles it was terribly rock and my pals caught me as I figured they would.

The climb was steep, as anticipated, but we finally got up that troublesome summit of Mt. Madison, 5,363 ft. From up there, we got to see the Mt. Washington we had missed in the fog. Looking back to the south, it stood with lofty majesty wearing a ring of white clouds for a crown. I'll bet it was still engulfed in fog. What a view!

Descending steeply on a rough and rocky trail was exhaustingly slow going to below tree line, usually 4,200 ft. An unscheduled break was needed at the Osgood Campsite. Coming off a ridge, we crossed Peabody Brook on a native wood footbridge, then over another ridge we walked a suspension bridge over the West Branch of the Peabody River.

Arriving at Lowe's Bald Spot, 2,860 feet, we stopped for lunch. From a rocky knob, we had a splendid view of the northern Presidentials and the Carter-Moriah Range of mountains. Of course we were looking up at the much taller mountains. Between the mountains was the Great Gulf Wilderness that we had made a horseshoe circle around. It was awe inspiring, and in that mood I sensed that Snapshot's attitude was changing in regard to me. I had been praying, more than talking, that this would occur. I think the Lord said that with patience and long suffering endure, but never force the will of man or for that matter, woman..

Well, good-bye, magnificent Presidentials. The trail had little change in elevation all the way to Pinkham Notch and it was still 2,000 feet. Tweety Pie waited with an anxious look in his eye. I gave him an encouraging wink as we went inside the lodge where I got my favorite, well-needed treat, an ice cream cone.

My knees were really aching after the steep downhill hike of 7.8 miles but fortunately my feet were doing extremely well because of my new boots. They had been tighter, so I only had to wear two pair of liner socks, instead of the heavy socks with a liner. It had made a tremendous difference.

It was 2:00 p.m. when Tweety Pie drove us back to the city of Gorham and the same hostel where we had stayed before. This time the owner let us have a motel room for the same cost as the hostel and it was on the ground floor, which I always prefer.

We ate our dinner out and enjoyed a good quality meal. I don't know if that's a compliment or not, anything usually tastes pretty good when you eat on the trail a lot. We capped that off with a half gallon of ice cream that we all shared back at the motel. It was almost like old times, but I dared not ask if Snapshot and Stickflipper had changed their minds about leaving me behind.

Nurse Without A Purse appeared at the most unexpected times and places. Straggling in with a big smile on his face, he told about catching a bus to get ahead on the trail. He was joshed a bit about cheating and we told him he had missed some marvelous rough hiking. He just said, "What a shame, I'll catch it another day and another way." I wished, in a way, I could have that attitude but the Den Mama was out to accomplish a dream and not one foot of that trail would be missed.

I went to sleep with a hope and a prayer that all the problems would be resolved for the short time and distance I had left. When sleep finally consumed me, I dreamed of being home on the farm with the A.T. completed. Weird, because I don't remember it being a satisfied feeling. I was getting worried that my infection may not have a cure.

JULY 26, 1995 - I felt great on our way back to Pinkham Notch. Following the valley beside the Peabody River on NH 16 was beautiful, with mountains rising to the sky on both sides of the highway. As we approached Pinkham Notch we noticed the Wildcat Mountain Gondola Ski-Lift off to our left and a clever idea took seed.

We had to hike out of Pinkham Notch and over Wildcat Mountain which was going to be a steep climb over five peaks. The gondola went up to the first peak (Peak E) after starting at the highway below. Why couldn't Tweety Pie take our full backpacks up the mountain in the Gondola? We stopped to ask the attendant and he said he could see no reason why we couldn't do that. It cost us $9.00 for the three backpacks and Tweety Pie and was the best $9.00 we had spent so far.

Arranging this brilliant plan took some time and it was 9:10 a.m. when we finally started hiking out of Pinkham Notch. Crossing a bog was done over a wooden bridge before turning to our left on a square ledge trail that led along the eastern bank of the Ellis River. We ascended slightly, then skirted Lost Pond for about a mile on a pretty level trail, which was deceiving for what lay ahead.

Just like that, we were on a steep, hazardous climb. My body felt light as a feather without the heavy pack, as we worked our way over rocks and ledges. Reaching the summit of Wildcat Mountain Peak E at 4,041 feet we had climbed over 2,000 ft. Tweety Pie waited outside the Gondola Terminal Building with the backpacks. It started raining, so we quickly carried them back inside.

Quite a few day hikers came in for shelter from, what became, a nasty little storm. As the thunder and lightening made its hostile statement outside, I could only think how lucky we were that we hadn't got caught on the climb up that peak. The nine dollar investment was looking better all the time because if we had been carrying the packs, we would not have arrived before the storm hit. We were proud as peacocks as we ate lunch and bragged about the wise decision we had made. The rain beat down for over an hour and when it began to let up, we decided to get it on.

Rain covers on the backpacks and good-byes to Tweety Pie over, we started hiking. It would be a roller coaster trail for quite awhile. It was only a short distance to the Wildcat's Peak D, at 4,063 feet. A wooden platform afforded a view that reminded we mortals that Mt. Washington may be briefly out of mind, but certainly not out of sight. Her ravines and cloudy peak stood above all, to our northwest.

Dropping into a col we ascended and topped Peak C, 4,298 feet. Several humps later, Wildcat Peak B at 4,320 feet was a wooded summit and we hiked in the trees to finally reach Wildcat Mountain's final peak. Even though it was small, 4,422 feet, compared to where we had been. It was, indeed, like one of the crests on a roller coaster ride. That one you look straight down into the loop, causing the heaviness in your stomach, when you rise even higher. Of course we were walking and not riding, so the speed and excitement was lacking. By that time the clouds broke away, exposing a much clearer view of Mt. Washington. Its 6,286 foot elevation was threatening, even at that distance.

We then turned to face the steep descent ahead that had to be made on switchbacks. Even the different levels were steep from one to the other. It took a lot of energy to drop into Carter Notch. When I say drop, that's exactly what I mean. Over a thousand feet to a 3,388 ft. elevation. We were still going down when we reached a lake.

We had to be careful to stay on the A.T. Many trails intermingled in that notch. We passed two small Carter Lakes and one, just before the Carter Notch Hut, was simply beautiful. It had a beach and large boulders surrounding the rest of the shore.

The Hut was not far. We again asked the Hut Master if we could work for our night's stay. What a relief when he agreed since it was such a lovely place to stay. It had cabins that were separate from the dining area which afforded some privacy, something you get little of, on the trail. After fixing our bunks and hanging our clothes to dry, we went back to the kitchen area.

Stickflipper immediately began cleaning the cook stove and grill. Snapshot and I washed the pots, pans and thoroughly cleaned the cabinets. That Hut was more laid back than the others and one of the smallest on the A.T. It was also the last hut on the trail. Quite a few guests were coming in, so the Hut Master fixed some of the tastiest baked fish I have ever eaten.

After dinner, we helped clean the kitchen and do the dishes. We worked so hard the Hut Master told us that if we would get up in the morning early enough to eat around 6:00 a.m. before the guests, he would allow us to get started hiking without helping clean up. We had only hiked 7.5 miles that day, but it was tough miles and we were more than willing to hit the sack.

JULY 27, 1995 - as promised we rose early, made up our bunks and got our backpacks ready to go. We were in the kitchen in time to eat breakfast with the nice young men of the early Croo. At 6:45 a.m. we started hiking. Our work was cut out for us that day and we started on the steepest and highest climb of the day to the summit of Carter Dome, 4,832 feet. Reaching the summit was a gentle slope and short climb to Mt. Hight, 4,675 feet.

We thought we had it made until we began descending steeply to Zeta Pass, 3,990 feet. I almost slipped but caught myself in time to avoid an injury. The climb to the nippled South Carter Mountain Peak, at 4,458 feet, wasn't to difficult. A walk in the park to Middle Carter Mountain, 4,600 feet and to the open ledges on Mt. Lethe, 4,584 feet. There was nice scenery there but I paid little attention.

We were coming to a boggy area. Crossing over the bog boards I was trying to watch where I put my feet, when down I went on one of the boards hurting my knee. I tested the knee the best I could in my precarious position and it seemed okay. Only twenty more feet and I slipped on another bog board. This time I was flipped over on my back between the logs. Envision a turtle with a pack on its back, laying upside down between two logs and you have the picture.

My first thought was "What the heck is a bog doing over 4,200 ft. up on a mountain?" My next thought was of the commercial where the lady said she has fallen and can't get up. Talk about feeling ridiculous. I tried several times to get turned to where I could get a leg, arm or some protrusion of my body in a leverage position to turn over, but to no avail.

The next thing I knew Snapshot was looking down at me. I knew she was concerned but was doing everything she could to hold back laughing. After pulling me up and seeing I wasn't hurt, she could hold back no longer. When she did burst out laughing, I laughed with her. It actually eased the pain and humiliation. There really must be therapy in comedy. Then a terrible thought crossed my mind. What if I had been all alone? What if the bog had been full of water? What a position I had gotten myself into. Well, it turned out all right and with Snapshot involved it was funnier than all get out.

Except for a few humps it was almost flat to North Carter Mountain, elevation 4,530 feet. All of a sudden, the mountain ended and dropped right into trees. Thank goodness for those trees growing that high up. It was steep for about a thousand or so feet before it became a little more gradual to the trail to Imp Campsite. The trees served as excellent hand holds. We all decided this was a good time and place to stop and eat lunch.   There were two backpacks with no one around. Two young ladies eventually came up a blue-blazed trail from the campsite. They had gone after water. After a short visit, we found out that they were hiking south. They had their dog with them, which again reminded me of fond memories of hiking with my lovely little pup.

Mt. Moriah, at 4,049 feet, wasn't the steepest climb we had but the threat of rain was causing more than a little concern. It was dispelled when it only sprinkled for a while. We had a long down hill hike that started out steep and rough and we certainly did not need for it to be slippery to boot. After about two thousand feet, the trail became a gradual slope all the way to Rattle River Shelter. The Rattle River ran very close by the shelter making an inviting place for a lot of hikers to camp. They were there in numbers.

I was glad no one wanted to stop. I was getting awfully tired and grateful when the trail turned into an old road bed making hiking a lot easier. After 15.2 miles of a pretty tough trail, I was relieved to see Tweety Pie waiting. The A.T. came out on U.S. 2 Highway just east of Gorham. It was only a short drive to the motel where we got the same room as before.

That was not all that would be the same. After we had a pleasant dinner out and caught up on our laundry, Tweety Pie told me Snapshot and Stickflipper were going to continue hiking with me after all. I felt we had resolved our differences and were hiking with a lot less stress but their decision, or lack of it, had been weighing heavily on me. Tweety Pie and I were elated and relieved.

In the darkness of night, a tear ran down my cheek. Before my eyes closed I was wondering what I had done to cause so much trouble. The last thought before sleep was the answer. *We humans must learn how to respect each other some day in the future.*

JULY 28, 1995 - a group of south-bound hikers that had been staying in the hostel, came over to visit with us. They came in handy since we were getting ready to hit the Mahoosuc Section they had just come over. The young men were eager to give us their opinion and even gave Stickflipper a guide book for Maine. They described what I believed was an exaggerated view of how tough the Mahoosuc Notch would be. I couldn't help but think,

294

"Wait 'til you guys get over those mountains ahead of you."

Naturally we were concerned because the section had a reputation for being some of the toughest miles on the trail. My problem was, I saw rough as being elevation, climbing and steep declines and this trail was certainly not as high as what we had just hiked. The thing that really caused me a little worry was, we would not be meeting Tweety Pie until the end of the section.

We finally got back to the trail on U.S. Hwy. 2 at 10:15 a.m. Tweety Pie hauled the packs over the Androscoggin River to Hogan Road, saving us about a mile of carrying them. Hiking across some railroad tracks took us to the Leadmine Bridge over the river. A small dam and power plant were on the left, almost creating a lake, actually a bulge in the river. To the right the river narrowed and split off into two forks, with little islands in each one.

Reaching Hogan Road, we donned our packs to get ready for whatever. My husband and I are not necessarily emotional people but on this occasion we hugged and gave each other a quick kiss good-bye. As we left the graveled road, I told him we would see him in four days.

It was only 760 ft. elevation when we started down a woods road. Shortly after leaving the road we ran into stone steps, steep stone steps. As I started climbing up the steps I glanced down at my muscled legs. I'm not prone to be obese but one of the benefits of this hiking illness is you will eventually have very strong legs and little body fat, that is, after you hike as many miles as I have. I needed my legs for the next steep three miles to the summit of Mt. Hayes, 2,555 feet.

As I expected, it was not as rough as what we had been over. The sky was hazy but we still had some pretty good views. Looking to the southwest and down on the Androscoggin River Valley, I could see Gorham N.H. nestled on the southwest shore of the river. Lancaster Village was only a few miles northwest on the same shore.

Descending into a col, which is a pass between two mountain peaks in the same range, there was a fairly easy climb to reach the summit of Cascade Mountain, 2,631 feet. As we passed over the last hump of the wooded mountain, it was a surprisingly steep descent into Trident Col.

We decided to cut the hike short so we took the blue-blazed trail, 175 yards to our left, to the Trident Col Campsite. There was water from a brook a short distance away, so we pitched the tents. It was no disappointment that there was an outhouse nearby either. It was only 3:00 p.m. but we stopped because the next campsite was another five miles up the trail and we wanted to get an early start in the morning.

As the bugs closed in on us, we opted to build a bonfire to keep them at a distance. So far, the Mahoosuc Range has not lived up to its wild and rugged reputation but we have only penetrated 7.2 miles into it. Two southbound hikers came in to make camp. They said the wet, boggy areas caused them the biggest challenges. Boy, bring on them wet bogs. Den Mama loves those. It was relaxing to know I would not have to hike by myself. The tension seemed to have disappeared so I was ready to turn in early and get ready for whatever the next day would offer.

JULY 29, 1995 - it rained during the night and left us with some very wet tents. Taking them down wasn't the biggest problem but carrying the tents before having the time to dry them out, undeniably caused our loads to be heavier. Regardless, we started hiking at 6:30 a.m. so it would be a few hours before the sun rose high enough to even cause a little evaporation.

In about a mile we, had traversed a ridge passing the three peaks that form the Trident Col, bringing us to the 2,232 foot high Page Pond. As we passed the south side, we came to the outlet of the pond. Stepping lightly, we crossed over the beaver dam that formed the large pond. I pondered how those little creatures can build a structure that could hold back such a large body of water.

Leaving the dam and the pond to the deserving beavers we started a gradual climb to the east that got steeper by the minute, until we reached Wockett Ledge which was a spur off Bald Cap that extended to the north. Crossing a branch of Peabody Brook led us to a small ledge. We had to climb around one end before descending gradually to Dream Lake.

Skirting around the northern edge of the lake we missed the other branch of Peabody Brook, that runs out of that lake joining the branch we had just crossed. Together they rush as one, headlong down the ridge to the river below. We did, however, cross the inlet brook to the pond twice before going steeply up and down with the low spots through swampy woodland. No, I did not slip and fall in the murky mud.

Passing around the northwestern edge of the small Moss Pond we descended in a "U" curve that took us around the southwest shore of Gentian Pond Campsite. The Gentian Pond Campsite was dead ahead at an elevation of 2,166 feet. It was a good place to stop for a break. When I looked at my watch, it was about 11:00 a.m.

Leaving the campsite, the trail took us through a spruce grove and then started getting a lot rougher to a ridge. We crossed another small col to, and over, a couple of steep humps. After the last hump, was a small brook running through another col. The wet packs were really bearing down as we began another steep climb into some woods. Emerging from the woods, we found ourselves on open ledges of the lower peak of Mt. Success.

The openness at 3,565 feet and the sun bearing down, was enough of an invitation to spread out the wet tents to dry, at least enough to lighten our loads a little. Big mistake. No sooner than we got them spread out on the warm ledges, clouds blocked out the sun and a shower of rain started. As we put the now, wetter tents away, I felt like the ants must feel when we swipe our feet across their hill causing them to have to rebuild it again.

Well, we had a hard climb to the summit of Mt. Success, which was 3,565 ft., due to the doubly wet tents. It was a steady decline to a deep col then over a hump to another col when we saw it. The sign said New Hampshire-Maine State Line, Elevation 2,972 feet.

For a moment we were all silent and then the silence erupted into shouts of joy. Only a hiker, who has walked over a thousand miles of sometimes unbearable terrain, could possibly understand. We were in the last state going north on the mighty A.T.! Our yells echoed up and down the col. No one was close by to hear us and if there had been they would have understood, or they wouldn't have been up there anyway.

It was a semi-climax and gave us the energy to tote those wet tents the 0.5 miles to the junction of the A.T. and Carlo Col Blue-Blazed Trail. Carlo Col was actually a small box canyon. It was only another 0.3 miles to the Carlo Col Shelter. It had beautiful trees that normally I would have appreciated. Where there are trees, there is shade and tents don't dry too good in the shade. We put the wet tents out anyway, since we really had no choice. I felt like I was doing a weird, slow-motion sun dance, moving the tents here and there trying to get them under the brightest sun rays the trees would allow. Finally between the sun and the friction of being moved, they were dry.

After all that, we were able to take a different look at the shelter, with a picturesque small stream gurgling close by. And my friend, it was in Maine! After hiking with the wet tent for 10.5 miles, I was really tired. The miles were as the young men had said, long and hard. But then as I lay pondering the fact that I just might complete the old A.T. after all, I realized that all the miles up to this point had been agony or ecstasy. What good is one without the other?

JULY 30, 1995 - coming alive early, we started hiking at 6:30 a.m. As I said we were in a box canyon, so there was only one way to go, up. The direction we were going took us to the steep climb to the open summit of Mt. Carlo, 3,565 feet. Entering the woods to our left we descended into a sag. I kept expecting the extreme bog areas with every descent.

The trail was not too bad even with all the ups and downs gradually taking us up to the West Peak of Goose Eye Mountain, with a height of 3,860 feet. The hardest part to the East Peak was a slight drop to a low sag and a hedge hop back up to 3,794 feet. As we made a fairly steep drop to another sag between two peaks, it led us on to an open alpine ridge before reaching the floor of the sag, that became another box canyon.

As we continued to descend, we ended up in yet another box canyon, only this one was pretty wooded. As with Carlo Col, it was back to climbing to reach the North

Peak of Goose Eye Mountain at only 3,680 feet. I shouldn't say *only* 3,680 feet because how high and how rough a climb can be, depends how low you start.

It wasn't too bad a descent to a sag where we found the Full Goose Shelter. Quite a few hikers were camped there, so since it was only 11:00 a.m., we decided to just take a short break before going on to take on the Mahoosuc Notch.

The climb, immediately out of the shelter to the bare crest of the South Peak of Fulling Mill Mountain, 3,400 feet, wasn't much of a challenge. But when we gradually descended through scrub growth to its north end, the bottom fell out, revealing a steep descent down to the west end and beginning of the huge, difficult and dangerous Mahoosuc Notch. At the bottom of the descent, several trails met. Our A.T. took off easterly with a sharp right turn into the Notch.

No sooner than we made that turn, we felt cold air coming from below the boulders. As we encountered some of the sharpest rocks I had imagined could be on the trail, it caused me a great deal of concern. Large chunks of boulders were everywhere. Carefully following the white-blazes and arrows, I hoped they would get us safely through. They directed us around the huge boulders as often as possible, but it was impossible to keep from having to crawl over many.

When we began ducking under them with our heavy packs, my back felt like it was going to break in half. Finally the clearance was so low we actually had to take the packs off twice, tugging and pulling them behind us. One crevice got so narrow, as small as my frame is, even I had to remove my pack to get through.

Just as I had begun to think I had taken on more than my poor body could take, we encountered slippery moss on the rocks. It was inevitable this was going to take its toll on at least one of us, when just that quick, Snapshot slipped and fell, striking her jaw on a boulder. We were fearful the worst had happened and her jaw may be broken. We stopped in the best location we could find, while all three of us evaluated the seriousness of her injury. Thank the Lord she was able to move her mouth in a normal way, with some soreness. After a rest, she felt it was okay and we proceeded, *very carefully*.

Looking into an ominous crevice, it was so cold, there was actually ice below us. That explained the blasts of frigid air we had felt at the beginning of the notch. I expect there are caves under that place but I never heard it mentioned. My concern for our well-being turned into a deep sorrow, as I looked upon a deer lodged between two boulders, eyes saddened with death. It was difficult to overlook the terrible odor. A macabre specter entered my thoughts when I contemplated what it would be like for a human being, with all their emotions, to be trapped in that terrible situation. Another reason for *never* hiking alone on the challenging A.T.

Even though it had only been a mile through that jumbled mass of rocks, it took us two and one-half hours to hike it. As I looked up at the rough walls of the Mahoosic Notch, I could only speculate the difficulty of getting out of this mysterious, miserable place. It was like a big giant had taken a chisel and hammer and just cut a huge notch into the peak of a mountain. A very sloppy giant, I might add. He didn't clean up all the rubble he had made. Believe it or not, old Den Mama made it through his messy artistry, almost unscathed.

At the eastern end of the Notch, we took a break in a small clearing. We felt the hard part was over so we decided to hike on to Speck Pond Shelter and Campsite.

Crossing a brook, we looked upstream to our left into two smaller versions of the main notch. I had no desire to explore them.

We began the nine-tenths of a mile climb up the Mahoosuc Arm. The steeper it got, the more grateful I was that it was fairly dry. A rain, at that time, would have been disastrous. There was even some hand over hand rock climbing. Believe it or not, it was so easy I was getting just a little bit cocky when it happened. At a point where we could walk upright, I tripped on a stubby protrusion. In that twilight zone instant, when body and rock are going to meet, I knew I was getting ready to feel pain.

I could not get my arms under me quick enough to avoid my face making contact. As a result, my cheek got a nasty scrape that disguised the skin peeling off my knee and hand. Strange how the brain blocks off instant pain to allow such thoughts as, "Boy I didn't break my glasses." I was thankful until that excruciating, burning hurt that one must inevitably experience with abrasive injuries, was manifested. Treating myself in that place would have been inconvenient, to say the least, especially with all the clothing I needed to remove. So we continued.

It caused some concern when we found a full backpack just lying beside the trail, with no one around. In that area, who knows what could happen to a lone hiker? After looking around to see if someone might be injured, we continued the strenuous climb up the Mahoosuc Arm. A desperate young man came toward us. We were relieved when he told us it was his pack on the trail. He had lost his water bottle and it was the only one he had, so he had gone back up the trail to look for it. He was truly worried, as he should have been. Water was scarce going south and he hadn't found his water bottle.

Knowing the plight he was in, I gave him my 1 liter bottle, since I had another one in the Jeep. Water is a top priority to any hiker.

The open summit of Mahoosuc Arm was a welcomed sight. It had been a steep climb to get to this 3,777 ft. perch but it was a steady descent now into woods. Reaching Speck Pond, a key land mark, and crossing its outlet, we circled the eastern shore. It was here we found the young man's water bottle. He had instructed us to give it to a young lady at the Speck Pond Shelter, if we found her there.

Upon arriving, she was there and were we glad to see the shelter. It was 5:30 p.m., much later than I care to push the setting sun. There was a caretaker there also and even though it cost us $5.00 per person, we were more than glad to pay, after an extremely rough 10.1 miles. All of us were completely wiped out. The lady inquired about the young man and we told her he was okay. The conversation was cut as short as was possible without being too ill mannered.

After that, I went to the pond to survey my injuries. Washing my face, hand and checking my knee, my body was better off than I thought it would be. I still felt like I had been in a train wreck. After getting back to the cabin I fixed my supper, medicated my scrapes and called it a terrible day. The bed felt good, unless I turned the wrong way rubbing a sore spot. A lot of hikers camped there that night and it took a while before they quieted down. Hush up, my brain cried out and then, even it was silent.

JULY 31, 1995 - it was 6:00 a.m. before I could make myself move. After adjusting to the aching and soreness, I finally crawled out of my sleeping bag to find Snapshot and Stickflipper not too eager to rise either. I had worked muscles I didn't even know I had. Crawling over, under and between those rocks was not something you run into on the trail every day and I hoped it would not occur again.

Four Canadian fellows, who had obviously dragged themselves into the shelter the night before, were chattering in French-Canadian. We couldn't understand them, which was just as well. We were not in the mood for conversation even though they needed some instructions. They were trying to cook their breakfast over an open fire and not doing too well. I didn't envy them, so I mumbled, "Good luck." I don't think they understood a word. We did determine they were going south and with the size of a couple of them, I couldn't help but wonder how they would get there big rear ends between those rocks.

Turning almost due east away from the pond, it was a gradual ascent. At the base of Old Speck, you could hear the trickling of a stream trying to remain qualified as running water. It got steeper along an old open scrubby slide then gradual along a ridge to the summit of Old Speck. It wasn't that bad getting up there to 4,180 ft. Skirting a peaceful meadow, we began the descent.

It was steep at first, down a long ridge. The trail became enough of a grade changing to switchbacks which made the descent much easier, but a greater distance to travel. We followed a brook a short distance, then after leaving it I discovered a familiar trademark scratched in the dirt on the trial. It looked like this: $\underset{TP}{A}$ The T.P. stood for Tweety Pie, but for some comical reason I always thought of toilet paper!

He had developed the habit of hiking in a little way on the trail to let me know he was waiting and we were about to end our day's hike. We found him at the Grafton

Notch State Park parking area. He cringed when he saw my face but didn't make a big to-do over it. A Ranger told him about a camp- ground not too far away that was a good place. He was right. A peaceful river ran through it, making it easy to find an ideal place to pitch the tents for the night. It was just close enough to the river to hear the rippling flow but not so close as to encourage bugs and crawly things that live in and around rivers.

Like a group of children, we decided to go for a swim in the river. I waited for the others to try it out, then with some hesitancy I waded in. The running water was like a natural massage to my beaten body and, I believe, caused my scrapes and scratches to heal quicker. Since the hike that day had been so short (5 miles) I had plenty of time to enjoy the water.

Putting on one of my last clean outfits, I joined everybody for a drive to the small town of Bethel, Maine. Of course, we all took our dirty laundry with us and found a laundromat. After looking the little town over. I got myself my favorite celebration treat, a vanilla ice cream cone. The short drive back to the campground gave me a chance to reflect on the fact that I was in the last stage of the A.T.

It was so peaceful in that camp, I was looking forward to the quiet, calm night. With my good old Tweety Pie with me, however brief, I knew I would sleep well. The Mahoosuc Mountain Range in Maine had been conquered by me, Den Mama, and was I proud! With Just 270 miles to hike, my dream would be fulfilled! I watched as my husband repaired the rubber tip on my hiking staff with black electric tape. With each round he made with the tape, securing tip to staff, I thought how grateful I was to him and all the people who had helped me get that far.

"Thanks Tweety Pie," I thought. "That tip might just make it the rest of the way. . . .if I can".

Under the starry sky I went to my sleeping bag. I lay there with the rustling of the river, the croaking of the frogs and I was indeed at peace. Sleep could only magnify that peace, right? Wrong! I had a frightening nightmare, where I was again in the Mahoosuc Notch. Snapshot was falling into one of those mysterious places where the cold air was seeping to the trail. She hit her jaw on a rock and it broke as I was trying to grab her to pull her away from the awful chasm. For a moment her body turned into that little deer, withering away into nothingness. I felt my flesh tearing as I was dragged down with her. Then I raised up in the tent screaming an awful gurgling sound. At least I thought I was screaming, but Tweety Pie had not budged. I was still shaking as I lay back. Fighting sleep, I realized that all things are not always our friend. Tonight sleep had betrayed me. Amnesia took over and sleep must have once again befriended me.

AUGUST 1, 1995 - back at Grafton Notch for a reference, we started at 1,550 feet elevation. At 6:30 a.m. we began the climb up to the West Peak of Baldpate Mountain. Crossing a stream at the base, we made it to the first plateau and it was steep in a few places. From the knob of the plateau, it was about a mile before we began the second stage, that was a steady steep climb to the partially open summit.

It was 3,662 feet up there. One thing I did notice right off, was Baldpate Mountain was like one, huge, round smooth rock, rather than the jagged things we had on the Mahoosuc Range. Hiking was a lot better now. I wasn't as fearful of being scraped and cut, should I fall. The two peaks on that mountain were separate and distinct protrusions as we descended into the sag between them, with a small canyon at the bottom.

Because of the drop into the canyon, it was about a half mile vertical climb to the East Peak of Baldpate, plus another couple hundred feet higher. This summit was all open and presented us with a 360° view of the spectacular, tall mountains we had crossed. Old Speck loomed high but visibility was so keen, we could see Mt. Washington looming in the far off horizon, with its apparently ever-present crown of white clouds circling around its royal peak. "Wear it proudly, wondrous mountain," I thought.

As we looked to the north, it was easy to see the mountains were getting lower. That did not necessarily mean it would be easier. One last peek over to the west, was a lot like looking back into my past. Those marvelous mountains had changed me. Before we dove off the steep drop to Little Baldpate Mountain, which was little more than a small cleft of the larger mountain, I had many reflections back on the woman who had started all this.

I was an introvert that many took as arrogance. Actually I had a very low self-esteem. To think I would ever enter a history of extraordinary accomplishment, was the last thing on my mind. Visions of the Grand Canyon, where whatever it was that touched me, infected me, or inspired me, tripped lightly before my eyes. "I am now Den Mama," I wanted to shout. "I am a woman of the mountains." That caused me to pause in my thinking. Was I now a piece of the pioneer past?

As we began the steep decline, I almost stumbled and fell. I had entered a world that made me more zombie than living creature and this is no place to be day dreaming. The weather was perfect and except for the breezy wisps that seemed always to frequent the higher peaks, the sky was blue as far as you could see.

A large cairn had marked the summit of East Baldpate specifying its elevation as being 3,812 feet. Almost vertical, we descended 1,437 feet in less than 1.0 mile with only a half mile plateau near the bottom, before the Frye Brook Valley. The Frye Notch Lean-to provided us a good place to take a well-needed break. The Brook was full and meandering through the valley to its last plunge west, to a branch of the Ellis River.

After tossing a few pebbles into the brook, we began the steep, but short, climb up Surplus Mountain. It was a gradual roller coaster type trail that descended to East B Hill Road. Old faithful, Tweety Pie, was there with his always wide smile to greet us. You know, now that I think about it, you rarely see him angry. I think it's because he's like a volcano. You don't want to see him erupt, but once every century.

It was a peaceful, relaxing drive into Andover, Maine, with the West Branch of the Ellis River running near the Pine Ellis Lodge. It was full of hikers, therefore, no vacancies. There was a campground on Ellis River, where we were able to camp. One of the few covered bridges left in the New England area made the campsite unique. Later on, in a very relaxing atmosphere, two hiking friends came by. Nurse Without a Purse and Water Witch had managed to get into the Pine Ellis Lodge and strolled over to our camp to visit.

It was as usual, a surprising, but pleasant experience. After sharing our different adventures, which involved the Mahoosuc Notch, I withdrew to enjoy a hot shower and to reflect on my own thoughts. It had been a normal but tiring 10.5 mile hike and I was eager to get ready for the next day, mentally and physically. Tweety

Pie is much more of a talker than I am, so he came to bed later.

I love the sound of running water in a stream. It always has a hypnotic affect on our human minds. As the evening shade drew lower, the covered bridge became a focus of my attention. I watched the shadows change the covered bridge from a normal scene in the sunlight, to a strange, almost spooky, scene the darker the night became. When the moon began casting its eerie glow over the river and bridge canopy, I was glad when Tweety Pie put his wooden leg beside him and I could hear his breathing.

The image of the bridge transformed itself into the recesses of my mind. Like a computer program I was able to decorate the scenery around it and along with the time machine in my brain, I was able to envision Model T's coming home to Andover, after a day out. Back even further in time, I replaced them with horses and carriages with surreys on top and gaily dressed women and dignified men arriving, after a party in a nearby mansion. I guess the little child in us, that retains the magic of fantasy, never really disappears. Then all was blank in the mystery of sleep, that seems never to recognize time at all.

AUGUST 2, 1995 - as we arrived back to East B Hill Road, it intersected the trail partially up the hill of the first stage of our climb to Wyman Mt. It was 6:45 a.m. and we were invigorated to the point that the two miles uphill went by pretty fast. When we topped a hump, we looked down on a wonderful campsite. There was a gravel road that ran right beside Surplus Pond and Ford Burroughs Brook running beside it, on its journey south. It was such an ideal campsite, we decided to have Tweety Pie take us back there at the end of the day's hike.

The rest of the hike up Wyman Mountain was a pleasant easy walk. Even though the summit was only 2,945 feet, it was partially forested. An easy descent and even easier small ascent brought us to Hall Mountain Lean-To, perched on top of a large knoll. Going over the rounded dome I looked down into trees and what appeared to be a shear drop. This is where switchbacks prove their usefulness. Without them, some of these mountains would almost require a mountain climber to get up and down them. Of course, it wouldn't be a challenge to those rugged individuals. They would use the trees for their rigging and I suppose it would be a piece of cake.

Nevertheless, we made the descent into the deep Sawyer Notch. Almost to the bottom of the notch, we crossed Sawyer Brook. Looking up the trail I couldn't believe it was as steep as it appeared, but it was. I was huffing and puffing after the near scramble, 1,100 feet up what was Moody Mountain. There was a good place to survey where we had just been, with a bird's eye view. Looking down into Sawyer Notch was fascinating, but looking across that deep gorge to the decline we had just taken, was nothing short of looking back into an expanse of time.

On the summit there was about a half mile to a big hump that took us down about 100 feet of steep decline, then leveled off somewhat before it turned to as much drop as we had down into Sawyer Notch. Black Brook was crossed and then it was only a short distance through woods to South Arm Road.

It was 1:00 p.m. and I was more than ready for the waiting Tweety Pie to take us back to Surplus Pond. We jostled and bumped over the dirt road that would have been a struggle for a regular car. As a matter of fact, it was so rough it would have torn one apart. But our good old jeep made it with flying colors.

The campground was as nice as we had expected, so we settled in for a restful evening. Snapshot fried her delicious potatoes with onions mixed in. Later, I carried the skillet and utensils down a dirt road that led to the pond. A piped spring was flowing freely, but certainly wasn't the ideal way to clean greasy cookware. Back in the old days, they used sand or dirt to remove the lard the best they could. Nowadays a little liquid Palmolive goes a long way.

As I moseyed back to the camp with my nearly cleaned cookware, a thru-hiker passed through going north. He stopped just long enough to be friendly. He called himself Salamander and even had a small rubber one on his pack. I wondered if he knew all the philosophy involving the little lizard-like creature.

The mythical version was supposed to be able to endure direct contact with fire and suffer no harm. Paracelsus even theorized that the animal lived in fire and actually was an element of it. Some portable stoves or incinerators are called Salamander. Well, this guy was never going to get caught standing still long enough to get burned by fire. I doubt that any salamander or lizard could keep up with him, as he turned and zipped up the trail.

Strangely, hikers are a lot like truck drivers. They don't look or act like they know much, but many are very educated and really are philosophers in their own right. In short, I'll just bet he knows all about the little soft-skinned things that he chose to honor with his trail name. He just didn't have time to talk about it. "Good luck Salamander and may the fire of life always be with you."

It was a pretty rough 10 miles that day, and I couldn't believe that Stickflipper had the energy to go looking for moose. He wandered down to the pond and I hoped he would let us know if he ran across one of the huge animals. We were entering into country where they frequent, so it was not beyond the realm of possibility. When Tweety Pie and I entered our tent for bed, there had been no call of the wild from Stickflipper. Tweety Pie drifted off and I listened to the routine of his deep breathing. Frogs, from the pond, chirped in providing another beat and I almost began keeping time with my foot. But the rhythm of the night only played me into the darkest of darkness, sleep.

AUGUST 3, 1995 - it wasn't just the fact that I was tired the day before that made the old road feel rough. It was just as rough then as we were jostled from left to right in the jeep. The only reason we were not bumping into each other was because we were rocking in the same directions. Finally, we reached the highway and eventually South Arm Road where we had left off. At 7:00 a.m. we said our good-byes and good lucks and immediately mounted the climb up Old Blue Mountain.

If you recall, I mentioned that the elevation of a mountain does not always dictate the difficulty of getting over one. Well, this mountain is 3,600 feet tall and I thought we were going straight up the first thousand or so feet. Over one hump we could get a little better grip. Over another and I felt almost horizontal again.

Trees were also hanging on for dear life, with their roots protruding above ground. Many roots were jutting up in the trail so we had to be cautious not to stumble on them. They have tricky ways of grabbing and tangling boots. That's one of the reasons Stickflipper always hiked in front of us. Unfortunately, this was not a good day to be the leader. As he passed over one root he disturbed a world that is always best left alone.

It started out like the hum of war planes and then the attack on three unwary hikers, clad only in shorts. This is certainly not the kind of garb one should be in, once a war has been declared. A few Yellow Jackets took aim at Stickflipper's legs, resulting in two hits.

Their nest was under the tree roots where they thought they were safe. Quite frankly, as far as we were concerned, they were. Snapshot and I, to coin a phrase, made a *beeline* which turned out to be a big loop around the tree root, taking us off into the brush. When we thought it was safe, we reentered the trail. One hotshot solo flyer, who wasn't willing to accept our surrender and retreat, came buzzing from my rear. Wham! He was a good shot and I felt him hit me in the back. However the cowardly, Yellow Jacket Red Barron had failed to hit open territory and was lodged under my pack strap.

I called for reinforcement and Colonel Snapshot came to my rescue. After her counter attacks ended, the battle of the Yellow Jackets seemed over. Courageous Snapshot escaped injury, so Stickflipper and I were the only casualties. I was in pain and I did not feel the least bit sorry for the little coward that stabbed me in the back.

Maybe Mother Nature heard my thoughts about that treacherous Yellow Jacket. Just as we started the steep climb to the peak of Old Blue Mountain, it became dangerously misty and foggy. When we reached the needle-like summit I felt like a blind person.

There was supposed to be a good view of the surrounding mountains including Clearwater Brook running to the west, making the bottom part of the trunk of Elephant Mountain. But we were cheated, so we felt our way down the descent, that was almost as steep as the ascent had been, until it swooped off to be gradually level and eventually flat.

We did have a close up look at what I would call the rump of Elephant Mountain. In reality, it was the eastern edge of the mountain. It was easy hiking compared to the steep climbs we had been experiencing. The rump we went over was about 3,300 ft. elevation and as we gradually descended into a loop, it was a higher climb to the main summit of Bemis Mountain, 3,592 feet. You could call it the West Peak, since this mountain has three other minor peaks.

From this point on, it was obvious we would be steadily working our way down. It was a fairly steep descent to the gully between West and Third Peak of Bennis Mountain. It was an easy walk up and over the hump of Third Peak at 3,115 feet. It was almost a level hike of about one and a half miles to the slight ascent to Second Peak, 2,915 feet. The descent was a little more difficult to the gutter-like separation, to a slight incline to the first and final peak of Bemis Mountain, 2,604 feet.

I hadn't realized how important the scenery was to me, until I was denied any at all. The misty, almost foggy atmosphere, had shut down all but the trail in front of us and 50 or so feet in all directions. Somewhere below and around us, streams, valleys, lakes and mountains were hiding.

A slight, short slope was easy to reach and the ground again became vertical. Way below, was an old railroad bed and Bemis Stream. The rocks, roots and what little dirt clung to the trail were getting extremely slippery. Not the best condition to be making a dangerous steep decline. Step by step, we cautiously made our way down to about 1,600 ft. elevation. It felt good to feel the trail curve back to somewhat level.

Crossing the railroad bed, we carefully maneuvered over rocks to get to the other bank of Bemis Stream. I was getting awfully tired as I looked up to where Highway 17 cut across the mountain. It was a steep 600 ft. climb, but I knew Tweety Pie would be waiting. Believe me, as we crawled up to the hard surfaced road, I was glad to see that jeep.

As we drove north to Rangley State Park, the weather and my weariness had caused me to be a little depressed. All of a sudden, just before we got to our campsite, a big, brown moose was arrogantly crossing the highway. I got so excited, my mood changed instantly. After all, this was the first moose I had ever seen, except on television.

Tweety Pie brought the jeep to a halt and we managed to get a good picture before the large, proud animal went into the brush. He paused long enough to look back as if to say, "What are you weird looking two-legged creatures looking at?" and then he was gone. Even though I was still worn out, my doldrums were gone as well.

After getting a tentsite, Tweety Pie built a big bonfire which helped to dry our clothes somewhat, but definitely warmed the old bones to the point of being tolerable. After a marvelous hot shower, I discovered that Tweety Pie had supplied Snapshot with potatoes and onions. She grinned and told him, "As long you buy em', I'll fix em'." She did and they were as good as ever. She is definitely one of those southern cooks you hear about.

It was a rough and tough hike of 13.3 miles that day, but I was much closer to the end of my dream trail.

AUGUST 4, 1995 - it was a rainy night in Maine, so things were dripping that morning. We barely ate our breakfast and got the tents down, when the skies opened up with a soaking downpour. My goal was getting close so I informed Tweety Pie to get us back to Hwy. 17.

At 7:15 a.m. we began climbing Spruce Mountain, reaching its summit of 2,530 feet on a slippery trail. As we skirted the north shore of Moxie Pond, my thoughts turned back to the feisty Moxie Turtle I had met on the trail back in 1994. Since she lived in Maine, I could not help but wonder if she had chosen her trail name from this little pond. Or, possibly, they had named the pond after her. I kind of doubt it, since the maps had been put together before she started nurturing her hiking illness.

Back up to 2,700 ft. over a fairly steep ascent and descent of a dome- shaped Bates Ledge. It was obvious, by then, that nature was going to pour water on us intermittently, the rest of the day. By the time we got to Long Pond and the Sabbath Day Pond Lean-to, she was even putting the blinders on us in the form of wet soaking fog. Yuck! The trail was slippery, we were getting soaked and now any view, we might have had, was all but gone.

Feeling our way up to about 3,000 ft. we found ourselves on a gradual up and down descent. Around noon, we came to an area where we could look down on a beaver pond. Snapshot was the first to see it as we were passing. It was the biggest bull moose I had ever seen. He was standing in the pond, with antlers that made the big creature look like he could fly, if he had a large enough runway.

He looked up and got an eyeball on us. Evidently he wasn't as curious about us as we were of him because he lifted those big hoofs and splashed water as high as I do, when I belly flop in a pool. Each time a hoof hit the surface, another splash ensued. He might not be able to fly, but he sure got through that water in a hurry. How can something look so clumsy and yet end up graceful?

Stickflipper was slightly ahead of us and rushed as fast as his hands would move to get a picture. Splish splash, splish splash and just like that, the big moose disappeared into the woods. Perhaps gone forever from our view, but he was locked in the camera and our memories, whenever we would desire to recall that wondrous experience on the A.T. By the time we reached Little Swift River Pond Campsite, it was apparent we were going downhill, big time. An outdoor privy, right beside the trail, presented an opportune time for a necessary, natural break.

The fog was clearing a little bit, enough to reveal that this was a lovely place. We were all relieved as we began the gradual step ladder descent. crossing a stream and passing another pond, we reached a knoll and looked down on the swooping last downhill to Hwy. 4 beside Sandy River. It was 2:45 p.m. and we were like wet packrats when we saw Tweety Pie.

As the jeep past four connected ponds formed by the river, the highway wound its way north by northwest to a town called Rangely. Not far on our left, we passed a huge body of water shaped like an upside down sea horse. I thought it was a lake but it turned out to be called Long Pond. I hate to keep repeating myself, but I have yet to figure out how they designate a lake from a pond, up in that country.

Arriving at the Hostel in Rangely I was starving so before doing anything else we drove to a little restaurant by Rangely Lake, where we got some juicy hamburgers that hit the spot. Down by the lake, ducks were bobbing and swimming while children tossed bread, and whatever items of food they could muster. It would be hard to describe which were the happier, the kids or the geese. It made me homesick.

Back at the hostel we set about putting the tents out to dry and getting our backpacks ready for, what I suspected might be, a pretty rough day tomorrow. All that done, it was time to reflect on the 13 miles we had hiked, with little or no cooperation from Mother Nature. Then it was the hot shower I had been waiting for.

Savoring every warm drop of water that melted my weariness into sleepy lethargy, I wondered why water was so marvelous at times and so cruel and miserable at others. I guess its that old adage, agony and ecstasy. You can't have one without the other. Tucked in my blanket, I told my brain to stop skip jumping about every subject in the world and eventually it obeyed.

AUGUST 5, 1995 - I felt like doing a reverse rain dance to get the clouds to roll back and give me a break from the terrible soaking moister that makes every aspect of hiking difficult. I don't really believe anyone makes Mother Nature change her attitude about anything. Talk about a stubborn lady.

Tweety Pie reminded us of another item that we all take for granted in everyday life. The jeep needed servicing. Even though we are a long way from our regular people who look after our equipment, it still had to be done. The first problem he had, was finding the oil that the jeep was used too. No one in Rangely had the correct brand.

I knew better than to risk asking my husband what difference it made. He had already informed me a long time ago that men never mix the oil brand. It has something to do with viscosity, molecular breakdown, whatever that means. One man told him there was a good old Wal-Mart in Farmington that had a wide variety.

The rain and this complication, made an ideal time to do some   shopping. We had enough of being soaked and having our views blocked out, so it wasn't hard to get a unanimous decision. Tweety Pie got his oil. I bought a supply of food items. Snapshot and Stickflipper picked up camera film and some special food items that appealed to them. We had a load when we came out of there.

After eating out, my two companions and I decided to go back to the trail on Hwy. 4. It was only 1:00 p.m. when we started hiking and Tweety Pie had his jeep to service anyway. It's important to stay in the hiking mode because when you have been out as long as we had, it's easy to get discouraged and head for home. Even though it was only 1.6 miles to Piazza Rock Lean-To, we were back on the trail.

You never know when or where your going to find an old hiking acquaintance. To my surprise, when we got to the Lean-to, that's exactly what happened. Looking surprised and as indecisive as we were, there in her sleeping bag, sat Water Witch. I liked her a lot so it was a fun meeting. Since heavenly waters started to dump on us again, it wasn't hard to decide to just stay where we had shelter.

A few day hikers stopped by to get in out of the rain but as soon as it eased up a bit, they moved on. Even though there was a caretaker, there wasn't any camping fee which never hurts. Piazza Rock Lean-to is one of the oldest shelters on the A.T., built back in 1935.

The continual rain made the temperature comfortable enough to snuggle into my sleeping blanket, so I crawled in early and let the steady, hypnotic drip, drop lull me into a fantasy-type sleep. It was about as relaxing a rest one can experience. The trouble was, the drip, drop turned into gushing, rushing deluge during the night and there is very little rhythm in that. But I slept.

AUGUST 6, 1995 - the hard night's rain made us slow getting around in the heavy wet morning air. As I have said, I now firmly believe the pressure of being on the trail so long was being manifested. Mentioning the subject would have been unwise, because I always felt like I was playing a delicate balancing act with Snapshot and Stickflipper, anyway. Negativity could have sent them off, helter skelter to finish, which would have left me behind. Life is all about selfishness and greed anyway, I believe. I never pulled any punches about my objective, finish the A.T.

At 7:45 a.m. we were finally able to get back on the wet, slippery trail. Surprisingly, it was easy walking on a gradual uphill slope until we got close to Ethel Pond. A steeper hill, up to a circle around the pond, was a threat of things to come. Crossing the swift running Saddleback Stream, the trail stayed fairly easy until we reached Eddy Pond and its outlet where we began the real climb up Saddleback Mountain.

It was steep and slick until the trees ended at 3,750 feet, then the humpback rounded off gradually to the highest summit at 4,120 feet. The final leg to that peak was not too hard, but it was smooth bedrock up there so we had to watch out for slips. When they named that mountain, they knew what they were doing. We were on the back part of the saddle and that meant we had a drop before the horn. The drop was much steeper than the ascent to the peaked horn. Trees were sparse for the next 2.9 miles and it was cold and clammy. It didn't take long before the familiar damp fog moved in on us. We were supposed to see Katahdin and Mt. Washington off in the distance and I don't doubt that on a clear day you could. All we saw was white to a greyish blur. Boring!

The deep valley, between the Saddleback Mountain's high back and its cantel (horn), was more like the deep Spanish or Brazilian saddles. Except for the horn, it was not too difficult a climb. When we almost slid down the horn to the valley below, we discovered that the horn formed the back part of Saddleback Junior. Its horn was much steeper and rocky to climb. Again, if you saw the mountains from a distance, Junior would be an even deeper Spanish Saddle, but lower in elevation, 3,655 ft.

It wasn't quite as steep dropping off Saddleback Junior but the rocks didn't make it seem any easier. In a valley, at the bottom, was the Poplar Ridge Lean-To. Since it was 2:20 p.m. and the temperature had dropped to only 58°, we were ready to call it a day. When my body's adrenaline came down off the steep descent and the inactivity set in, I became chilled. "Lord," I thought. "I hope its just the temperature and I'm not coming down with something."

After crawling into my sleeping bag, I got my body temperature up and I was relieved enough to fix myself a meager supper. Close by, a little brook was flowing pretty good and bubbling over small boulders. It made a safe, cold water supply. Everyone was more than ready to turn in. As I lay in my warm sleeping bag, I said a prayer that the plaguing weather would end and brighten things up a bit. Depression is bad enough when it's in your own mind, but when a gray mystic cloud of depression is following you all over the mountains, it seems even more out of your control. "Oh well," I thought, "there is tomorrow." Then I shivered once more and the switch tripped consciousness off.

AUGUST 7, 1995 - I dragged my body out of the sleeping bag and entered the cold morning air. Hurriedly, we prepared to leave the lean-to at 6:00 a.m. It was a short hike to the edge of Poplar Ridge, where we looked down into the misty darkness and mysterious trees below. We were standing on the ridge at 3,120 ft. Somewhere below, was a cut through the mountains and an old railroad bed. That somewhere was at an elevation of 1,500 ft. It didn't take a mathematician to figure this would be a long drop.

We reached the treeline quickly, which always helped in case one should slip. The first thousand feet was steep until we reached a fairly level plateau. The last 500 ft. was a bearcat. Orbeton Stream lay at the very bottom of the canyon and was flowing at a good clip, due to all the moister the mountains had been receiving.

Snapshot and Stickflipper, with their long legs, entered the crossing first, stepping from one exposed boulder to the next. From the bank it looked pretty easy. On the other side they signaled it was my turn. Forgetting how much shorter my legs were than theirs, I reached one span of boulders in the middle of the swift running water that provided a reminder, one moment to late.

It must have looked ridiculous to see me balancing on the one boulder while the ruler in my eyes was telling me that distance and leg length did not compute. Immediately my brain took the knowledge and started calculating another landing. There it was, a smaller rock within my leg's span. The only problem was, it would be like landing a Boeing 707 on a Piper Cub runway.

Too late to worry about that, as off I went. Everything that could go wrong did, in those split seconds. The little runway was slippery as grease on a hog's back. The legs of my jet were trying to go in every direction at the same time. All that was left was to pick the softest landing smack dab in the middle of the stream. So down I went.

There I was, sprawled in the water in a sitting position. The fast moving water was treating my body like a paper sailboat with a stabilizer dragging on the bottom. Every time the water built up behind me, I felt a surge push me further down stream with my rump scraping along on the rocky bottom.

Stickflipper, seeing my plight, was about to come in after me, so I hollered "Wait, let me try to get out by myself." I managed to work myself over on my hands and knees. Pushing myself up, I waded on an angle with the current to the other bank. At least I was the only soaked rat in the group. The 50° temperature started to make its effect felt immediately. I knew if I started hiking, I would probably warm up and dry my boots and shorts quicker. Everything in my backpack was wrapped in plastic, so I hoped it remained dry.

It was straight up hill across the old railroad bed, which was no more than a rocky road now. My boots squished and were even more slippery than usual, as we climbed alongside Sluice Brook that dumped into Orbeton Stream, now 700 ft. below. It, too, was running as if it had a late appointment to keep with my less-than-favorite swimming hole.

Just after crossing our friendly brook on an up hill grade, we came to a big plateau that served well as a breathing place before continuing our climb to the summit of Lone Mountain. After reaching that place, we crossed an old logging road where we found a single tent. A head emerged with a big smile and a cheery good morning. Water Witch had obviously expected us to catch her and was not as surprised as we were. I asked her if she was ready to go on up the mountain. She answered she was still too tired and would maybe catch us later. We were anxious to make time so we moved on crossing another stream and road. Soon after crossing the old road the trail sloped upward, and then again steeper as we neared the summit.

It was almost level across Lone Mountain, except for a few rolling knolls. A gentle slope brought us down into a valley where the Spaulding Mountain Lean-to had been erected. After the break with Water Witch we were in no mood to stop, so we immediately began the long climb to the needle peak of Spaulding Mountain. The climb up the summit, 3,988 feet, went well, but was steep and rough, going down.

We circled around a familiar mountain, that almost everyone has heard about in the ski reports on the boob tube. At the base of Sugarloaf Mountain, which is considerably above 3,500 ft., we found a ski resort kept open for hikers in the summer months. A side trail led to the summit which was 4,237 feet high. It was only 0.6 miles to the summit, but I was willing to pass it up, knowing the view would have been spectacular.

Descending on down from where we were was going to be difficult enough. Wearing the wet boots for as long as I had, was a violation of any hiker's rules. My poor feet and legs served as a reminder. The pain was getting worse, especially in my right leg. At first the descent wasn't so rough, more like rounding the top of a globe and then we went down, and I mean almost straight down.

The view into this deep ravine wasn't too shabby with the South Branch Carrabassett winding its way at the bottom. Caribou Valley Road crossed through at the base of what appeared to be a very steep Crocker Mountain. Finally, the trail sloped down to the river bank.

South Branch Carrabassett River was not as full as it could have been but we still had to cross on rocks. Would you believe I made it across without taking another cold dip? A welcomed site was waiting at the Caribou Valley Road. Desperately hugging Tweety Pie and almost shifting too much weight onto his wooden leg, I told him about my aching legs. We decided to pitch our tents right there by the road. It really wasn't a bad campsite with the river running below and Crocker Mountain in our background.

All in all, a pretty good 13.2 miles, even with the steep climbs and my unexpected bath. The weather had been about as good as you could ask. I looked back on it with a good attitude but hiking in those wet boots was not my idea of a walk in the park.

Water Witch and a new companion, Box Car Jerry, came wandering by our camp. Late in the afternoon with Crocker Mountain looming ahead, they decided to pitch camp with us. Tweety Pie made a big warm bonfire to help keep the bugs away, while I unpacked my sleeping bag, barely wet from the dunking in the stream. My Band-Aids were not in a Ziplock plastic bag so they were soaked. They are an important item on the trail so I laid them out to dry in the sun. After a fireside chat with everybody I turned in, looking forward to dry clothes and boots the next day.

AUGUST 8, 1995 - feeling pretty good, I helped take the tents down. Afterwards we had a standard breakfast of oatmeal, pop tart and tea. While donning my pack, I looked up at the steep Crocker Mountain and its twin peaks looming up there somewhere in the dawn. As we crossed the gravel Caribou Valley Road I glanced at my watch, 6:30 a.m., right on schedule.

It was uphill from the road and things were going good to the side road to Crocker Cirque Campsite. A cirque, in this case, is a cut in the side of a mountain like an amphitheater. One last short slant and it got steep, very steep and rough. The trees were clinging to the side of this mountain as desperately as we were, which really saps your energy and makes a short distance feel like ten miles. At last it curved into an incline, that I handled somewhat better.

At 4,010 feet I made the last lunge to the snub-tipped needle peak. Actually, the highest point of South Peak was little more than a rocky outcrop. Descending into the saddle between the peaks was easy and the climb up to the higher North Peak (4,228 feet) went pretty well.

From the more rounded peak, I looked to the east at the Bigelow Range of mountains with the beautiful Carrabassett Valley winding its way between the many mountains. I was savoring those views because I knew, near the end of the trail, we would be traversing lowlands and they would only be a memory.

Looking down the trail, there were lots of trees whose tops revealed a gentle slope on the descent. As we began the exit from the peak, it wasn't long before we came to a small stream running through a lovely grove of white birch. I hated to leave such a peaceful place behind.

A little ways further we topped a small hump that signaled an easy hike down to Maine Highway 27. Tweety Pie was there and asked us to hike on over to Stratton Brook Pond Road. It was only 0.8 miles, so no one gave him any static, besides it brought our total day's hike up to an even ten miles. It was a short drive for Tweety Pie to the road. From there we went to Stratton, where we checked into a motel.

A nice little restaurant provided us a tasty supper, after which it was wash the laundry time. That went fast so I went back to the room to enjoy a hot shower. Boy, do we take our luxuries at home for granted! If I have not gained anything else out of this hiking illness, I have learned to love the comforts most of us have available to us in our everyday lives.

After drying my hair, I went out to where the others were talking to a delightful thru-hiker. Tweety Pie had met her earlier and they had enjoyed a nice visit. She then left him to wait for us. Holly, a petite school teacher, was hiking all by herself. Listening to her tell about her experiences, one could detect a truly jolly attitude. I told her that a good trail name for her would be, "Jolly Holly."

Not being much of a talker I went back to my room to catch up on the news. The television took about an hour to lull, or bore me into a peaceful sleep that was only disturbed briefly when my husband decided to call it a day. In case you have any misunderstanding, Tweety Pie is, hands down, the talker in our family. . . . but things they are a changin'.

AUGUST 9, 1995 - there was a tension in the air as we drove back to Stratton Brook Pond Road. I had noticed it yesterday. The large peaks are fading away and each one, from here on in, will be a major mark to the end of a dream. At 6:15 a.m. we began slackpacking.

Bigelow Mountain hovered above with a promise of new adventure. Make no mistake, I knew it was still going to be rough for some time to follow. The initial climb started a lot like it had up Crocker Mountain except a gentler slope. We made our way across Stratton Brook on a wooden foot bridge. The cool water of the brook below and the morning air made my skin tingle but not for long, as adrenaline built for a steep climb.

The farther we went, the steeper the slope and the warmer my body temperature became. Passing an interesting slab cave system I kept expecting the worst, when just like that we came over a knoll onto a large ledge. Only a short walk further, we looked down on the second highest pond on the A.T. (3,250 ft.) The Horns Pond had two lean-tos named after it, nestled close by on an eagles perch. A very friendly caretaker, who was stationed there, showed us platforms that could handle six tents each. Water was available from a small spring or from the pond itself. The experimental solar privy was an interesting thing, at least for hikers.

Immediately after leaving the Horn Pond Lean-tos, it was almost a vertical climb on a steep and rocky trail to the South Horn of big Bigelow. On the way up there was a boxed-in spring right beside the trail. It was like nature had put a luxurious water fountain here for a refreshing break. No water fountain ever had water like this . . . ice cold and pure. I never drank so much water at one time in my life. Indeed, the elixir was so good I couldn't get enough. If we had water like this at home, I think the soda pop business would be in danger.

Easy to see why they call the minor peaks, horns. That's exactly what South Horn, at 3,805 feet was. I don't understand why they name these horns at all, unless, back in the old days it was for landmarks to keep the settlers from getting lost on those huge mountains. South Horn presented us with a bird's eye view of The Horns Pond below.

Dropping off the horn on a short decline into a rolling valley, it was about a mile before we climbed West Peak, which was nothing like climbing South Horn. From there we looked down into a narrow cleft with the Avery Memorial Lean-to tucked into it. We could also look straight across at Avery Peak, that we would climb later.

It was steep and rocky down into the cleft for a short distance. The Myron H. Avery Lean-To accommodated six tent platforms with a small spring nearby for water. I was honored to be there since Myron H. Avery was the first person to section hike the entire Appalachian Trail. He completed the A.T. in 1936 and continued to write guide books and design shelters for dreamers, like me.

This shelter was built in his honor in 1953. The man's contributions to hikers cannot be listed or overlooked. The A.T. was his life. As I looked at the plaque embedded in a rock to honor his memory, I had never associated a mortal with my gratitude for this trail, as I did at that moment. Climbing Avery Peak was not as difficult as I had anticipated, but it would not have mattered. That one I did gladly for Avery.

We were on the East Summit of Bigelow Mountain which was only slightly lower than West Peak at 4,088 ft., the last high point of Bigelow Mountain. I was glad they named this one after Avery, rather than West Peak, because the view was outstanding.

The Barren-Chair Range was off in the distant Northeast Appalachian Chain, including Mt. Washington, to the southwest. In that, almost complete, panorama you could even see the Canadian Border Mountains. Couple that with the Northeast view of Flagstaff Lake sprawling below us and you had a peak worthy of the memory of Mr. Avery. What a sight and what a man!

Hikers were gathering on this memorable spot, so we decided to leave it for them to admire the awesome view. The weather was so clear, as we made the launch off the peak, that you could see Sugarloaf Mountain in the distance.

Descents like that one were getting farther and fewer between. It started out extremely steep and rocky and about a thousand feet down, near a place called Old Man's Head, its incline lessened to Safford Notch below. Boulder caves were here and there in the notch, but it was only a small steep climb to the easy hike up Little Bigelow Mt.

It was more like climbing out of a creek bed to a long rolling walk uphill. When we reached Little Bigelow Mountain, at 3,040 feet, it was easy to see how much lower it was, by looking up at Avery Peak. A rock outcropping gave us an unexpected reward. The more than friendly Canadian Gray Jays gave us another visit. Digging in my day pack, I found some cookie crumbs and as I held them out, the little birds ate right out of my hand. I loved that experience! It just made me feel so warm inside, as I wondered if they were the same ones we had fed earlier. After all, as the birds fly, it is probably not as far from one peak to another as it was for we earth bound mortals.

Little Bigelow was a long gradual, easy decline so we made good time to the East Flagstaff Road. Tweety Pie had staked out a nice campsite near an inlet of Flagstaff Lake. It didn't take long for each of us to work our way down to the shore to wash up.

That section was lowland for the next several miles, actually working from below 2,000 ft. to slightly above sea level and yes, I had awful mixed emotions. Shortly, we would be seeing Katahdin Mountain with his majestic peak of 5,267 ft. signaling the end of my dream trail. I was tired after hiking 16.4 miles. It was 4:35 p.m.

and fairly quiet, as far as conversation. A good time to enter the other dream world called sleep.

AUGUST 10, 1995 - circling our branch of Flagstaff Lake at 6:15 a.m., Tweety Pie waved his good-luck sign and gave me a kiss. Crossing Bog Brook on a foot bridge, it wasn't long before we headed east toward Roundtop Mountain. We went over a 1,700 ft. hill that did not qualify as a mountain. In between there and the mountain was a low ridge that Long Falls Dam Road crossed through. Jerome Brook graciously provided us with another foot bridge to cross on the way to the summit of Roundtop Mt., which, by the way, was a round top.

On a gradual slope, West Carry Pond and its lean-to lay below. When we reached the West Carry Pond Lean-To, we stopped for a short break. Very pleasant there, with a slight breeze blowing across the water. We were on the southeast shore of West Carry Pond, which would have easily qualified to be a small lake in Missouri. On the map, it is shaped like a large teardrop falling from the north, northwest sky. For some distance we traveled its shore going north, before heading east again.

Welcome to the lowlands, I thought, as we arrived at Arnold Swamp. Bog bridges provided us a fairly dry path through, and you can bet, I really watched my step on those. Falling into a clear rocky spring was one thing, falling into that muck would have been an entirely different ball game. "No Thanks!"

Off to the south of the bog was Middle Carry Pond, an extension off the muddy swamp becoming a haphazard water pool from the runoff. Our trail had been easy, not much ascending or descending. Arriving at East Carry Pond, we crossed more muck until we came to a clear shore that was like a sandy beach on an ocean front, minus the waves and salt. It was there we stopped for a lunch break.

Snapshot and Stickflipper couldn't resist going for a swim. Watching them shiver in the cold water was enough to deter any desire I might have had to join them. I still had memories etched in my brain of my dunk in that icy cold stream. After the two had decided they had been in the liquid icebox long enough, they emerged, dried off and we were on our way the 1.7 miles to Main Logging Road.

Tweety Pie waited patiently for our arrival. Even though it was only 12:00 noon, after a few minutes rest and discussion, we called it a day and started looking for a decent campsite. We headed east down Main Logging Road. In only a short distance, we found a partially grown-over road. Out of curiosity, Tweety Pie turned the jeep to the left and we went exploring.

Immediately we discovered a smooth spot right near a flowing stream, coming out of a marshy area. Like Brigham Young, when he discovered the Great Salt Lake Valley, we all exclaimed, "This is the place," and pitched our tents.

Later on, in the afternoon, it was strange to see hikers through the trees, heading south. We knew we had to be at least a quarter of a mile from the A.T., that is, if the trail continued north as it had appeared from the road where we left off earlier. Our first thoughts were that someone had seen us go in there and was advertising our secret campsite.

Upon closer examination of our map, we found that the trail took a direct right turn soon after Main Logging Road. That put our campsite almost smack dab back on the A.T. Now Stickflipper, Snapshot and myself are all, what is termed *purist* hikers, so that would never do. What that simply means is, we set our feet down every foot of the way on the A.T. or we would not have accomplished our goal of hiking the entire trail.

What to do? None of our team could possibly go to sleep until we backtracked over the trail, which was no big deal because it only involved a mile at the most. Arriving at Main Logging Road, I found exactly where I had come out on the road before and planted my feet in the spot. When I turned to start back to the campsite, Snapshot and Stickflipper were both laughing. They then proceeded to put their feet where they thought they had entered the road. There is humor in all things, but there are some who probably think I don't find comedy in enough situations. They're probably right. I will work on that and I did crack a smile as we headed back to camp.

The weather had been almost perfect that day but we had only hiked 9 miles. That still bothered me and before the setting sun turned off the lights, I took another look at the trail map. There was a road that led up to the Pierce Pond area and it sounded like a hiker's dream for a place to camp. Camping is one of the real pleasures of hiking. That is why you pick your locations so carefully. The more luxuries and beauty surrounding your camp, the better it is to unwind from the day's hike. It was too late to hike the short distance to the pond, so I kept my trap shut. But this site was not as good as I had thought, earlier. Picky, picky.

AUGUST 11, 1995 - days were getting shorter so it was imperative that we got earlier starts. As quickly as possible, we packed the tents. After a hurried breakfast, we were back on the trail at 6:15 a.m. The stream that passed to the east of our campsite turned out to be a branch of Carrying Branch Stream. Fording the stream was necessary before we could cut out for Bates Ridge.

Actually we had a small climb to a saddle, through the ridge, at only 1,500 feet.

Not long before we came to the Pierce Pond Lean-To where I wished we had spent last night. We stopped for a short break there, anyway. The Lean-to was located on an arm of Pierce Pond and was built in 1970. It accommodates six, has a nice brook for water, scenic waterfalls and good swimming in the pond. I never claimed to know more than A.T. authorities about camp sites and this was proof concrete. We had just not paid close enough attention to the map. Okay, I've degraded us enough and I am humbled.

I left ahead of Snapshot and Stickflipper and it was not far until I discovered a side trail that led 0.3 miles to Harrison's Camp Ground. There was a road that led right up to the campsite, so Tweety Pie could have easily spent the night with us. Doggonit, I have to get my mind off that subject. It was past tense and over, right? Besides, I came to a wooden dam over Pierce Pond Stream, the outlet of Pierce Pond. It did not look like the sturdiest structure I had ever seen, so crossing looked kind of iffy.

I glanced back to see if my companions were coming. Seeing a clear trail, I gingerly stepped on the dam and very carefully made my way across. Further down, I came upon an open ledge almost right over the top of a waterfall. While I listened and watched the water fly into the air and fall to the stream waiting below, Snapshot and Stickflipper caught up with me.

It's always a treat to see waterfalls but it wasn't far until we came to even larger ones. The trail followed Pierce Pond Stream east with more falls than I have ever seen in one area. A blue-blaze trail led us to the base of a large waterfall with a pool rippling and glistening as the water did its dance before falling into it. The kind of

334

peaceful beauty you would like to imagine lying beside every night, as you drift off to sleep.

Walking beside the stream, the falls became smaller until we reached a point where a large tributary, called Otter Stream, merged with Pierce Pond Stream. It was necessary to wade that stream, in order to continue our course to a ledge overlooking several more high waterfalls. Unbelievable!

Soon the answer, to why so many waterfalls on this busy little stream, was clear. From the top of Bates Ridge, it was one continual drop to the Kennebec River. Pierce Pond, where Pierce Pond Stream started its dash to the river below, was 1,200 ft. above sea level. The river was only 450 ft. That's a pretty good drop in a very short distance. Just before we got to the Kennebec River, we topped a little hill where the river ran directly below. We had a good view of the river and even saw Tweety Pie waiting on the other side.

We also witnessed something that sent chills up my spine. A south-bound hiker was fording the 70 yard wide, terribly swift river, in spite of the fact that there are strict warnings not to wade the river. The reason is obvious. It is the most hazardous non-bridged crossing on the entire 2,100 mile A.T. Even in ideal conditions, its current is dangerous. Couple that with the unpredictable release of huge amounts of water from a hydro facility up stream and you have a disaster in the making, when you do what this foolish man was doing.

There is no set time when the water is released and is impossible to cross the 70 yards before the rushing water rises. No matter how good a swimmer you are, you will be swept away, along with your heavy hiking gear. Several souls have drowned and met their maker by hiking through this river, and as I said, warnings abound all over the place. I was happy to see this thrill seeker emerge safely.

As he came toward us with his boots sloshing I wanted to give him a good lecture. When he said "Hi" as he passed us, the lecture just stuck in my throat. Friendly and unwise, I allowed him to stay in that condition. Well, he would be hiking in wet boots for quite a while and that is not the most enjoyable circumstance for hiking. I wanted to tell him that he may not care about his life, but I didn't need to be an eye witness to what could have been a traumatic tragedy.

In case you wonder how you do get across, I must say it is unusual. The A.T.C. actually provides free canoe rides across the Kennebec River. Arriving at the river's edge the canoe was not working, so we had a break. Only 9:45 a.m. and the canoe would not be active until 10:00 a.m.

Finally the operator of the canoe arrived and I volunteered to be his first passenger of the day. He was a nice young fellow to have such a strenuous job. As I watched his powerful arms paddling, he actually took time to point out a loon on the river. I had never seen one of these birds before so he explained that they are divers and make a sound like they are laughing and crying, at the same time. He made my trip across the Kennebec River, a memorable one.

While he went back across to get Snapshot and Stickflipper, I talked with Tweety Pie. He had parked on U.S. 201 and hiked 0.3 miles to the river to meet us. He got bored if he had to wait very long and he, like all men, loves rivers so I had expected him to be right where he was. He said the old boy that waded the river hadn't given it a second thought, before he entered. We all bid farewell to the canoer, who didn't seem to be the least bit winded from the two crossings. I got the feeling he liked what he was doing. Then, off to the city of Caratunk for ice cream and pop. While we were eating our ice cream, Holly arrived. This gal never dilly-dallied, so after a brief visit she was on her way.

After that treat, we located an outfitter with a laundromat and proceeded to do the dirty work, our laundry. The place also had free showers and we took full advantage of them. That made me hungry, so we inquired about a good eating place and were referred to a little pizza place beside the highway. We bought two large pizzas to go and went back to the A.T. parking lot where we decided it was a good time to set up camp. The pizzas were either awfully good or we were very hungry, but they didn't last long.

It was warm and clouds were moving in with a promise of rain. I felt pretty good, even though we had only hiked 8.4 miles and that was mostly due to all the beautiful waterfalls along Pierce Pond Stream. Those scenes would probably have been my image for sleep, had it not been for my thoughts of that careless man fording that dangerous river. I wonder how many people do such things because they are suicidal anyway.

AUGUST 12, 1995 - rain passed us during the night, but left a wet dew that soaked the tents anyway. Tweety Pie had taken on the job of seeing that they were as dry as possible, while we prepared ourselves for the day's hike. Maybe they could finish drying out in the jeep, since we would not be carrying the heavy packs. I always appreciated his efforts and I believe Snapshot and Stickflipper were realizing the convenience of having me along, if for no other reason than the benefits they received from my husband and the jeep.

Slackpacking, we fully anticipated making good time. Tweety Pie still had the tents spread out as we began the easy hike to the Pleasant Pond Lean-To. It was apparent that we were on a steady incline as we gazed at the sandy beaches of Pleasant Pond. As a matter of fact, we noticed we were getting a better aerial view of the pond as we climbed almost vertically. Near the summit of Pleasant Pond Mountain, I glanced down and realized the pond was shaped sort of like a giant squid without the tentacles. We had passed around the head on the way up the 2,477 ft. summit.

The hovering clouds began to manifest their anger that we mortals had not sought shelter, rather than arrogantly ignoring them. I didn't see the first lightning but the loud thunder clap woke me up. Then, as if an argumentative conversation had begun, lightening hissed and more thunder boomed its loud voice. Not having any desire to be a part of the discussion, we hurried over a hump called Middle Mountain.

After a short steep drop, the trail became a ripple rather than a roller coaster up and down. It was pretty easy trekking until the sky ended its loud discussion and began pouring its tears on us in a steady drizzle. No time to get careless, because no matter what surface you're walking on, it gets slippery with rain. Watching every step made me aware that my right leg was still hurting a little from my last fall, so I sure didn't need another tumble. When we arrived at Jake's Hole, a part of the long slender eel like Moxie Pond, the trail ended up on a road with a convenient parking area.

Tweety Pie had rushed ahead and was there with tents already set up. Now this is something he never does, so I was becoming suspect of his motivations. Maybe he was trying to keep my companions happy for the rest of the hike. Anyway, my tent was a Flash Magic, which is very easy to pitch, but Snapshot and Stickflipper's, on the other hand, was much larger and more complicated to put up. He had done a good job, except he put the rain fly on backwards.

Believe me, he received no complaints. Even the leaves were dry under the tents, which feels good when you crawl into your sleeping bag. Though the dampness doesn't touch you directly, you still get that clammy feeling underneath. An early supper seemed to usher in more rain so there wasn't much to do but lay in the tents. With 11.7 miles behind me, I was ready to go to bed early anyway. After the rain locked me into my tent with its ever wet blanket of semi-imprisonment, I found it hard to drift into my usual peaceful slumber. I listened to Tweety Pie breath after he got himself ready for bed. Between that, the rhythm of the raindrops and my thoughts, sleep finally came like a veil within a veil. The wet one outside and the dark one over my eyes.

AUGUST 13, 1995 - The aching in my body was loud compared to the silence outside. The rain had stopped so my eyes squeaked open to another new day. Often, when I dragged my aching body out of a wet-tent night, I wondered what I was doing out there, so far away from my comfortable bed. Well, it was cool and that promised a nice day for hiking.

Shaking the stiffness out of my poor old body, I then worked the negativity out of my puzzled mind. It was early and everyone was showing an eagerness I could identify with. After all the packing and putting food in our mouths, it was time for another adventure.

Even though it had been at least 5:00 a.m. when I awoke, it was 6:15 when we started hiking. Baker Stream, across the road from our camp, was running full. Rocks protruded above its surface often enough to make a precarious bridge. Believe it or not, I got across without taking another spill. Tweety Pie cheering me on in the background might have helped. I managed to crack a smile and blow him a kiss good by.

A gentle sloping incline led us past Joe's Hole Lean-to and a small brook that was much easier to cross than Baker Stream had been. Joe's Hole was named after a famous fishing guide. The gentle slope ended and we began a steeper climb, that was not so challenging, to the summit of Moxie Bald Mountain (2,629 ft.). From the open ledges the panorama in all directions, was like being in a helicopter that hovered above the miles and miles of lowland to the east and the sprawling Bald Mountain Pond below. Back to the west, I could see a better view of the long slender Moxie Pond with Pleasant Pond Mountain rolling up behind Joe's Hole. There were many other ponds and mountains to the northeast and it was easy to see why a guide for fishing would be needed and if he was good enough, would gain fame.

The wind picked up in intensity and there was a chill trying to pierce through my skin to my bones. This was enough signal to exit that peak, but not before surveying the trail ahead with several streams feeding the West Branch Piscataquis River. Blueberry crops dotted the country side. As we began the steeper descent, my thoughts drifted back to my friend Moxie Turtle. Moxie Pond, Moxie Bald Mountain, I was sure she must have taken her trail name from that area.

The trail was exceptional and almost level all the way to the shore of West Branch Piscataquis River. We crossed a bridge over Marble Brook that emptied into the river, a hop, skip and a jump north, among the fir and

340

spruce forest.   We still had to ford West Branch Piscataquis River.

Unlike that careless fellow we met back at the dangerous crossing of Kennebec River, I took off my boots and tied them together.   After that I put on my all-terrain sandals, put my boots around my neck and entered the river. The rain had made it pretty deep and swift and the rocks on the bottom were slimy slippery, so it was one step at a time.

At one point, my feet slipped and I thought I was on my way down river. With the help of my hiking staff, I was able to get them back under me. I was glad to exit on the other bank, wet, but none the worse for wear and tear. For that matter, it was kind of refreshing. Drying my feet off , I put on dry socks and slipped into my boots.

As I shook myself off like a bandy rooster, I gave one last thought to that poor guy and his sloshing boots, as we headed down a trail with a few ups and downs. We followed the west branch of the river for about 5.4 miles to where it merged with the East Branch of the Piscataque River. Looking across the 50 foot wide water I thought, "Come on, where's the bridge." Well there wasn't any, so off came the boots and socks. . . on went the sandals and. in I went behind my daring companions. It was between my knees and hips deep and the other bank looked a lot further than 50 feet away and a lot steeper.

As luck would have it, a cutbank had been made into the river and it wasn't as hard to get out as I had first thought. Quickly drying my feet again, I donned my dry socks and boots and followed Snapshot and Stickflipper up a steep climb to Shirley-Blanchard Road where I was glad to see my Tweety Pie. I needed help to put my gear in the jeep before we were off to our room with meals included, at Shaw's in Monson, Maine.

It was a famous place where hikers routinely stayed and we were treated like royalty. The cold rivers had left me stiff, so a hot shower felt even better than usual. The fact that we had our meals fixed for us, didn't hurt either. After the delicious supper, Mr. Shaw took the camcorder and gave us an interview of the day's events. It was a special day and I am proud to say this old Den Mama had stuck it out for a whopping 18.5 miles. At that rate, my dream hike would not last much longer.

The many hikers there indicated how popular the place was. It wasn't long before Holly came packing in. She wasn't a bad looking little lady and always pitched her tent where other hikers couldn't see it. This is good on one hand and bad on another. We had passed her along the trail and had no idea where. If she had needed help, we would never have known. Scary, when you think about it, especially since she would have been welcome to join us at anytime.

Hikers are funny people and you don't always know what their motive for being out there is. Perhaps some are driven to solitude. Obviously, she wasn't making any better time than we were. I am not a nosy person, so whatever her story, it will remain a secret. My bed was my only interest tonight and Kings and Queens may go their way, my dreams are for the trail ahead and the vision of Katahdin rising at the end.

AUGUST 14, 1995 - like a child taking its first steps, I swung my body out from under the covers to plant my feet on a real floor. After dressing myself in some nice clean clothes, combed my hair and tried to feel normal. It made me feel pretty good, so I thought I was ready for whatever that day might throw at me.

The owner, Mr. Shaw, was a stocky man and extremely friendly. He fixed all the hikers big breakfasts paying close attention to each request for doneness and choices. Stuffed is the word that best describes how I felt afterwards. I was eager to get back on the trail to walk it off. Rarely, do I ever eat that much in the morning.

Tweety Pie was more than willing to haul us back to Shirley-Blanchard Road. I think he was getting a little eager to get back to Missouri. Leaving the road over a hump, it was easy hiking to the north shore of Lake Hebron. Following the shore for a ways, we could hear the loons crying. The canoest, back at the Kennebec River, was absolutely right about the sound . . . a mournful sound that made me wonder if they knew something we didn't.

Changing our eastern course, we turned straight north away from the lake and its apparent sad residents. We had been told a ridiculous story about a beaver pond we would have to cross up ahead, over *floating boards*. The way the story had been told by the party, is that you couldn't keep from falling off the boards into waste deep water.

Shoot, it turned out to just be a great big rumor. As ridiculous as it may seem, I was disappointed. All we had to do, was circle around through a little bit of brush. Over a few small hills, we arrived at Maine Highway 15. Tweety Pie took us back the short distance to Monson where we had decided we would get some more spoiling.

That time, though, we did do the manual labor of throwing our laundry into the washers and dryers. This was also a good time to get our packs ready to hike the 100 mile wilderness, as it is called by hikers. If it was as rumored, it would not be too pleasant, with lots of climbing and wading.

Tweety Pie, as usual, had been talking to people at Shaw's. It seems that there was an inventive young man, named John, who had a large 4X4 truck. John was as husky as his truck, 18 years old, with a real New England accent. Along with this labor of love, he also worked at the local hospital. He made a business out of hauling hikers from a strategic point, called Long Pond Stream on an old logging road in the wilderness, back to Shaw's. After picking his customers, he told Tweety Pie he would take the hikers back to that same spot on the trail. It was not only a labor of love, but also lucrative. He charged $20.00 to pick us up and another $20 to haul us back to the trail. The fact that Tweety Pie had tried to run the trip with our jeep and had hit high center on that old logging road, guaranteed a steady clientele. For that matter, Tweety Pie was lucky to get the jeep unstuck and back to Shaw's. So it was a great idea and allowed us to slackpack one more day, saving unnecessary wear and tear on the jeep. The weather had turned hot, so spending another night in Shaw's was certainly appealing. The deal was made and we settled for hiking a leisurely 6.3 miles. We stayed in an upstairs bedroom supplied with three beds. However, there was a bunk house with several bunks, in case it became too crowded. The huge, family-styled meals were served at a large dining table, making the place a warm extended family-type atmosphere.

AUGUST 15, 1995 - waking in a place that caters to hikers made it difficult to have a bad attitude. Businesses along the Appalachian Trail make most of their living off hikers, like truck stops make profit off the truckers. You will notice that truckers are treated special at the truck stops and all the establishments along the trail, treat hikers pretty doggone good. The fact that we had another well-prepared and more than enough breakfast at Shaw's, testifies to that fact. His establishment is a credit to all business people.

Eagerness was the word of the day, when Tweety Pie drove us back to Highway 15. Need I say I felt a little shiver go up my spine as I read the sign at the beginning of this section? It was a big sign, and read, "Starting 100-mile wilderness, through some of the most remote mountains and forest traversed by the A.T. Carry at least a 10-day supply of food."

At this point, I have to admit that section had not been scouted by Tweety Pie, so we had no certain knowledge of how often he would be able to meet us. Thanks to John and his big 4 by 4 we, at least, knew that day we would be able to slackpack. We missed the trail right off the bat. Nearly thirty minutes of precious time was spent to find it. Just about the time you think all is well, mistakes like that will happen.

We did not expect to have to wade a brook at the very beginning of the section and even have to search for a decent place to cross. Never take the A.T. for granted! With the fording of Goodell Brook out of the way, I discovered, in the process, that it was an outlet for the Spectacle Ponds that strung off to the north. Finding the blazes, we were finally on our way at 6:30 a.m.

Boy, after that problem was solved, a short distance up the trail it started raining. Skirting Bell Pond, I was like a pony heading for home after a long trip. I reigned myself in, when we arrived at some open ledges at the top of a ridge. Dropping off the ridge into a small canyon past the north shore of Lily Pond, I noticed rain drops hitting the ponds surface. They must have felt like they had gone to heaven, to be accepted into the pleasant little pool. A slippery knoll rose up immediately in front of us, but after

345

a small slippery decline, we were at Leeman Brook Lean-to, above a small slate ravine.

What a welcome sight. We stopped just long enough to get rid of the clammy, wet feeling, when "Lo", the rain almost stopped. I was fighting an anxiety that was not familiar. When Tweety Pie was to meet us at designated locations I hardly gave it a second thought, but having to meet John was an entirely different matter. Would he wait for us if we were delayed too long? After all, we were carrying the light packs with few supplies. Tweety Pie had almost become psychic when it came to our rendezvous.

"Enough of that," I thought, as we left the lean-to and headed up the trail. Just 0.8 miles later, we came to a long narrow cove of North Pond and had to step lively over a swift running outlet stream. Water from above and water below. Enough already!

I was becoming increasingly aware of the pain in my right leg. Fortunately hiking was easy to Mud Pond, until we had to climb up to some small ledges about 500 ft. high and traverse the rims. The pain increased when we crossed the small James Brook and a gravel road. It was like being an injured football player in a championship game. "Don't take me out now coach. Whatever it takes, I *must* finish my dream."

The pain was forgotten for a while when I reached the awesome, and often talked about,Little Wilson Falls. They dropped 60 feet, one of the highest falls on the entire A.T. Two lady hikers were there and one was writing a book on the trails in Maine. As she took pictures of her partner below the falls, I told her I was contemplating writing a book on my experiences while hiking. As soon as the words came out of my mouth, I realized how foolish they could have sounded. I have a limited ability to write or to speak but she seemed to be impressed. I was flabbergasted at my audacity, until I remembered my calling on Mount Mooselauke. As I write, I am indeed amazed.

Working our way down to Big Wilson Stream was hazardous, as usual, especially near a waterfall. It was necessary to ford the Little Wilson Stream but we made it okay. A 200 yard long beaver dam fascinated me and we crossed with little or no difficulty. Walking on a gravel road was a welcome breather for about the distance of a football field.

Leaving the road, we found a long, open, slate ridge that took us eventually into a deep rock gully. There we crossed Thompson Brook and met up with Big Wilson Stream. It appeared to be a safe place to cross, but we could have hiked 1.5 miles downstream to a bridge. Then we would have had to come back the same distance, to the trail on the other side.

It was a swift stream and the boulders were terribly slick. I watched as Stickflipper made it across. Snapshot was following him, when all of a sudden she slipped and fell on the hard rocks in the stream. I could tell she was in pain as she grabbed her right arm. Upon following her, I immediately stopped at the river's edge, where I took off my boots, put on my sandals and carefully step by step, made it to the other bank. Snapshot made it out and was looking at her arm. Stickflipper helped her move it around, then gave it the thumbs up.

I truly wished we had hiked the extra distance to the bridge. Needless to say, I thanked the Lord that my good friend had not broken her arm. She had a nasty scuff, but on that trail, such abrasions are par for the course. The steep climb up to the Canadian Pacific Railroad tracks seemed mild compared to that river crossing. It was an active track so we crossed it carefully and dragged ourselves uphill to the Wilson Valley Lean-to, which turned out to be a good place to eat our lunch and contemplate our hiking to that point.

After leaving the shelter, the drizzle kept badgering us off and on and finally turned into a harder downpour. Crossing an old logging road, we soon came to open ledges and looked straight across through the rain at Barren Mountain waiting patiently. Stumbling over a rocky slope I thought, "Later, Barren Mountain. I'll deal with you tomorrow."

Wilbur Brook and Vaughan Stream was all that lay between us and our ride back to Shaw's. Personally, I was looking forward to being spoiled rotten. By the time we stepped out of Vaughan Stream, the road was in sight and the rain had taken a time out. Relief was in all our eyes when we saw Tweety Pie and John waiting in the big 4X4, however, it was a bumpy, hour long, ride back to Shaw's.

We hiked 14.5 rough miles and that was to be our last night at Shaw's. My leg was swollen in front, just above my ankle; red and hot to the touch. I tried to figure out what was causing the flare up, but who knows? I could have banged it on a rock or maybe all the wading was causing an arthritic reaction. Just in case, I had an antibiotic that my doctor had given me before I left Missouri. I contemplated taking one but decided to hold off. After all, I only had nine more days to hike.

AUGUST 16, 1995 - reluctantly leaving Shaw's at 6:30 a.m. in Johns truck, Tweety Pie and Stickflipper rode in the back with the backpacks, while Snapshot and I rode in front with John. With a New England accent he spilled off stories about his adventures with people and the wilderness of the area. Obviously the road he guided his

348

big truck over, picking up and delivering hikers, had presented some exciting adventures. I was as fascinated with his accent, as the stories. Being used to the old, slow speaking Missourians, I missed a lot of what he was saying, but it was entertaining anyway.

Often, the truck was down to a slow creep along the old logging road. It was steep enough to require all four of the wheels to be engaged. The truck tilted precariously over some big boulders, that had been too much trouble to be removed by whomever had built that old road.

Long Pond Stream ran near the road to the east all the way to our drop off on the trail. Finally, we were back where we had left off. Quite frankly, I would just as soon have hiked, as to ride, over those rough roads. It renewed my respect for what Tweety Pie experienced when he had to meet us in remote areas. I hoped my companions respected that fact too.

Tweety Pie hiked in the short distance with us to Long Pond Stream. He took pictures of us while we forded the stream. Consequently, I had hiked the 0.1 mile from the truck to the stream in my sandals in anticipation of fording the swift running Long Pond Stream on its twisting journey down to Lake Onawa. That way, I didn't have to remove my boots.

The water was above my knees, tugging at me as if to say "Come along with me, frail little lady, and I will show you sights not often seen." Naturally, I fought to refuse the invitation. When you are crossing those rain and snow fed streams and they say the average depth is knee deep, add at least another six to eight inches automatically, if you are a *shorty*. Please be especially careful, if you take young children with you.

At 8:00 a.m., I was putting my boots on and getting ready to get down to business on the opposite bank. I waved good-bye to Tweety Pie before turning to face the immediate incline up Barren Mountain. The temptation to take the short trail to Slugundy Gorge and Waterfall was passed up because the pain in my leg was getting a lot worse, especially when I moved my foot up and down.

I didn't want to make too much of it for fear I might discourage Stickflipper and Snapshot, but it was obviously slowing me down. The trail was steep all the way to Barren Ledges. Before we topped the level ledge, there were lots of rock slides to our right.

The weather was clear and we had some great views below us to the west and south. Bodfish Intervale rolled alongside the Long Pond Stream which led into Slogundy Gorge and its falls. From that point I scanned south, at Lake Onawa, with an island on its north end. A good fishing lake, I assume. Close to the summit of Barron Mountain, 2,670 feet, they had built rock steps into the trail. My aching leg really appreciated them.

Talk about taking a belt in the old pride zone. Snapshot and Stickflipper had gone ahead and were waiting patiently for me to catch up. Don't get me wrong, I really appreciated them. But Lord, I hated holding anyone up. They allowed me enough time to take a break when I reached the summit, which gave me some temporary relief. I knew when they decided to stop for the day at Cloud Pond Lean-to, it was for my benefit. Even though we had only hiked 5 miles, I guess they figured it made sense to stop and let me rest my leg. Hopefully, if I kept the pressure off, the next day would show improvement.

Cloud Pond was beautiful at 2,500 ft. elevation. I went down and soaked my leg in the chilly water of the pond. Afterwards, I rubbed it with mineral ice. Lounging around the rest of the day, I decided when I got back to the jeep, it would be time to start taking my antibiotics. Perhaps they would make it better. If not, I would be in a world of hurt. It was foolish of me to have left the drugs behind with my extra supplies. I tossed and turned during the night, mostly with the anguish that anything could jeopardize my finishing the trail. I prayed for relief and drifted into fitful slumber.

AUGUST 17, 1995 - I was not in peak racing form at 6:00 a.m., but with the Lord's help, I was able to slowly drag myself into the sag between Barren Mountain and Fourth Peak, with my companions. It was a peak like the base of an ice cream cone and the sag was a fairly gradual slope to a bog, at about 1,900 ft. Fourth Mountain looked like it was straight up and it was, all the way to 2,383 ft. The summit was heavily wooded, blocking any possibility of a view.

Third Mountain, 2,061 feet and shaped like a mini butte, was a lot easier. There were views to the west of the streams and ponds below, especially a large two-phase pond called Long Pond. One part was fatter than the other, with a narrow part connecting them like somebody had put a belt around what was once a large body of water and squeezed it, as tight as they could.

A slight decline led us past West Chairback Pond. As we ascended the steeper incline up to the open ledges of Columbus Mountain, 2,326 feet, I kept looking back to see if that pond resembled a chair back. From what I could tell, it didn't. Maybe from an airplane. Again, there were some good views of the valley below with mountains in the background. There was another lean-to in the gap between Columbus Mountain and Chairback Mountain called, yes, Chairback Lean-to. Someone, who named that area, was obsessed with chair backs.

The shelter was unimpressive and I was glad we had stayed at the Cloud Pond Lean-to. Ascending Chairback Mountain, 2,219 feet, was steep but no major challenge. The descent was another matter, with rocks and boulders just waiting to trip me with my bum leg. Immediately off the summit, it was a blessing when it sloped down a gentle upsweep on a knoll past East Chairback Pond. Admittedly, it sort of resembled a lounge chair but it turned out the chair back name was derived from the unique cliffs and ledges on the east side of the mountain.

The trail took a long slope down to a logging road with the West Branch Pleasant River running below. The old road led directly to Katahdin Iron Works and had been unofficially named after the plant. Actually it was one of the major logging roads in the area. Because of that, Tweety Pie was able to meet us there and take us to the entrance to the historical Katahdin Iron Work Site. A fee of $8.00 is charged to use the logging roads, but since Tweety Pie was 70 years old, he got in free. Some of the old iron works were still standing and a description of its history was posted.

The gate keeper told us of a campground where we could spend the night. We had passed a nice looking stream, so we backtracked and took advantage of it, to wash off the trail dust. The campground turned out to be more than adequate. It even had a picnic table and outhouse. All in all, it was more than satisfactory.

Tweety Pie had bought some more potatoes, a hint to Snapshot to practice her southern cuisine for supper, once more. I started taking the antibiotics and, with the Lord's help, was able to hang in there for 15 miles that day. Golly Moses, less than 100 miles to Katahdin. I slept better with that knowledge.

AUGUST 18, 1995 - things were somewhat normal, since the point where John had picked us up and delivered us back to the trail. Anytime you break up a system, there is always a degree of confusion and stress, no matter how beneficial that break in the system may be. Tweety Pie drove us back to the trail and we were able to get started at 6:30 a.m.

It was 0.5 miles when we reached the West Branch of Pleasant River. Taking off my boots could have been avoided if I had left my sandals on until I reached the river. Boots don't come off easy and anyone who has worn a boot that must fit comfortably, knows what I mean. Boots off, I entered the river behind my two companions. A river that is supposed to be knee deep, was low so I had no problems crossing.

Carefully I emerged on the other side, put my boots on and we were off to climb the last high mountain before Katahdin. The incline was steady to the Hermitage, a protected stand of beautiful, tall, majestic pines. The incline got somewhat steeper after that and it was no illusion that we were going steadily upward.

Reaching the Carl A. Newhall Lean-to, built in 1986, it got a lot steeper. "Hang in there, girl," I kept telling myself. The leg was doing a lot better, but I was glad when we reached the first rippley peak called Gulf Hagas Mountain. Actually, it is just one of the peaks on one big mountain. I found that confusing and wished they would just name a mountain by its highest peak, which in that case was White Cap Mountain.

We were below 850 ft. elevation back at the river and at this point we were at 2,683 feet on a partially open summit, climb by climb, working our way upward. The inevitable decline came into a narrow gully where lay the Sidney Tappan Campsite. It was a good spot to stop for lunch. Stickflipper went to a spring, that was the very beginning of Gulf Hagan Brook, flowing swiftly down to the river below. It was as cold as ice water right out of the refrigerator.

The campsite was a smooth grassy area, an ideal setting for several tents. Looking up at a needle peak, we began the struggle to reach it. It was another partially open summit called West Peak. The elevation there was 3,178 feet. The drop wasn't too bad into the valley between West Peak and Hay Mountain. Climbing was much easier to the completely wooded, rounded summit of Hay Mountain where we were then at 3,244 feet.

We then hiked into a loop and after a steep climb made it over a ledge and a short gradual incline to the top of White Cap Mountain (3,645 feet). Emotions were high when I looked out over nothing short of inspiring. Everything was lower and too vast to describe. Everything that is except one, far off in the distance.

Katahdin stood majestically like a welcome beacon or a seductive temptress, so close and yet so far. I was sad and glad, all at the same time. A tear caught me off guard as it gently rolled down my cheek. You see, I was looking at a dream not yet realized but almost, just almost ready. It wouldn't be long before I would be back in Missouri, with the alarm beside my bed waking me to the other world of Mary Twitty. My leg reminded me of my reality and that it was not over yet.

It was a steep descent to Logan Brook Lean-to, not halfway down that mountain. I was more than a little relieved to get there. I went to the brook in front of the shelter and soaked my leg in the icy water, but it was too cold to leave it very long. While I was contemplating giving the aching limb one more numbing dip, three thru-hikers came in. They called themselves French Tickler, who was hiking with his dog, Ben, and the other was Ghost Hiker. Ben was a beautiful husky and extremely well-behaved.

After they moved on, I mustered the energy to dry my tent, putting it back in its stuff sack. The shelter accommodated six, so the tent would not be needed. Located in a little ravine between two humps of the mountain and with a brook running close by, it was a nice shelter. The 12.2 miles today had drained me so much, I was unable to walk upstream to see the cascades and look into the deep ravine. Stickflipper and Snapshot would tell me about their experiences tomorrow.

I crawled into my bag early and closing my eyes, I could faintly hear the wild water. The numbness wore off and my leg gained relief from the other power of nature, called warmth.

AUGUST 19, 1995 - you go to bed early, you get up early; as was the case that morning. I ate a meager breakfast and headed down the trail leaving my two swifter buddies to catch up later. It was 6:00 a.m. when I reached an old logging road. Snapshot and Stickflipper were already beside me. A nice gradual slope would have made going downhill a piece of cake, if it hadn't been for that nagging pain in my leg.

Four miles of hiking brought us to the foot of the mountain at about 1,200 feet and the East Branch Pleasant River. The most difficult task of fording the river was removing my boots and putting them back on. We had to climb steeply back up to 1,700 ft. to reach Mountain View Pond, where we crossed its outlet stream.

Continuing on up, we reached the wooded summit of Little Boardman Mountain, 2,017 feet. After a 750 foot drop, we arrived at Kokadjo-B Pond Road. Tweety Pie was there working his tail off clearing brush and weeds from around the area, where white-blazes were grown over. This not only helped us, but also made it easier for other thru-hikers to stay on track. Gladly, we loaded our heavy backpacks in the jeep. After eating a quick lunch and having a cold can of pop, we were off slackpacking, feeling light as a feather, which didn't do my leg any harm.

Steadily downward we came to Crawford Pond with a nice sandy beach. Two young ladies, taking advantage of the large pond, were enjoying a refreshing swim. Crossing the outlet of the pond, we found ourselves on an old logging road that ran alongside Cooper Brook, all the way east to the Cooper Brook Falls Lean-to, built in this strategic location in 1956. The brook bounced gleefully right in front of the lean-to with a large tributary emptying into the brook directly to the east. Beautiful cascades were doing a fairy flight dance just up the tributary. It would have been a knockout place to spend time but instead, we crossed the tributary. Why? Because our long awaited date with mighty Katahdin was drawing nigh.

In 3.7 miles, we circled Church Pond and shortly thereafter, Jo-Mary Road. This is a major logging road and ol' Tweety Pie was there doing his self-appointed trail maintaining job, with a lady named Chris and her husband. Chris had informed Tweety Pie about a good campsite just across the bridge, over the Brook. These trail-maintainers deserve a big pat on the back for the hard work they do, making life better for hikers.

After getting set up in the camp, I went down to the brook and washed. I soaked my leg in the cold water again

and I believe it was feeling much better. Ghost Hiker, French Tickler and his dog, Ben, had found another friend and came straggling into camp a little later. It was just cool enough to feel good, sitting in the sun.

We had a fun supper, more entertaining with the company of Tweety Pie's. It didn't take me long to get ready for bed after 15.4 miles. All the really tall mountains were conquered between me and Katahdin and I was still up to the task. My husband, my hiking companions, what more could I want? I snuggled in my sleeping bag, like a fluffy teddy bear in a little girl's arms. "I hear your windy voice, big mountain. I am coming."

AUGUST 20, 1995 - according to the map, we would be passing a series of lakes and ponds. Refreshing as they are, they created a lot of variances in the trail adding more miles for us to circle around them. At any rate, we broke camp around 6:30 a.m. Heading east on the old road bed, slackpacking. Yes, this meant we would make good time!

The first of the series of ponds and lakes was Cooper Pond, which lay off in the trees, out of our vision. Then we crossed a gravel logging road right next to a log bridge, that had long outlived its usefulness over Cooper Brook. At the east end of Mud Pond, shaped like a skinny chick, just meeting the world out of the egg, we had to ford several outlet streams. During this nasty activity, I kept hearing an occasional slap on the pond that I assumed indicated an active beaver residence.

Leaving Mud Pond, we turned so far north, it became northwest. The reason for this is, we had worked our way over to the northwest shore of the big Lower Lake Jo-Mary. In a jut out into the lake was Antlers Campsite in the middle of a beautiful grove of red pines. Circling the northwest end of the lake we had to wade an inlet brook. I thought I heard another slap on the lake. Boy, what a wonderful place that was for beavers! Leaving that lake, we cut straight north across a gap of Potaywadjo Ridge that actually took us up to about 950 ft.

After that gentle climb, the trail sloped down to the Potaywadjo Spring Lean-to built in 1957, that got its water from a unusual source. It was a 15 ft. diameter spring with the water bubbling, as if a giant was below blowing his heart out. The bubbling was pressure from an underground spring and pressure, not heat, caused the reaction; a good place for a break. Chris and her husband were responsible for maintaining that section and to their credit, it was one of the cleanest lean-to's that I had seen.

In a mile, we came to Twitchell Brook emptying into the huge Pemadumeook Lake. Of course, we had to wade the stream but the lake was beautiful. A little ways further we had to wade Deer Brook just below a small beaver pond before it, too, emptied into the gigantic Pemadumeook Lake.

Stickflipper asked me to look north. I suspected what I would see. With an almost bashful feeling, I gazed off in the distance at the huge gentleman, Katahdin. What a mountain! "Was that the finger of a big white cloud waving at me tauntingly? Watch it Den Mama," I thought. " Don't lose it now." When my two friends had turned their heads away from me, I managed a wave at the mountain and my imaginary pesky cloud, "I'll be there soon."

The trail became rougher and all the water in this area was causing a plague of mosquitoes, with their irritating little "eeeeee" sound around our ears. I had to stop to put on a long sleeve shirt. We had to wade two more streams in succession and it didn't help things a bit.

Our wet legs just seemed to make us a more appetizing target. Meanwhile, we had began to follow Nahmakanta Stream and strangely, the little blood suckers eased off. It was awfully pretty and seemed to be inviting us to have lunch. We accepted.

Back on the trail, we came across a mysterious 74 year old lady laying beside the trial. Her knee replacements were hurting her. She had been flown into Kahmakanta Lake by a seaplane, no less, in order to try to finish hiking the A.T. She was determined to make it to Katahdin Iron Works Road to complete her hike. She made me a little fearful of Katahdin, when she said she had made two tries at climbing the great mountain before making it.

As sorry as I felt for this courageous lady, I looked north and thought, "If you think this frail messenger will discourage me, your plan has backfired. If she made your steep side with those knee replacements, I know I can." We told her there were lots of good hikers back that way and if she needed help, they would give it. To be frank, I was humbled after complaining so much about my leg.

Tweety Pie was waiting for us at Nahmakanta Lake. He was parked up on a gravel road. Taking the backpacks out of the jeep, we took a trail to the lake shore and made camp. We were far from being the only ones there and out of the many hikers, one was a nurse. I told her about my leg and she looked at it. Her opinion was that it was probably bruised and it wouldn't hurt to take the rest of my prescription to keep the infection down. Call it psychosomatic, or whatever, but my leg felt better.

It felt so good, I went swimming in the lake with Tweety Pie, Stickflipper and Snapshot. The water was warm and felt marvelous. Our tents were in the sun, soaking up the warm sun rays.

Snapshot and Stickflipper sometimes reminded me of a couple of otters. They scouted around until they found some clams. Yeah, they decided to fix them for supper. Yuck! I couldn't eat any. Tweety Pie, on the other hand, will try anything but when he spit it out, I felt pretty proud of my intelligence. Snapshot, I think mostly out of pride, downed the most and this was the lady whose hands I had trusted my life and appetite to. Stickflipper, for some reason, wasn't hungry and left them alone. My kind of guy.

I crawled into my tent early and laid there watching the sun set below Nesuntabunt Mountain. It was calm and beautiful. Later in the night, I looked out and the stars were shining like diamonds in the black sky. Oh what a beauty God creates. We had hiked 15.1 miles.

AUGUST 21, 1995 - tension was building each day, replacing the thrill of the high mountains with a different kind of excitement. We will not be above 1,600 feet until we reach Katahdin, which only served to make it even more majestic than all the rest, except one, my Mt. Mooselauke.

One thing impressed me was the tremendous amounts of water they had access too in that part of Maine. Breaking camp and carrying our backpacks to the jeep, we managed to get a 6:20 a.m. start. The temperature had warmed during the night and we were hoping it wouldn't get any hotter. Even though we were in the low lands basically, did not mean we wouldn't have some strenuous climbs.

Following the west shore of Nahnakanta Lake we crossed Prentiss Brook in a small valley bordering the lake, before coming to another sand beach. Evidently, a lot of hikers liked the area and were camped there. The small spring between the trail and the lake was struggling to provide drinking water, but personally I would not have trusted it without boiling. I was happy we had camped where we did.

Weaving away from the lake a bit, we crossed Wadleigh Stream and found Wadleigh Stream Lean-to nestled between the trail and the stream. Built in 1981, it has had plenty of time to suffer some abuse. It slept six, had the stream for water and only 0.5 mile to excellent swimming in the lake. All in all, it wasn't that bad. There was a log book, so we all signed in, writing our personal statements.

A little ways on up the trail there was an unusual rock formation with, I guess you would have to call it, a rock roof. Made a good nucleus for a house. I'll bet a lot of Indians camped there in the old days. Crossing over a long rounded hump we dropped into a slight gully and looked straight up, at least 500 to 600 ft. to the summit of Nesuntabunt Mountain.

They were building rock steps into the trail, but hadn't completed them yet. It was just enough construction to leave loose rock all over the place. It was an irritating, steep climb up this little peak and I had a strange feeling of resentment that it dared stand in my way, that is, until we reached the stub needle top. The view of the lakes was marvelous, with some of the small peaks off in the distance.

I slowly turned toward the north and looked upon a Mt. Katahdin, disguised in a white cloak of thick clouds. "That's all right. I can wait to see you eye to eye, oh Greatest of Mountains," which is what Katahdin meant in the Abenaki Indian language.

A clear view showed us a seaplane as it gracefully circled Nahmakanta Lake before lightly landing, creating its own swells. There, it taxied to a lodge specially constructed for the water-faring airplanes. I'm sure I shared the thoughts of my companions in thinking, "It must be nice to be able to afford such luxuries."

It was a steep descent immediately off the summit, then becoming a gradual sloping exit to a gravel surfaced logging road that was, in essence, the north, northwest base of the mountain. After a small hump we circled the inside edge of the crescent of Crescent Pond, then came to a blue-blazed trail that led to Pollywog Gorge. I was tired and didn't want to put any extra miles on my leg, so I continued on, while Snapshot and Stickflipper visited the Gorge. Coming to a bridge over Pollywog Stream, I spotted another logging road and Tweety Pie.

We decided to make camp in a wide spot beside the road. Pollywog Stream provided us a lovely place to wash up. Tweety Pie had cleaned the weeds around the white-blazes on the bridge over the stream, so hikers could see them. French Tickler came by and we told him there was plenty of room for him to camp. He decided to spend the night with us.

The atmosphere was friendly, with adventure stories being bandied around. Tweety Pie's description of his roll as backup and chase for our little group, I believe, had French Tickler convinced to hike with us for a while. We'll see. It was an easy hike that day and I cannot figure why we had only made 8.3 miles. I suppose it could be a desire, subconsciously, to prolong the end. Sleep was becoming a little more difficult for me. I knew it was the anticipation and vision of going home, with the dream over.

AUGUST 22, 1995 - poking my head out of the tent, I could have sworn I smelled smoke. It was early and

I certainly didn't want to get caught in a forest fire. There were no signs of fire out of control, but I couldn't go back to sleep. Tweety Pie, seeing that my sleep was over, began preparing himself to get the day started. Breakfast over and breaking camp done, there was still no signs of smoke to be seen.

At 6:00 a.m. we were ready to embark and guess what? French Tickler was putting his gear in our jeep so he could slackpack with us. Can't say as I blamed him. It did make it more pleasant. Tweety Pie was going to haul the packs to Abol Bridge and would have to backtrack to Jo-Mary Road, then catch Highway 11 into Millinocket, then take the road to Baxter State Park to get where he needed to be. These large bodies of water did create a problem, just like our lakes in southwest Missouri.

We crossed Pollywog Stream to the trail and the jeep began its long winding trip north. We met Rainbow Stream quickly and followed its friendly west bank all the way past a small pond. Crossing its outlet stream, we found the Rainbow Stream Lean-to. Built in 1971, it was easy to see why it was built in that location. Sleeping six, it had water from the stream and an old log and rock configuration upstream, creating a sluice that made a wonderful old fashioned swimmin' hole.

It was such a pretty place, in an old Huck Finn sort of way. I was disappointed that we had not gone a bit further to spend the night there. Maybe I would have slept better. I didn't dwell on the thought because I still felt the smell of smoke in my nostrils. Everyone was sticking their noses in the air now and the smell was getting stronger when we crossed Rainbow Spring. It took our attention off some small droplet-like ponds, all in a series, called Rainbow Dead Waters. Still no fire, but the smoke was visible, dispelling the thought that it had been imagination.

The droplet ponds became a long slithering pond, before a dividing stream between it and Rainbow Lake Dam. This was called the north end of the Rainbow Dead Waters which, for this old Missouri girl, is just a dramatic way of saying this series of streams and water holes are just spill off from the lake's dam. The lake, itself, seemed to be shaped like a big bowed Northern Pike fish, as we worked our way to the inside of the bow to follow the east shore.

It was a sight to behold all the campsites along the shore, with hikers and other segments of humanity clinging to that desirable area of nature. It was a massive area of water and, as I have mentioned, seemed to draw humans like a magnet.

Southbound hikers were expressing their concerns about the drifting smoke. They had surmised that a forest fire across the lake, near the west shore, was the source. With that suspicion, we decided we would be safe to proceed on between the lake on our left and Rainbow Mountain on our right. We followed the shore line north, deeper into the bow, until it curved around east, eventually going southeast to, what would be called, the south end of Rainbow Lake, with an emphasis on the word bow.

Curving around the south end of the lake, we headed east and that took us away from the lake, past two beaver ponds and the Rainbow Ledges. A climb over a hump allowed a gradual climb to two humped ledges, which rose slightly above 1,500 feet. At the highest point we should have viewed Katahdin, but it was still cloaked in its billowy, cloudy disguise. Remnants of barren areas were still visible on the ridges, of a fierce forest fire that happened clear back in 1923. Nature heals slowly in some places.

Like King Kong blowing his breath on his fair maiden, I felt Katahdin was blowing its cold breath on me. Eyeing that huge cloud bank to the north, I put my arms in my jacket, pulling it tightly around me. This is so wonderful to have this opportunity to tell the strange things that occupied my inner thoughts. I never dared reveal them to the people on the trail, involved in that adventure. Some thought I was crazy enough as it was. I wished I had taken up writing a long time ago.

A youth group passed us going south, while we were eating our lunch. They chattered their excitement until it became only murmurs in the distance. The descent off the cliffs was a steeper slope and became more exaggerated as we dropped down to the crossing of Hurd Brook, between two large ponds. Hurd Brook Lean-to was on the other side of the stream. We wrote in the shelter long book, realizing that it was the last one before Baxter State Park.

A south bound hiker came into the shelter and relayed a story about how he had climbed Katahdin with Holly, our secretive little hiker, who always camped out of sight. He said they had accomplished it two days before. Boy, she must have shifted gears! It was about August 13, when we had passed her somewhere on the trail, or maybe she had been too far ahead for us to catch her. "Good going, Holly."

Reaching an extensive cedar bog and an interesting combination of boulders, mixed with some big hemlock trees, we arrived at Abol Bridge on a main logging road. Tweety Pie had made his long swing around Rainbow Lake, which was a relief to me, since he had been on the opposite side of the lake and had driven much farther north. I asked him if he knew where the smoke had been coming from. I knew if anyone had a more inquisitive mind than he did, I hadn't met them yet. He said there was a large forest fire burning around Montreal, Canada. I was relieved that wasn't a problem for us, however, it was sad to hear that more forests were becoming ashes. He had inquired about campsites in this area. Someone informed him about a good one.

We took advantage of a little camp store at the bridge campground. A deli sandwich and pop was a refreshing, luxury at that stage of the game. Ready and willing to end the day, we picked a site in the campground and pitched our tents. French Tickler and his dog spent the night with us, again.

Later in the evening, Ghost Hiker came into camp and Tweety Pie pulled more potatoes out of the jeep. We were treated to fried potatoes and onions, *for the last time.* Even though it had been a fairly easy 17.4 miles, I was pretty worn out, but the meal was delicious as always and I was refreshed afterwards. It had been a privilege to have our own southern cook hiking with us and I was to miss Snapshot terribly when that moment would only be a fading memory.

Refreshed as I was and only 1:15 p.m., I took a shower, then looked around the campground. It was close to an inlet of the West Branch Penobscot River and the noisy Golden Road. I walked down to the river to pay my respects to my nemesis, Katahdin. This huge mountain could hide no longer. When I got back to camp, an energetic conversation was in process. I just didn't feel like taking part. From where we were, there were only a few miles of gradual ascent, before the beginning of elevation to the big monster. The sun set in a lonely foreboding way for me and my emotions were going

Tracy, Trip, Rita,
Carla, Leslie,
Sonya.

Back Row: Paul, Jr.; Jeannie, Lori, Della, Jason.
Front Row: John, LeNae, Jeff.

Mary, Wanda, Jeff, Jason, Bill, Jeannie, Karen & John.

completely haywire. I finally ignored the noisy trucks above on Golden Road, let eyelids meet cheeks and my friend, sleep, calmed my frayed nerves.

AUGUST 23, 1995 - no one was in a hurry to crawl out of the sack. I suppose there had been no particular reason to be in a hurry. It was sort of like the calm before the storm, an anticlimax, so to speak. Unbelievable as it seemed, there was only 10 miles left to hike. I waited as long as I could stand for something that may, or may not, happen.   At 7:30 a.m. I struck out on my own   I knew Snapshot and Stickflipper would have no problem catching me.

This was to be our last day to hike together, since they were going to wait for their daughter, Kathy, to come from Tennessee to climb Katahdin with them, six days from now, on August 29. Those thoughts were plaguing me as I passed a ski trail and eventually a bridge over Abol Stream. Pausing briefly, I looked into water that had come from who knows where and entering a new element in a larger river not far from the bridge, taking it to who knows where?

Was I selfish, wanting us to all climb the great mountain together? After all, we had gone through a lot, in over 900 miles of hiking. If it was not to be, I shouldn't really have any complaints. Without them, I may never have come that close to finishing my dream hike. For that matter, as I reflected back over the terribly rough country we had hiked, I probably wouldn't have made it. Talk about mixed emotions.

My friends caught up with me and we crossed Katahdin Stream over a road bridge on a trail that was just too easy. Of course, up to that point, we had been walking on a road that ended abruptly, soon thereafter. We had to cross a small brook, then Foss and Knowlton Brooks on a footbridge, before coming to the bed of Foxbow Lake, that was normally full in the spring. We were able to cross over, with no more than a little mud here and there.

The West Branch Penobscot River forked off to the northwest and left us to follow Nesowadnehunk Stream that fed into the river. It was almost as large as its soon to be host. As the stream became narrower and narrower, it also got swifter, the farther we followed it. Something spectacular usually happens when water does that. After fording a lower branch, that rushed into the main branch, it did. Just 150 foot off the trail, we found some wonderful water falls called Big Niagara. As if that was not enough, a little further we left the trail to see the Little Niagara Falls. The water, hurdling over the rocks, took my mind off my immediate worries. Above the walls was an old toll dam, that was used to control the flow of water during log drives.

Soon we arrived at the Daicey Pond Campground. Tweety Pie was already there and introduced us to the Ranger who helped us check in and rent space in the shelters for two nights. There, mostly for thru-hikers but available to all hiking the A.T., the shelters came in handy for us, in case the weather was too bad to climb Katahdin the next day.

Finding our designated shelter, we claimed our bed space by rolling our sleeping bags out. The shelters were small and designed to sleep only four hikers. A great view of Katahdin, from Daicey Pond, served to cause my fears to rise. It is an awesome mountain and has a weather system of its own. How would I hike that monstrous thing, rising into the clouds, by myself?

Leaving our sleeping bags in place, we decided it would be a good idea to hike on to Katahdin Stream

Campground situated at the base of the big mountain. That way I would not have to hike that section on the same day that I climbed Katahdin. It wasn't very far and actually flat, for the most part, with a few grassy ponds and some outlet streams to wade. Tweety Pie met us there and drove us back to Daicey Pond.

Well all that was left, was the big guy and the weather was not cooperating at all. The forecast was for rain during the night and all the next day. It would have been extremely dangerous for me to hike that mountain alone and in the rain. I spent a lot of time finding reasons to be by myself, with all the wild things that were rushing through my mind.

Elated, and oh my gosh, it is impossible to describe how I felt. Disappointed? Yes! What had become my life's accomplishment was near the end. All the expectations I had been experiencing each year to prepare to hike the A.T. . . . what would replace that? Sad. Lord, I have never been so sad in my life. I had made some of the most interesting and unusual friends that a small town lady could ever hope to meet. They had broken my heart, then made me laugh. I would miss them desperately.

As if on cue later on in the evening, a thru-hiker named M.A. from PA. came into the shelter. She was a pleasant lady and only a year younger than me. She was going to climb Katahdin the next day by herself, by golly, come hell or high water. When she found out that I was of the same character and would have to climb alone, two determined allies joined forces for the assault.

Before the sun set, leaving the mountain in darkness, I went back out to view it. I raised my fist in arrogant defiance and in privacy of my brain screamed, "You will not have me at your mercy all by myself." Then in opposite humility and calm, I thanked my invisible friend, my Heavenly Father, for coming to my aid again and sending me this stalwart lady. Upon my entering into the seeming reality of the camp, I found that this was my new friend's second thru-hike. She was quite a lady but neither of us suspected the hell we would go through together.

French Tickler came in to get shelter. His family had met him at the Abol Bridge and he had left his faithful friend, Ben, with them. You see dogs are not allowed in the park. I wasn't even allowed to have Tweety Pie stay with me, since they were very strict about allowing *only* hikers. Strange, huh? The reason is logical. They are simply trying to keep as much space restricted for the people who dare to hike this huge trail. We were both disappointed, to say the least, but he was able to find a place at Roaring Brook Campground in the park.

My new friend and I talked for a while and it helped to calm me down, but I was beginning to realize this lady was more rambunctious than me. I don't remember if I slept or not, but I do remember when the torrents of rain began. "How long was that rain to prolong the agony and ecstasy?" The agony of my leg had eased off and I was able to move my foot up and down without too much strain. In short, I knew I was ready for the climb. But obviously, nature had a different opinion.

Tweety Pie was going to be in the park to take us back to the base of the mountain. I hoped we could get an early start, but they didn't open the gates to the Baxter State Park, until 7:00 a.m. .

AUGUST 24, 1995 - it rained hard all night and I didn't see how I could make the climb that day. All the rocks and boulders would be a bearcat and I knew it. A

370

normal human would not give it a consideration. M.A. from PA. was not normal. I heard her up and around at 5:00 a.m. and it appeared to me she had no doubt as to her plans, with or without me. I couldn't believe I was crawling out of the sack and going through the motions of beginning a hike, but I was.

Hike alone or follow this headstrong lady. It wasn't really a choice. If she was going, so was I. Even though Tweety Pie was unable to stay with me, he checked with me at the camp at 5:30 a.m. When I told him we were obviously going to finish today, he just shook his head. When he did that, I wondered if I wasn't more like M.A. from PA. than I had realized. Regardless, he drove us over to Katahdin Stream Campground where I grabbed a pop tart, snarfed it down and afterwards hoped I was ready to hike with M.A. from PA. A trail registry was there for all campers going up and coming down the mountain. The reason is obvious. It is dangerous up there and they want to know who is on the mountain, for their safety. If you are not back down in a reasonable time, the rangers will look for you.

At 6:00 a.m., we started up the mountain. It is the crowning jewel of all the mountains we have conquered. If I had any doubts before, I had none now, as to why the Indians named it the "Greatest Mountain". Only 4,200 feet straight up and my hike is over. At that moment, it might as well have been a hundred miles. It is a dangerous mountain and the weather can change in a minute up there and me and this strange lady are taking off, in what looked like less than ideal conditions. She didn't bat an eyelash as we started.

It wasn't so bad and the climbing was gradual as we followed the Katahdin Stream racing down to the river. Then we came to a side trail that led to the Katahdin

Stream Falls. It wasn't hard to hear the 50 ft. cascade. My interest was in the trail that took a marked change to the vertical.

There were slippery boulders and rocks that we had to climb over and the thought crossed my mind as to why the trail authorities had not made an easier trail. While I pondered this, I realized I had started the climb in my shorts. "Man, what was I thinking?" We crossed, what was probably a small brook normally, but now, a swift running stream. It presented no major problem going up and I hoped it would remain that way going down.

By the time we reached The Cave, actually a small slab type cave that provided some shelter from the elements, I knew shorts were not going to work. Shortly up the trail, we left the treeline at almost 3,500 feet and came to some huge boulders. A cold wind hit, biting right into my bones. I knew I had to put on my rain pants, jacket and gloves, just to keep warm. As I made the change, I was concerned about my companion. Being a seasoned hiker, she should have known to carry her protective clothing. She hadn't even brought any long pants, so all she had was shorts and her rain jacket.

The climb was almost straight up and had it not been for the boulders, I don't think hikers, who were not mountain climbers, could make it. They even embedded re-bar into the boulders, in certain impossible places, for you to pull yourself up.

We innovated our system to scale that area. I would push M.A. from PA. up a level and then she would, in turn, pull me up. The difficulty was magnified by the fact that we both were short in height, with even shorter legs that wouldn't stretch. I kept trying to remember the map and if it was as I recalled, it would get a little better at a place called Hunt Spur at 3,750 ft.

Stopping for a break was out of the question, due to the severe cold. When we reached a steep plateau, there was a definite change from the almost perpendicular to a very steep slant. I knew that had to be Hunt Spur and I thought out loud, "Not too far, now." I think I heard my buddy say, "Yeah." Regardless, we were making better time.

We met French Tickler on his way down. He told us that we weren't far from The Gateway and it got a lot easier to the summit from there. Those were encouraging words. He was regretting going up so late, since he had wanted to see the sun rise from the summit. You see, Mt. Katahdin is the first place in the United States that the sun hits when it rises over the horizon.

Not long after that meeting, M.A. from PA. and I struggled over The Gateway and it did get a whole lot easier. As we crossed the intermittent Thoreau Spring a shiver, of either the cold wind or excited expectation, rippled up and down my spine. Table Land was at the very base of Baxter Peak on Katahdin at 4,750 ft. Only 560 ft. from the end!

The climb was not too bad. All I can say is, it was a sight to behold when we reached the Katahdin sign at 5,260 feet. Many times I have said I am one of those people you hear about, who rarely ever cries. It isn't that I am without emotions, it's just that I lock them inside me. Not so, this day. One tear and then another trickled down the weathered lines in my face, that the A.T. had helped to create. I was happy. I was sad. I was, indeed, experiencing agony and ecstasy, all at the same time. Everyone needs to experience that, at least once in their lifetime. My DREAM was finally fulfilled. *I had hiked the 2,160 miles of the Appalachian Trial.*

There were other hikers up there that had come up the Knife's Edge Trail and, seeing our emotions, congratulated us when they found out I was finishing the entire A.T. today and M.A. from PA. was starting her second hike. They took our picture by the Katahdin sign. I was warmed by all my emotions for a while, but Katahdin would not let that last long. The weather was rapidly going downhill and when I looked at poor M.A. from PA., shivering in her shorts, I decided it was time we head in the same direction.

Sure enough, on the way down it started raining and sleeting. The wind began blowing its icy cold breath, and I thought "Rave on Katahdin. Your glory may be the end and the beginning for many but, in the end for me, Mooselauke has my heart." I could have sworn the wind picked up in strength as we scooted down to The Table. Almost skipping over Thoreau Spring, we slowed abruptly at The Gateway. No time to get ourselves seriously injured. I had a lot of bragging to do back home in Missouri.

Carefully, we made it to the Hunt Spur in the cold wind, rain and sleet. Then, trying to be careful, we literally slid down the rocks that we had helped each other over, on the way up. In some places I could have sworn I felt ice on the boulders. I prayed that I would not gain such momentum, as to not be able to stop before smashing into the boulders and trees below.

Like magic, the boulders ended and I felt my hand grabbing a pine tree. Gaining my composure, I entered the trees and the wind immediately ended its war against us. It was a good feeling and we both fought the urge to stop and eat. We were eager to get off the mountain. I did get a couple of views as the clouds broke and even though Katahdin was greedy about allowing visions from on top, the scene from here was awe inspiring. Only God could create such beauty and only pain and suffering can bring you to a place to see its full splendor.

At 2:45 p.m. we reached the trail registry and checked out. Tweety Pie, with his weathered face and wide smile, was waiting anxiously. He gave us both a great big hug and kiss. You see he has lived the hiking part of this adventure by proxy, through me. M.A. from PA. helped me finish my last 11 miles in style, 5.5 miles to the summit of Mt. Katahdin and 5.5 miles back down. She was a gutsy lady, as she prepared to head south, when we got back to the Daicey Pond Shelters to pick up our backpacks. Tweety Pie even asked her to come back to Missouri and hike with me. Well, you can bet we are going to keep in touch. Snapshot and Stickflipper left with French Tickler. After all the miles we spent together, I didn't even get to say good-bye.

Ghost Hiker had made it into the shelter and was sound asleep in his sleeping bag. "A calm ending," I was thinking as I shivered in the cold. I slipped into some dry clothes to get warm. Quietly my husband and I loaded my gear in the jeep before turning to the waiting M.A. from PA. and the last farewell. It is an irony that the person I spent the least amount of time with, was the only one there at the end. Thanks, M.A. from PA.

Tweety Pie and I, in silence, headed to Millinocket, Maine, where we got gas and a big, juicy hamburger with fires. Then we drove to Stratton, Maine, and a motel. I was up and down in my emotions. There should have been fireworks on the mountain and all my friends and I should have had fond good-byes. It was a rude awakening that many great things happen in complete solitude. Great discoveries of healing and inventions were conceived in dreams. I was humbled. Yet, it was good that Bill and I were alone again. It would be a long three days of driving to get home. In calm sleep, the night ended back in civilization where I had begun. It was over.

You made springs and fountains flow; You dried up large rivers.
You created the day and the night;
You set the sun and the moon in their places;
You set the limits of the earth; You made summer and winter.
Psalms 74:15-17

HOW I PUT MY MEALS TOGETHER

Each meal is prepared individually at home and placed in a plastic bag. I have what I call my *KITCHEN BAG*. It is nylon. I put margarine, (I use squeeze Parkay in the small plastic bottle) salt, pepper, sugar, (I use Sweet and Low because it is lighter in weight) tea, waterproof matches and anything else needed for personal cooking preferences. This must be kept light!

I *Coffeemate* to mix with my oatmeal. It tastes like cream and takes the place of milk. I pre-mix the instant pudding with instant milk at home. Put this mixture into a small baggie. On the trail, just add water. The amount of water added is less than the amount of milk normally called for in the recipe on the pudding package. Pour water into baggie, zip it closed and mix by kneading with hands. By the time you have your meal cooked, the pudding is ready to eat.

To start a hike, I would put three breakfasts, three lunches and three dinners in my pack, plus one extra meal. This would be just in case of an emergency. When I stopped for lunch, I would take a lunch meal from my pack. Everything I needed was there, except my drinking water.

I allowed two snacks for each day's hike.

I mixed my own trail mix with - - - -

       1 jar of peanuts

       1 # raisins

       1 # M & M's

Mix together and put in separate plastic bags. An interesting taste to this mixture would be various types of dried fruits, also.

I take along little sticks of fire starter to start a bonfire easier and quicker.

BREAKFAST	**_LUNCH_**	**_DINNER_**
Oatmeal Pop Tart Tea or Coffee	Spreadables Trail Mix Crackers	Mac & Cheese Cookies Tea Ham Stick
Oatmeal Pop Tart Tea or Coffee	Peanut Butter and/or Jelly Crackers Candy Bar	Noodles & Cheese Pudding Tea Ham Stick
Breakfast Bar Pop Tart Tea or Coffee	Spreadables Crackers Candy Bar	Spaghetti Cookies Tea Ham Stick
Breakfast Bar Pop Tart Tea or Coffee	Peanut Butter and/or Jelly Crackers Trail Mix	Chicken Noodle Dinner Cookies Tea Ham Stick
Breakfast Bar Pop Tart Tea or Coffee	Peanut Butter and/or Jelly Crackers Trail Mix	Potato Dinner Pudding Tea Ham Stick
Oatmeal Pop Tart Tea or Coffee	Cheese Crackers Trail Mix	Motor Home ☺

GLOSSARY OF TRAIL TERMS

THRU-HIKER. . . . . . One who is hiking from Springer Mountain, Georgia to Mt. Katahdin, Maine or visa versa, in one continuous hike.

SECTION HIKER. . . . . . . One who hikes sections of the A.T. over a period of time, trying to become a 2,000-mile   hiker.

2,000-MILER . . . . . One who has hiked the entire A.T.

SLACKPACKER. . . . . . One who hikes without carrying a heavy backpack.

PURIST. . . . . . A hiker who does not miss a white blaze.

WHITE BLAZE. . . . . . A 2 inch by 6 inch painted white blaze on trees or other objects, marking the A.T. pathway.

BLUE BLAZE. . . . . . A 2 inch by 6 inch painted blue blazes on trees or other objects, marking a side trail of the A.T.

CAIRN. . . . . . A pile of stones, stacked high, to mark the trial above tree line.

LEAN-TO. . . . . . A three-sided shelter, usually with a raised floor for hikers to sleep overnight.

USFS . . . . . United States Forest Service

SWITCHBACK. . . . . . A zig-zag trail going up or down a steep mountain to cut down the steepness of the climb.

May the road rise to meet you -

May the wind be always at your back -

May the sun shine warm upon your face,

The rains fall soft upon your fields -

And until we meet again,

May God hold you in the hollow of his hand.

---------author unknown

ORDER FORM

Please send _____copies of
" The Dream Trail".

Please include $2.95 shipping and handling for
each book. Thank you.

Send Cash, Check, or Money Order to:

Mary L. Twitty
Rt. 1 - Box 131E
Verona, MO 65769

INCLUDE:

NAME:_____

ADDRESS:_____

CITY:_____

STATE:_____   **ZIP:**_____